Don Osborne was raised in the Melbourne suburb of Preston, in the shadows of the mighty Pentridge Prison. He obtained a primary teacher's certificate at Melbourne Teachers College and later a Special Teacher's Certificate at the same Institution. His teaching experience covered some thirty years and included terms in several primary schools, a secondary school, and a special school as well as the institutional school at Pentridge Prison.

He has always spent much of his leisure time reading and researching true crime, and has been an avid court watcher for many years. The murder trials he has attended include the sensational Supreme Court trial of Ray Bennett, Vin Mikkelsen and Laurie Prendergast for the murder of Les Kane, when police marksmen lined the roof of the court.

Don's sporting interests include football, cricket, horse-racing and lawn bowls.

PENTRIDGE

BEHIND THE BLUESTONE WALLS

DON OSBORNE

echo

echo

Echo Publishing
An imprint of Bonnier Books UK
4th Floor, Victoria House, Bloomsbury Square
London WC1B 4DA
www.echopublishing.com.au
www.bonnierbooks.co.uk

Echo Publishing acknowledges the traditional custodians of Country throughout Australia. We recognise their continuing connection to land, sea and waters. We pay our respects to Elders past and present.

First published 2015.
This edition first published 2018. Reprinted 2023.

Printed and bound in Australia by Pegasus Media & Logistics

MIX
Paper from
responsible sources
FSC® C008194

The paper in this book is FSC® certified.
FSC® promotes environmentally responsible, socially beneficial and economically viable management of the world's forests.

The paper this book is printed on is certified against the Forest Stewardship Council® Standards. Pegasus Media & Logistics holds FSC® chain of custody certification SGS-COC-005088. FSC® promotes environmentally responsible, socially beneficial and economically viable management of the world's forests.

Edited by Jenny Lee
Cover design by Luke Causby / Blue Cork
Page design and typesetting by Shaun Jury
Cover and all internal photographs of Pentridge Prison, except
for the aerial view, by Donna Squire
H Division floor plan on page 46 by Brett Squire

NATIONAL
LIBRARY
OF AUSTRALIA

A catalogue entry for this book is available from the National Library of Australia

ISBN: 9781760681029 (paperback)
ISBN: 9781760069605 (ebook)
ISBN: 9781760069612 (mobi)

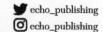

echo_publishing

echo_publishing

echopublishingaustralia

CONTENTS

FOREWORD

Growing up in the 1970s and '80s, we three children loved to sit with Dad and talk crime. Our father hadn't only spent many years following famous cases and attending criminal trials, but he'd even worked at the infamous Pentridge Prison. Pentridge – the name itself still holds a dark mystique. As youngsters, we were hooked!

Dad's stories included famous cases such as the brownout murders, the escapades of William O'Meally, the disappearance of Christopher Flannery and the murders of the Kane brothers, but our favourite story was that of the Great Bookie Robbery. My brothers Peter, Stuart and I would sit and talk for hours with Dad about the cases. We'd debate what could have happened to people he once knew, especially those who had mysteriously vanished. It's an interest we still share.

When I talked with friends over the years, it would invariably come up in conversation that my father had worked at Pentridge as an education officer. People would look shocked. They probably didn't believe that prisoners deserved an education, but we knew how important Dad's work had been to him, and how many lives he and my mother, who often attended evening sessions at the prison, had touched over the years.

Pentridge prison was formally closed in 1996. Many years have passed since then, but my brothers and I have never forgotten the hours we spent talking about criminal cases, and about Dad's time at Pentridge. We all urged him to write a book about the prison. We thought at the time that it would be something we could keep as a family – stories of the past that one day we could read and reflect on to our children. Once we all began reading, though, we could see this was an important book, as well as a good read.

After a time, Dad decided to contact the owners of the Pentridge site to explain that he was writing a book and ask if it would be possible for him to visit. Thankfully, the owners gave permission.

As we stood in front of the towering bluestone walls, some still with razor wire running along them, we could understand how this would have been such a frightening façade for the many men and women who were sent here. Right now, though, we could hardly contain our excitement at the thought that we were about to walk through those infamous gates to hell.

We were greeted by the head of security, Marty Ryan. As we walked through the first checkpoint, Dad pointed out where the guards had once stood and where visitors' vehicles had been searched. He spoke of which prisoners had been housed where, and told us some of the history of the buildings.

Dad was taken aback by how different the prison now looked. Where once there had been beautifully tended gardens, there were now mounds of dirt, dust and weeds. Many structures had been completely demolished. We tried to imagine what the place had looked like before the farm and sports oval were replaced by blocks of flats. What took me by surprise was the silence that enveloped the surviving bluestone buildings and the feeling that they held many stories, most probably long forgotten.

All of us, including Dad, were keen to enter B Division. This is where he spent most of his time, holding his daily classes in the division chapel. To go in there with him was almost like stepping back in time. Dad looked around the division and explained his daily routine, but when we entered the chapel, he became emotional, recalling his time in that room. Now totally bare, without its pews or altar, the chapel still evoked vivid memories. It was a day I will always remember.

On a subsequent visit, we met Ray, who was a student in A Division when Dad was at Pentridge. Ray went with us to H Division, one place in Pentridge that Dad had never been able to enter, and Ray and I climbed the steep steps to the H Division guard tower. While we were up there, Ray asked me what I thought of Dad working at Pentridge. I said, 'I am very proud of Dad's work here,' and Ray replied, 'You should be proud of your father. I owe a great deal to him and the other teaching staff that followed.' I have never told Dad what Ray said that day, but I know that reading this will mean a lot to him.

I hope that through reading this book, you too will become interested in Pentridge, and that it inspires you to help preserve what remains, so that future generations can appreciate the history behind those bluestone walls. Well done, Dad, and happy reading everyone, from three very proud children!

Tania Bainbridge (née Osborne)

INTRODUCTION

In early 1970, I took a position as an education officer at Pentridge Prison in the Melbourne suburb of Coburg. Assigned to the high-security B Division, where the chapel doubled as the only classroom on weekdays, I became tutor, confidant and counsellor to some of Australia's best-known criminals.

I'd previously taught adult students at Keon Park Technical School for several years, but nothing could prepare me for the inhospitable surrounds I faced in B Division. No bright and cheerful classroom or happy young faces here – just barren grey walls and barred windows, and the sad faces of prisoners whose contact with me was often their only link to a dimly remembered world outside. The eerie silence of the empty cell block was only punctuated by the occasional approach of footsteps and the clanging of the grille gate below.

Although it's some forty years since I taught in Pentridge, the place and its people have never left me. In recent times, my adult children encouraged me to write an account of my experiences there, and this book is the result. Its primary focus is on the 1970s, which were years of rebellion in Pentridge, as in jails across the Western world. These were also the years when I worked at Pentridge, feeling tensions rise across the prison.

The first chapter maps the prison's evolution from its origins in 1850 until 1970, and the prison authorities' struggle to adapt to changing philosophies of incarceration over that time. The forbidding exterior of Pentridge was a sign of what lay inside; once it was constructed, this nineteenth-century prison was literally set in stone, a soulless place of incarceration that was nevertheless the only home that many of its inmates had known.

The second chapter describes how an inmate experienced Pentridge as he travelled the well-worn path from the grim remand section, D Division, with its appalling exercise yards, into one of the divisions of the prison itself. These divisions were named alphabetically, and each housed a particular class of prisoner. In time, the prison established a range of industry yards that provided prisoners with daily employment and made the prison substantially self-sufficient in many of the essentials of life. The prison came to constitute a world of its own.

For prisoners who further infringed while incarcerated, Pentridge from the late 1950s had a punishment section, the dreaded H Division, which is the subject of chapter 3. The operation of this division has been the subject of much controversy, as the penal authorities' version of what took place there was far more benign than the picture painted by many of its inmates. All agreed that the division operated under a strict military-style discipline, but prisoners insisted – and the prison guards denied – that this was accompanied by daily violence. H Division was totally isolated from the rest of the prison, and my interpretation of what happened there has been constructed from personal contacts within the jail and written accounts by ex-prisoners, all of which portray a consistent picture.

Chapter 4 outlines my own experiences as an education officer in the proverbially tough B Division, where inmates constantly lived under threat of being relegated to the punishment section for even minor infringements. The small educational provision in B Division was a sign of how low a priority was assigned to preparing prisoners to operate

2

effectively in the world outside. Understandably, while most inmates were desperate to get out, a very high proportion reoffended and wound up back in jail.

The prison's fortress-like construction was a great challenge for its more daring inmates, who dreamed of escaping the harshness of life there. Chapter 5 outlines some of their more ingenious attempts – though almost all were ultimately doomed to fail.

Pentridge was also the site of all executions in Victoria after 1924, and these are the subject of chapter 6. The last Australian execution of a woman and the last of a man, Ronald Ryan, were both conducted there. Ryan's hanging was met by a storm of protest that ultimately brought about the end of capital punishment in Australia in 1975.

The following chapters focus on some of Pentridge's more notorious inmates during the period when I worked there. They include some of the best-known criminals in the annals of Australian crime, from William O'Meally, the last man flogged in Australia, to 'Mr Rent-a-Kill', Chris Flannery, whose experiences in H Division set the scene for a life of violence, only brought to an end by his unexplained disappearance at the age of 36.

The final chapter of this book begins the story of Pentridge's metamorphosis after the prison was closed and the site sold off to be redeveloped for housing. This has been a fraught process, and is likely to remain so. The developers' desire to maximise their returns from the site has periodically brought them into conflict with those interested in retaining the heritage of the place. In the time since I began writing this book, plans for the redevelopment have been repeatedly redrawn, and there have been heated campaigns to protect Pentridge's historical landscape. Long after it ceased to operate as a prison, Pentridge's history remains a bone of contention, the focus of a story that is still being written.

CHAPTER 1
THE DEVELOPMENT OF PENTRIDGE

THE STOCKADE

Early on the morning of Thursday 5 December 1850, a group of sixteen prisoners set out on foot from the Melbourne Gaol in Russell Street. Handcuffed, some in irons, and connected by a running chain, they were all dressed in white hats, jackets and trousers, on the legs of which were stamped the initials 'PRG' for Pentridge Road Gang. Their destination was a new stockade at Pentridge, a tiny village some eight kilometres north of Melbourne. Sentenced to hard labour by the Supreme Court, they'd be put to work constructing the road leading north towards Sydney. The stockade was to act as an outstation to house them as they did so.

The prisoners were guarded by warders on each side, and were accompanied by six armed police constables, a sergeant and two Aboriginal troopers. Leading the procession in a horse-drawn cab was the superintendent of Pentridge Stockade, Samuel Barrow, formerly a magistrate at the notorious penal establishment on Norfolk Island. The prisoners made their way to the rough track known as Pentridge Road, then trudged north through the bush until they reached the stockade.

The site for the stockade had been chosen because there was plenty of bluestone, which could be quarried and broken up by the prisoners, who were soon put to work spreading gravel along Sydney Road. Over the next few months, the workforce was strengthened by the addition of more convicts from the Melbourne Gaol. Prisoners in the stockade were held in two dozen hardwood slab huts, which resembled animal cages on wheels. These were originally designed with the intention of moving them along Sydney Road as required, but instead they were used to move the prisoners from one quarry to another as the bluestone was located.

The residents of the district were greatly concerned by the scant number of officials sent to guard the stockade, which was contained only by a log fence little more than a metre high. To assist with supervision, Barrow was provided with a number of Aboriginal police, who guarded the road gangs during the day and patrolled the perimeter of the stockade at night. Many of the police deserted and were replaced by members of the military. Gold had been discovered in central Victoria, and it was increasingly difficult to find men willing to work as guards.

The gold rushes brought a dramatic increase in crime. The Victorian population doubled in just a few years, and the numbers of people committed for terms of imprisonment leapt. To reduce overcrowding at the Melbourne Gaol, some of the more unruly prisoners were sent to the 'hulks' – prison ships moored off Williamstown. Additional stockades were also established at Richmond, Collingwood and Williamstown.

Samuel Barrow was a firm believer in hard work and discipline as tools for punishment and reform. At Pentridge Stockade, prisoners slept on wooden benches in their rough wooden huts. They rose at 6 am, and within an hour they were set to work on the road construction. If they refused, they'd be punished by being made to wear heavier chains or placed in solitary confinement on a diet of bread and water. They were also employed cutting bluestone pitchers, building living quarters for staff and constructing walls and culverts. Those who worked industriously had their sentences shortened, and Barrow also allowed them to make straw hats for sale in their spare time.

Local residents were alarmed at the frequency of escapes. In March 1851, eleven men were flogged for attempting to escape. Five months later, Pentridge experienced its first fatal escape when 31 men made a rush for freedom and one was shot dead as he ran through the bush north of the stockade. These and other escapes, including some from the road gangs, resulted in Barrow abandoning the use of prisoners in road gangs in 1853.

Early the following year, Barrow relinquished his position as Inspector-General of Penal Establishments. On 5 May 1854, he was drowned when a sudden gust of wind overturned a small boat in which he was sailing off Williamstown. Few prisoners mourned his passing.

His successor, John Price, had been Civil Commandant at Norfolk Island prison for seven years, and brought to Pentridge a reputation as a tyrant who enjoyed the sufferings of others – particularly prisoners. In their book *Fifty Years Hard*, Denton Prout and Fred Feely wrote of Price's term on Norfolk Island: 'It seems undeniable that his rule of six-and-a-half years was marred by some of the most cold-blooded debasement of fellow humans ever known in this part of the world'. Price was to be Inspector-General of Penal Establishments in Victoria for a little over three years, during which time he disciplined many a poor wretch with great cruelty.

Price was highly critical of most things penal in Victoria from the start. The prisoners, the warders and the police all came under fire from the Inspector-General. He quickly banned smoking by prisoners, saying that on his first night at the stockade, he couldn't see the faces of the prisoners for tobacco smoke.

In an endeavour to improve discipline and security at the stockade, Price had a two-acre area near the entrance surrounded by a wall made of hardwood planks, with elevated platforms from which the armed warders on duty had an unobstructed view of the quadrangle beneath. The area had eight huts on wheels, each holding about ten men, with a peephole at each end to assist surveillance. This crude structure was painted black to set off its forbidding exterior. The area became known throughout the stockade as the Crystal Palace, because the domes of the huts resembled those of London's Crystal Palace Theatre.

This fearsome place struck terror into the most hardened prisoners. Its inmates were never out of chains, and their hard labour consisted of quarrying, cutting, breaking and hauling bluestone by hand. They were often flogged, and many developed physical deformities from their chains. Some malingerers were 'put to the stone' – a bluestone boulder weighing almost a tonne, positioned close to one of the wooden huts. The stone was flat on one side and had a long bolt in the centre. Prisoners were fastened to the bolt and chained to the wheel of a hut, or were forced to sit on the stone for up to six weeks at a time. Other prisoners were placed in small wooden cells in solitary confinement for 23 hours a day; this punishment lasted from ten to thirty days, and was worsened by the terrible stench that permeated the cells. Prisoners in the Crystal Palace had two things in common: constant rock-breaking and an absolute hatred of the Inspector-General.

Price also came under fire publicly for the methods of discipline he was using throughout the jails and hulks. The hatred came to a head at Williamstown on 26 March 1857, when he was listening to prisoner complaints. During the meeting, a group of convicts, unable to contain their anger, attacked Price and his guardians, hurling rocks at them as hard as they could. Initially, the officials were able to fend off their attackers, but then Price inexplicably turned and ran. He was knocked to the ground, hit with a shovel, kicked and stoned. Satisfied that Price had been dealt with, his attackers fled.

In an attempt to assist Price, a couple of prisoners put him in a barrow and took him to a nearby lighthouse. A doctor was called but was unable to revive him. There was much rejoicing around the stockade when news of his demise reached the inmates. A month later, fifteen men were tried for his murder. Seven were found guilty and hanged at Melbourne Gaol.

THE PRISON TAKES SHAPE

Price's successor as Inspector-General of Prisons, William Champ, had previously been in charge of the penal settlement at Port Arthur, and was briefly Tasmania's first Premier after the State gained responsible government in 1856. Champ was a disciplinarian, but he was appalled by many of the measures Price had used to break the prisoners' will.

He persuaded the Victorian government to replace the stockade with a modern English-style prison. Using prisoner labour, Champ oversaw the construction of several major buildings at Pentridge. As each stage was completed, he was able to reduce and then eliminate the use of the hulks. The new buildings also allowed Champ to introduce a system where the prisoners passed through three stages of imprisonment, intended eventually to achieve rehabilitation. In the first stage, prisoners were absolutely secluded; in the second, they were permitted to associate with others only at work; and in the third, they were allowed to associate under supervision at all times.

Near the entrance to the jail, Price's Crystal Palace was replaced by a completely new building, a bluestone structure known as the panopticon, which was completed in 1859. The idea of the panopticon – literally a place where 'everything is seen' – was the brainchild of the eighteenth-century English philosopher and social reformer Jeremy Bentham. The concept was that a single warder could observe all the prisoners within a building from a central observation point, but they couldn't see him, so they wouldn't know if they were being watched at any given time. The panopticon at Pentridge accomplished this by having three aisles of tiered cell blocks radiating from a central observation hub, which was encased by a great skylight. The building contained 176 high-security cells, each three metres long by two wide. Within the panopticon, Champ was able to implement the first stage of his system, employing the 'separate and silent' method popular with penologists of his time. His predecessors' philosophy of using hard work and physical punishment to assert control over the prisoners was replaced by one that aimed to teach prisoners to discipline themselves through psychological punishment.

In the panopticon – initially named A Division, but later changed to B – the prisoner was kept in total isolation in his cell for 23 hours a day. During his one hour of supervised exercise, he had to wear a white canvas mask to conceal his identity. Communication with other inmates, either by word or sign, was strictly forbidden. The theory was that a prisoner kept in silence and isolation would become so desperate for companionship that he'd readily obey the prison regulations. To complete the atmosphere of absolute silence, warders wore slippers to ensure they made no sound as they did their rounds. In the nineteenth century, all newcomers to Pentridge were sent to 'solitary', as the panopticon was known. The term of confinement depended on the length of a prisoner's sentence, but it was normally from three to nine months.

The outside exercise yards were also built to Bentham's design. These one-man, wedge-shaped yards – known as 'airing yards' – were formed like the spokes of a wheel around a guardhouse. Each yard was about six metres long and had very high walls to prevent any sort of communication between prisoners in adjacent yards; there was a small shed attached to the wall at the end away from the guardhouse so prisoners could shelter from inclement weather, and the complex accommodated ten or twelve men at a time.

On release from solitary – or 'model', as it was also called – the prisoner was sent to complete the second stage of his sentence under less restrictive conditions in another new building constructed in the late 1850s. This was B Division – later called C Division, the name by which it was known until it was finally demolished in 1974. Here, inmates could work and exercise with other prisoners, though still confined in separate cells.

At the third stage of his incarceration, the prisoner was transferred to dormitory accommodation in what was initially known as C Division, renamed F Division at the turn of the twentieth century. Prisoners in this division worked in one of the prison's industrial workshops in association with others. This was actually the first of the new buildings opened while Champ was Inspector-General; it had been started under Price, who intended to use it as a hospital, and was completed about 1858.

During the construction of the prison, the last escape for many years occurred. In January 1859, nine convicts leapt the low wall at the northern end of the stockade, hotly pursued by several armed warders. Scattering in all directions, the escaping prisoners were fired upon. One of them was shot in the head and died later that night. In less than an hour, the rest of the escapees had been rounded up. They were later sentenced to extra imprisonment in irons.

The last of the major buildings that formed the prison complex under Champ were a new infirmary and a separate prison at the northern end of the site, built to accommodate female prisoners. Both were forbidding bluestone structures. The women's prison had 120 cells, each about three metres by two. It was begun in the late 1850s and completed in 1864.

By that time, the central structures that would dominate Pentridge for the following century had mostly been completed. Surrounded by a great wall stretching for almost four kilometres, the prison occupied about 57 hectares (140 acres). Its buildings and walls – including the great edifice at the entrance – had largely been constructed by prisoners from bluestone quarried on the site. The main gate building contained an armoury, administrative offices and warder accommodation. There were three large divisions for male prisoners and one for females, an infirmary and various workshops.

As well as overseeing the construction of the new prison, Champ attempted to find employment for prisoners on release, but his efforts didn't receive much support from the business community. He also introduced chaplains and schoolteachers to provide for the prisoners' religious and educational needs. By December 1868, when he retired to a farm in Meredith, he'd transformed Pentridge from a collection of makeshift huts into a penal settlement set in stone. The road to the main entrance would later bear his name.

The system of separation and silence was continued at Pentridge until just after the turn of the twentieth century, with some sinister elaborations that weren't part of Bentham's original design. Prisoners who breached the strict rules of 'solitary' could now be sent to 'blind' cells, where they were kept underground in total darkness and fed only bread and water. For those considered incorrigible, some of the 'blind' cells also contained a pit into which the prisoner could be lowered. Prisoners sent to the 'blind' cells went to considerable lengths to keep themselves occupied and fend off insanity. An inmate would often smuggle in a pin or some other small object, toss it into the darkness and then go down on hands and knees to find it. When he found it, he'd toss it again and repeat the search. To spend time in a 'blind' cell was the most feared punishment of all.

NEW ORDERS

In 1870, the residents of Pentridge voted to change the district's name to Coburg in an attempt to dissociate themselves from the prison that had come to dominate their locality. In the same year, a Royal Commission was held into prison discipline, chaired by the former Chief Justice, Sir William Stawell. Its recommendations brought much change to the administration of the prison.

Believing that the dormitories were a breeding ground for crime, Stawell recommended that women prisoners be moved and that male prisoners in the dormitory section go into single-cell accommodation in the former women's prison. Exercise yards similar to those at the panopticon were now built there as well.

The Stawell Commission's other major recommendation was that the prison authorities adopt a modified version of the Crofton or Irish system. When this system was implemented at Pentridge, inmates would pass through three stages of imprisonment. In the first stage, a prisoner would be housed in the panopticon for six months of solitary confinement, during which time he could only work in his cell. At the second stage, he was still housed in a single cell but was employed in one of the prison's workshops, which were upgraded and relocated to accommodate the new system. There were tailors', bootmakers', carpenters' and blacksmiths' shops, and a timber yard. Inmates at this stage of their imprisonment were given marks for work effort and behaviour. Prisoners in this stage received a money allowance on a graduated scale and were rewarded for good work with 'permitted indulgences' such as tobacco.

Once the second stage was completed, the prisoner entered

the third stage, where he could be employed on public works. Again, prisoners operated under a 'marks' system. When this system was introduced in 1873, it marked the first time that prisoners had received payment for their daily work.

A further consequence of the Royal Commission was that Pentridge became a centre for child welfare, with reformatories for both boys and girls established in 1875. What was later called G Division opened in that year as the Jika Reformatory for Protestant Girls, the name under which it operated until 1893. The Jika Reformatory for Boys was established in the old dormitory section and operated between 1875 and 1879. These reformatories housed children as young as nine who had been imprisoned for such offences as vagrancy. Discipline was severe, and included solitary confinement and corporal punishment.

Labour yards were also built on the eastern end of the former women's prison. These were used for stone-breaking, either for prisoners sentenced to hard labour or as punishment for a prison-related offence. The yards were used for rock-breaking until the 1970s, when the practice was finally abandoned.

In June 1894, a contingent of female prisoners serving sentences of three months or more was transferred to Pentridge from the Melbourne Gaol. Unlike the first men, who had to go on foot, the women were transported in vans under police escort. They'd occupy a new three-storey building, which was built to accommodate 195 female prisoners.

What became known as the Female Prison at Coburg was under the control of a governess, who oversaw a female staff. It consisted of three sections – the new building housed ordinary prisoners; Jika, the old dormitory section of Pentridge, was used for habitual offenders as well as for the elderly and infirm; and the former 'Reformatory for Protestant Girls' was renamed Coburg and used for first offenders and those judged to be more promising. The women in Coburg were segregated from the rest. Most of the women were in jail for petty offences such as vagrancy, prostitution and drunkenness.

Conditions in the female prison were very harsh. Few of the prisoners even had beds to sleep on. First offenders were issued with a mattress and spent their days washing and ironing. Many of the others slept on mats, and their daily employment consisted mainly of washing and sewing. Conversation was only permitted occasionally at work. All women prisoners were required to serve the last four weeks of their sentence in separate confinement. Female prisoners were to be segregated at Pentridge for the next sixty years in a prison within a prison. It was only when Fairlea Women's Prison opened in 1956 that there was an improvement in the treatment of female offenders.

In 1901, a successful escape by Edward Sparks highlighted the great security weakness of Pentridge prison – the unguarded eastern wall, over which he made his escape. This wall was easily climbed by outsiders, including ex-prisoners, who could easily plant tobacco, spirits, tools, money and escape equipment. These items were collected by the farm workers and distributed to adventurous prisoners throughout the jail. It was half a century before this weakness was fixed.

By the turn of the twentieth century, the authorities had finally recognised that the solitary system had no reformative effect, and adopted a more humane approach to punishment and reformation. This new philosophy had two essential elements: each inmate was to receive individual attention, and all prisoners were to be gainfully employed. Part of this process was that prisoners were classified, and two new classes were created – the 'specials' and the 'restraints'. The 'specials' were mainly first offenders; they were given relatively light day work and nightly lectures. The 'restraints', chiefly young offenders, attended school each morning, then worked on the prison farm.

At about the same time, the divisions of Pentridge changed their names and functions. The original women's prison on the northern end of the site was renamed A Division, while the bluestone panopticon was renamed B Division. The panopticon also ceased to be used as a place for solitary confinement, but was simply used to house hardened prisoners in single cells. Inmates of B Division were now able to work and associate with other prisoners. Until the prison closed, B Division was used for long-term high-risk prisoners.

Another innovation was that indeterminate sentences could now be served on inmates in 'reformatory prisons'. Two of the oldest and most primitive sections of Pentridge were classified as reformatory prisons: C Division for men, and Jika for women. Indeterminate sentences were mainly given to habitual offenders, who would only be released when they were judged to be reformed. Indeterminate sentences became known as 'the key'.

REORGANISATION AND REFORM

In 1924, Joseph Akeroyd, a former inspector of primary schools, became Victoria's Inspector-General of Prisons – a position he was to hold until 1946. He took charge of a system in the throes of a major reorganisation. The Melbourne Gaol was gradually being decommissioned and its prisoners transferred to Pentridge, requiring a significant reorganisation of the Pentridge site. The three-storey building constructed in the 1890s to accommodate women became the Metropolitan Gaol for male prisoners on remand, known as D Division. There were now three separate prisons on the Pentridge site: Pentridge itself, the Metropolitan Gaol and the female prison. It was about ten years before the three were amalgamated under a single governor and became officially known as H.M. Prison Pentridge.

Akeroyd brought much reform to Pentridge, particularly in prisoner education and prison officer welfare. He immediately introduced entry examinations for warders and selection procedures to assess their suitability for the work. The prison soon had a school staffed by qualified teachers where young offenders received instruction, and adult prisoners were encouraged to do correspondence courses and study at night.

Electric power was now being used at Pentridge, increasing the output from the prison's industries. Under Akeroyd, the system of grading prisoners by marks was abolished and replaced by a system of sentence remissions. The labour yards, however, remained in use to enforce physical punishment on recalcitrant prisoners; hard labour still meant breaking rocks.

During the 1940s, Pentridge came under pressure from several directions. Akeroyd himself recommended that the prison be given an upgrade and that C Division be demolished. There was also a push from the citizens of Coburg for Pentridge to be closed down. At one stage, the mayor of Coburg claimed that conditions for prisoners at Pentridge were worse than those of the animals at Melbourne's zoo. 'At least their living enclosures are free from vermin and lice,' he added. But Pentridge survived the pressure – as did the increasingly archaic C Division.

In 1947, Akeroyd was succeeded by Alexander Whatmore. Whatmore believed that prison had a twofold purpose – it should protect the rest of society, and also had a moral obligation to rehabilitate its inmates. He argued that prisoners should be provided with training to fit them for their eventual return to society. He appointed a Chief Education and Training Officer to oversee the training of prison staff, as well as to supervise voluntary daytime correspondence courses for prisoners.

Whatmore oversaw a considerable liberalisation of prison life. His reforms included the introduction of a parole and probation system, the abolition of indeterminate sentences, and the use of a system of minimum and maximum sentences to give prisoners an incentive to behave and give them greater certainty about the duration of their sentences. He had headphones installed in the cells so prisoners could listen to radio programs, and he permitted recreational activities such as weekend sporting matches. He also encouraged evening activities such as toy-making and printing, where the prison made substantial contributions to charity.

Whatmore also allowed prisoners to use their wages to purchase tobacco and other goods from a prison canteen. Like Akeroyd before him, he unsuccessfully proposed the demolition of C Division. He also suggested that the labour yards be demolished, but C Division remained, as did the labour yards. Another of his initiatives was the establishment of Fairlea Female Prison, which opened in Fairfield in 1956 and took all the women prisoners from Pentridge. The former female reformatory was now converted into a psychiatric assessment area and renamed G Division.

But Whatmore was publicly criticised for 'going soft' on prisoners, and his term in office was beset by a spate of escapes and incidents within the jail. In 1952, a prisoner named Kevin Joiner was shot dead by a tower guard when escaping in company with prolific escapee Max Skinner. Two years later, 'lifer' James Walker held up warders in B Division with a pistol. He was aiming to kill the warders and some of the other prisoners, whom he'd placed on a 'death list', but his plan was foiled and he committed suicide in his cell.

One of the most notable escapes from the prison during the 1950s was a breakout spearheaded by John Taylor. In August 1955, Taylor and another prisoner named Peter Dawson produced a rifle and a shotgun and used them to take three unarmed prison guards hostage after a football match at the prison oval. Taylor, Dawson and William O'Meally escaped along with two other B Division inmates, and Taylor and Dawson remained at large for ten days. It was the fourth escape in a single year, and it brought the total number of escapes since 1949 to nineteen.

The government responded by appointing a board of inquiry headed by Charles McLean, a retired magistrate. McLean found many security problems associated with the match and the supervision of prisoners. He reported that the governor of the prison hadn't been sufficiently rigorous in vetting the list of men allowed to attend the match, which had recently been moved from an area inside the main prison to a less secure oval on the prison farm. He was especially critical of the poor security along the farm wall, which was almost certainly the route through which the escapees' guns had made their way into the prison. McLean also pointed out that the warders were carrying old rifles and weren't trained in their use.

As a result of the escape, the guards' weapons were upgraded, but more importantly, Whatmore proposed that 24 hectares (almost 60 acres) of the farm area be removed from the prison grounds. The proposal was put into effect in 1958, when the area was given over to a high school and a teachers' training college.

Two years later, Taylor and O'Meally escaped again. This time, Taylor shot a guard at the main gate as they made their dash for freedom. The escape was short-lived, but the consequences were dire. As well as receiving an additional ten years imprisonment, Taylor and O'Meally were sentenced to receive twelve lashes from the cat-o-nine-tails. Amid much public protest, they became the last men flogged in Australia.

As a further consequence of these escapes, the old labour yards at the rear of A Division were rebuilt into a new, heavily fortified maximum-security punishment section named H Division, and O'Meally and Taylor became its first inmates. This new division contained 39 cells to house and punish rebellious prisoners. It was a jail within a jail, totally isolated from the rest of the prison. For the next several years it would serve as a punishment section, though later it was officially described as providing 'security'.

Pentridge also became the site where all Victorian hangings were carried out. When the Melbourne Gaol was closed in the 1920s, the gallows beam and trapdoor were installed in the eastern wing of D Division at Pentridge. In all, Pentridge was the site of eleven executions, including those of the last woman and the last man executed in Australia. The woman, Jean Lee, was carried to her fate in 1951. The last man hanged was Ronald Ryan, who met his fate at Pentridge sixteen years later.

In 1965, Ryan had been involved in a widely publicised escape, in the course of which a prison guard was shot dead. Ryan was sentenced to death for his murder, and was hanged amid much public outcry on 3 February 1967.

This execution brought the prison to public attention. Protestors took to the steps of Parliament, participated in street protests and signed petitions against the hanging. Even members of Ryan's jury campaigned against his execution, stating that they wouldn't have convicted Ryan if they'd known the death penalty would be carried out. Thousands more gathered outside the prison in a peaceful vigil of protest on the night before the execution, and many police were in attendance to oversee the large crowd gathered there the next morning. A persistent public campaign eventually led to the abolition of capital punishment in Victoria in 1975.

CHAPTER 2
FROM REMAND TO PRISON

ON REMAND

The Pentridge prisoner usually began his prison experience with a stay in D Division, the Metropolitan Gaol, which was located at the southern end of the Pentridge grounds, separate from the prison itself. The jail held accused men who had had their charges heard by a magistrate and had either been refused bail or failed to raise the necessary funds. They were then taken in a prison van from court directly to D Division.

You can imagine the prisoner's sense of foreboding at the grim appearance of the high bluestone walls and the loud clanging of the prison gates as they closed behind the van and its human cargo. After alighting handcuffed from the van, the new inmate was ushered into a large bluestone building – the Metropolitan Gaol. This place would soon become quite familiar to him (if it wasn't already, as many of the inmates were repeat offenders). Men usually spent several months on remand before they had their day in court, and those facing capital charges might have to wait for a year or more. Guilty or not, the remand prisoners were held in primitive, inhuman and degrading conditions. In order to survive, they had to adjust quickly and learn the rules of the Pentridge jungle.

The newly remanded prisoner was immediately put through the reception procedure, beginning with the confiscation of all personal property in his possession. He was then fingerprinted, photographed and strip-searched – a degrading and frightening experience. At the completion of this procedure, the prisoner was taken to his cell – a space three metres long by two metres wide, where he'd have to spend sixteen lonely hours each day. He was provided with two blankets, a pillow and a lumpy kapok mattress. The cell contained a single bed, a lidless toilet bowl and a cold-water hand basin. There was also a Bible and a set of headphones through which he could listen to the radio program broadcast to that section of the prison. D Division had 198 of these cells on three levels, running off a central hub.

At night, the prison officer on duty in D Division usually turned the lights off about 9.30 pm. The nights were long and stressful. The stillness was often punctuated by the sounds of inmates weeping, or calling out in fear in their sleep. Others screamed abuse at the prison officers on duty and got an earful in return, or banged on their cell doors in frustration and anger. Depending on the time of year, D Division could be bitterly cold or oppressively hot. Obtaining a night's sleep was a difficult task.

To relieve the monotony of their nights in the cells, Pentridge inmates had devised a way of pushing water out of the toilets so they could talk to each other through the empty sewer pipes. One prisoner would create a plunger, using a blanket or pillow to push up and down continuously until the water was pushed out of his toilet bowl and along the pipe. On hearing the toilet gurgle, his neighbours, who were connected to the same pipe, would simultaneously push the water from their toilets. Once the pipes were empty, the prisoners could talk to each other by putting their heads into their empty toilets. They used blankets to cover themselves and the toilets so that the guards couldn't hear them speak.

Occasionally, word filtered through that someone had

committed suicide during the night. Quite a few inmates were kept on suicide watch on the ground level, in observation cells with open grille doors where they could be kept under constant supervision. Prisoners in these cells had no privacy at all. Men were clad only in underpants or left naked. Each cell had only a mattress on the floor and a bucket for a toilet, and the cells were bitterly cold in winter.

At 7 am, the prisoners were woken by the ringing of a bell. No matter how tired they were, they had to get up, make their beds and tidy their cells. Fifteen minutes later, all the prisoners were counted as part of the regular morning 'muster', and at 7.30 they were released into the division's exercise yards, where they'd spend eight hours a day, every day of the week.

The yards were surrounded by a six-metre bluestone wall topped with rolls of barbed wire and steel spikes. Inside the wall, high wire fences had been used to subdivide the area into four separate yards connected to a semicircular hub. There was a yard for prisoners under 21 years of age, a general remand yard, which held about a hundred men, a classification yard, which held about fifty prisoners, and a yard for condemned prisoners, which was much smaller than the others and sometimes empty. The yards were triangular in shape, with open showers and toilets and a covered section at the end. These covered sections were very small, so most of the men spent their days exposed to the elements, sweltering in summer, freezing in winter, and being thoroughly drenched when it rained. Each yard had bench seats for about twenty men. The rest of the prisoners just paced up and down the concrete.

With so many men crowded together under harsh conditions, there was constant conflict in the yards. Fights occurred regularly, almost non-stop. There was no segregation between hard-core repeat offenders and first-time prisoners

– known to the seasoned campaigners as 'squareheads' – and newcomers were often exploited, attacked and abused.

Not yet having been convicted, remand prisoners couldn't be put to work, so all they could do to occupy themselves of a day was to walk up and down, clad in their 'civvies', mostly in groups. Their conversations naturally centred on crime, and many a young prisoner honed his criminal skills in D Division. The long, dreary day in the exercise yards came to an end at 3.30 pm. The men were again mustered, then given dinner and locked up in their cells for the next sixteen hours.

Visitors were allowed to give remand prisoners two ounces of tobacco per visit. In prison, tobacco was a form of currency, particularly on weekends, when prisoners used it to place bets on the football or the races with the division's SP bookmaker. Cash was obviously the most desirable currency, and there was some of it about, but it was contraband, and the prisoners had to exercise extreme caution when using it. Cigarettes were a precious commodity in the yards and were always in great demand, as almost all the prisoners smoked.

The classification yard was for sentenced prisoners, who had already been tried and convicted but hadn't yet been assigned to a particular prison. This yard was also exposed, overcrowded and squalid. In the 1970s, sentenced prisoners were permitted to purchase a limited range of goods at the canteen – up to five blocks of chocolate a week, plus two ounces of tobacco, cigarette papers and matches. Remand prisoners, however, had to get their tobacco from outside. Unless they had regular visitors supplying them with tobacco, the remand prisoners were often 'on the bot' with their fellow inmates. The bookmaker was usually a great source of supply for 'lends', though he'd demand prompt repayment with interest. To make their allocation of matches go further, canny prisoners would split them into two, or even into four.

All prisoners were allowed two 30-minute visits a week

from family or friends. Remand prisoners were also entitled to unlimited mail, but sentenced prisoners were restricted to two censored letters a week. Apart from that, they had no direct contact with the outside world.

Prisoners on remand weren't necessarily destined to progress to Pentridge or any other prison. At least a third of them would eventually be found not guilty in court. But after release, they were never compensated for the harsh and degrading treatment they received in D Division. Among those who were found guilty and remained at Pentridge, there was common agreement that conditions in D Division were so bad that to be transferred to one of the mainstream divisions was a reasonable substitute for release.

The first stop for remanded prisoners who had been sentenced to a term of imprisonment was the classification section of the Metropolitan Gaol, where they were held until the Classification Committee had decided where to send them. If they were assigned to Pentridge, the committee also decided which division they'd be housed in and which work gang they'd join. The committee – referred to throughout the prison as 'Classo' – would take into account an inmate's age, criminal record, type of offence and term of imprisonment, as well as other factors such as whether he needed protection from other prisoners and whether he constituted a security risk.

The sentenced prisoners in the Metropolitan Gaol weren't yet part of Pentridge proper, but they were subject to its rules and regulations. If they were found guilty of a prison-related offence, they could suffer a loss of remission – losing credit for time already spent on remand – or even be sent to H Division, Pentridge's notorious punishment section.

INTO PENTRIDGE

Prisoners who were classified to a term in Pentridge were taken in a group under escort from the Metropolitan Gaol to the prison itself on the northern side of the site – a fairly lengthy walk along a gravel path. Even for seasoned offenders this was quite a nerve-racking experience, but it was many times more so for the first-time offender, and nervous chatter and tension would fill the air as they trudged along. Massive bluestone walls topped with razor wire ran as far as the eye could see around the perimeter of the jail, with armed guards staring down on them from the sentry boxes strategically placed along the walls.

Off to their right, the new inmates could see the prison sports field and in the distance were endless rows of vegetables being tended by prisoner gangs. To their left lay the governors' residences. Manicured lawns and splendidly kept garden beds helped to beautify these otherwise drab buildings.

As the central section of the prison appeared, the group would become tense and apprehensive. Eventually, they reached a large iron grille gate, which opened to let them into the industrial area of the prison. Here, the air was full of the sounds of the looms in the woollen mill and the hammering from the boot shop on the right. On the left, several prisoners were at work in the mat yard.

A little further along the roadway that ran through the centre of the jail was a second arched gateway, manned by an armed guard. This was opened to allow entry into a large courtyard known as the Square. Directly ahead stood the main gate, clock tower and administration buildings, while on the left were the clothing store, the boiler house, which supplied the prison's hot water, and the imposing bluestone B Division. To the immediate right was the antiquated double-storey C Division, which stood next to the kitchen and bakery. Completing the Square was E Division, the bluestone edifice originally completed as an infirmary in 1864. As the tower guard closed the gate behind them, the newly arrived inmates could feel the claustrophobia that was part and parcel of life in Pentridge – along with a sense of going back a century or so in time.

Having now entered the prison proper, the new inmates were marched to the clothing store, where they were required to exchange their civilian dress for new prison uniforms: a greyish-white-striped shirt, grey jacket, blue denim trousers, thick woollen socks and heavy black leather shoes. Their civilian clothes were taken from them and placed in storage until they'd completed their sentences.

Now in full prison garb, the newly arrived inmates were assembled and marched off to their assigned divisions. Each division was labelled alphabetically, housing a particular class of prisoner.

Adult first offenders who had received lengthy sentences would more than likely be sent to A Division. To reach their destination, they'd march from the clothing store across the square and down a narrow pathway between high stone walls until they reached a gateway that gave access to the northern section of the prison. Accompanying them were the young offenders group, known throughout the prison as the 'Yogs', who were held in the modern J Division.

In A Division, 140 prisoners were housed in single blue-stone cells about three by two metres, each containing a bed, lidless toilet, a tap with cold water only, a table and a stool. Like most of the prison, A Division had very little natural light, though its gloom was somewhat brightened by the constant polishing of its bluestone floors by the billets, whose job was to clean the prison and distribute prisoners' meals.

Forbidding though it looked, A Division was probably the most relaxed part of the prison. The inmates were mainly first offenders, and the emphasis was on rehabilitation. Prisoners enjoyed more freedom and had a wider range of activities than those in other sections of Pentridge. They were allowed out of their cells – though only ten or twelve at a time – for film nights. Most of the films were of football matches obtained from Channel 7.

The division had a shared television set, and a very few select inmates had sets in their cells. There were concerts by well-known performers, including Roy Orbison, as well as play nights. Plays weren't only performed by outside groups but also by a group of inmates, the aptly named Players Anonymous, who were listed simply under their first names and initials. Players Anonymous provided high-quality productions and sometimes performed to 'outside' audiences.

Other groups active in A Division included a debating club, the Jaycees, which raised money for needy causes, and the Ryder–Cheshire group, which did screen-printing to raise money for homes in India. Some prisoners did woodwork, helping to brighten what would otherwise have been a long, drab evening.

Almost directly opposite the entrance to A Division was the modern J Division, which was opened in 1970 to house young men aged 18 to 21 years. Until then, young offenders had been housed in a section of A Division or sent to the archaic C Division. By Pentridge standards, J Division offered its youthful inmates luxury accommodation. It contained six dormitories, which fanned out from a central office where a prison officer sat behind a glassed-in desk each night from 4 pm to 8 am. But the authorities didn't realise that its design had created a monster. The open dormitories were very difficult for a single officer to supervise at night. The division held some particularly vicious and cowardly young thugs who had progressed through various boys' homes and youth welfare institutions. When the guard wasn't watching, these predators attacked the division's weaker and newer inmates.

The young first-time offender sent to the 'Yogs' had to fend for himself in some fearful situations. Night-time bashings were common, and there were incidents of rape.

For inmates of J Division, the criminal cycle usually began at the boys' homes, many of which were terrible places. Youths who had been incarcerated there were often at the mercy of those who had them in their care. Sadists and paedophiles sexually abused and generally brutalised these boys. Of course, this treatment only hardened and embittered them, making them a bigger menace to the community on release. When their criminal activity advanced them to J Division in Pentridge, the wheel turned and they became the predators, collectively hunting newer, inexperienced inmates. The youth who began as a delinquent finally graduated from the 'college of knowledge' as a hardened, vicious criminal.

The products of the boys' homes would make a significant contribution to the 'Who's Who' of Australian crime. Daryl Suckling, Christopher Flannery and Laurie Prendergast, whose stories are told in later chapters, were all products of this system. J Division just completed a long line of failed institutions for the young offender.

* * *

After the 'Yogs' and the A Division prisoners had marched off, a miscellaneous group of offenders was left in the Square. For prisoners assigned to B, C and E divisions, it was only a short walk from the clothing store to their cells. Those who had previous convictions and had received lengthy sentences were likely to be sent to B Division – particularly if they were considered a security risk. Shorter-term prisoners with prior convictions were sent to E Division, leaving a few petty offenders to head off to their antiquated – and soon to be condemned – quarters in C Division.

B Division prisoners were kept under lock and key at all times, even at work. A short distance along the passageway leading from the entry to the division was a locked, barred grille gate, manned by a guard who controlled the comings and goings in the division. The cell block consisted of 176 high-security cells – 24 of them on each of the double-tiered floors along the outer sides of the building. Each cell had mud-brown walls, a barred window, a bunk, a toilet bowl, a table and a stool. The steel door had a security lever and a padlocked sliding bolt; there was a steel 'trap' 25 cm square – a small panel that could be opened and locked from the outside – and a 'Judas' hole for observation. Around the top tiers, a waist-high metal barrier ran parallel to the walls, encasing a walkway about a metre wide.

B Division held many of the most dangerous and unpredictable men in Pentridge. Its prisoners were locked up in their cells for sixteen hours a day during the working week, and again at the weekend. Their working day began at 6.30 am, when a bell signalled that it was time to rise, clean and sweep their cells, and have breakfast. At 7.30, the cell doors were opened and the prisoners would assemble in the exercise yard for muster. They were then marched off down the central roadway to their industry shops. These were like small factories. Each was supervised by an overseer and contained a central 'cage' in which stood a guard.

Long-term prisoners would work in one of these shops every day for years on end. Nothing altered – neither the workplace nor the routine. A break for lunch back in the cell was the only relief from the constant grind – and was followed by a return to the workshops at 1 pm. Work ceased for the day at 3 pm, when prisoners were mustered, searched and returned to the division for dinner. At 4.30 all cells were locked until the following morning. Lights out was at 9.30.

The monotony continued of a weekend when the prisoners

spent most of their day in the exercise yards and had to devise ways to while away the hours spent there. However, some prisoners were permitted to compete in inter-division football matches on the jail oval. The B Division players wore black-and-white-striped jumpers, and would celebrate their victories with a rousing rendition of 'Good Old B Division Forever'. Normally, though, the only weekend diversion was to attend the Sunday service in the chapel, which was especially well attended on sweltering days in summer, or on freezing days in winter.

As B Division was where the prison 'heavies' were housed – the gunmen, murderers, bank robbers, safe crackers and all-round professional criminals – there was a hierarchy among its inmates, who also had their own lingo. Here a safecracker was a 'tankman', a hold-up man was a 'gunny', and 'murderers row' – consisting of a whole wing of 40 cells – had a distinction of its own. On the other hand, the 'rock spider' – as paedophiles and child murderers were known – was considered a cur by his fellow inmates.

Prisoners of B Division lived under spartan conditions. They were always locked up, whether at work or in their cells, often in oppressively hot or bitterly cold conditions, and were deprived of virtually all the privileges afforded inmates elsewhere. Having no freedom of movement within the prison, quite a few sought to relieve their total regimentation by attending educational classes and Sunday worship. Pentridge chaplain Father John Brosnan conducted services in the upstairs chapel, which doubled as a classroom through the week.

Directly opposite B Division, across the main driveway, stood E Division, originally the prison hospital, which was now used to house medium- to long-term prisoners who weren't considered to be a high security risk. It was a two-storey bluestone building that held inmates in six dormitories.

Prisoners here were still kept under tight security, however, and didn't enjoy the nightly activities available to A Division prisoners. In the dormitories of E Division, there was a lot of homosexual activity, consensual or not. Many of the E Division inmates were repeat offenders who regarded Pentridge as home.

Next door to E Division was the rundown section of the prison known as C Division – and for primitive conditions in Pentridge, it stood alone. Built in the late 1850s, its greatest claim to fame was that Ned Kelly had been housed there in the early 1870s. Apart from its historical significance – which was ignored when it was summarily demolished in 1974 – there was little to commend it.

C Division prisoners were generally considered to be the derelicts of the jail. Most were petty criminals – habitual drunks, vagrants and fine defaulters – and they included a disproportionate number of Aboriginal prisoners. Conditions here were appalling. The division consisted of two double-storey buildings , one on each side of a brick-paved exercise yard. All the cells opened directly on to the yard. At each end was a wooden staircase giving access to the top tier of the building via a wooden landing with a safety rail. The cells were very small, with poor ventilation, no running water or sewerage and no electricity until the last few years of the division's existence. Flooring was wooden and there were no beds – just a kapok mattress on which lay five neatly folded blankets and a pillow. Lacking sewerage, each cell had a wooden pot that held a steel bucket. To hold his nightly supply of water, each prisoner had a small plastic bottle, which had to be filled by lockup at 4.30 pm. Lights out was at 8.30 pm.

As C Division was lit by candles, wags around the prison referred to it as 'Candlelight Alley', though it was more generally known as 'Dodge City'. Each morning, prisoners could be seen carrying the toilet buckets from the cells and emptying them into the open sewerage channel that ran east and west along the northern end of the division's exercise yard. The stench there early in the morning was absolutely foul. The worst cells in the division were those on the northern end of the ground floor, adjacent to the open sewer. Then again, residing on the top tier and having to carry your bucket downstairs wasn't a particularly inviting prospect either. The appalling conditions in C Division had a lot to do with the general perception that Pentridge was uninhabitable.

There were two other divisions in the southern section of Pentridge, quite close to the Metropolitan Gaol – F and G Divisions. F Division, the original bluestone building at Pentridge, was used as a dormitory area for prisoners convicted of relatively petty crimes. All of Victoria's vehicle registration plates were manufactured here.

G Division, in the far south-western corner of the prison, served as Pentridge's psychiatric hospital. Inmates were imprisoned there for a variety of reasons. Some had been referred by the courts for a pre-sentence psychiatric report. Others were undergoing treatment and could only be released with a psychiatric clearance. The division also housed those sentenced to imprisonment at the 'Governor's pleasure' – an indeterminate sentence used for violent or mentally disordered offenders. This was preventative detention – protecting the community from the offender until such time as it was believed he was no longer a threat.

There was still one further division – the feared maximum-security punishment section named H Division, situated at the rear of A Division. The newly arrived Pentridge prisoner would hardly be familiar with H Division, but he most certainly would have heard of it. This was a part of the prison that was only referred to in hushed terms and was held in dread by all. Officially, it was a place to house the 'worst of the worst' – the incorrigibles of the prison system. It contained 39 cells, twelve labour yards for breaking rocks, and two industry areas – a brush shop and a button shop.

As well as being housed in a particular division, the newly arrived prisoner would have been allocated to his daily work gang. Normally this would be in one of the industry areas on the eastern side of the prison. Collectively, these industry areas contributed to the prison's self-sufficiency and earned it additional income. The woollen mill produced the prison's blankets, the tailors' shop produced the uniforms and the bootmakers manufactured the prisoners' shoes. Cooks in the various kitchens prepared the meals, and the billets distributed them, as well as cleaning the divisions. The mat-yard workers manufactured all the coir matting used around the prison and in various government buildings, boiler-house attendants produced the prison's hot water supplies, and carpenters and sheet-metal workers produced various items used around the jail. Meanwhile, the F Division workers were making vehicle number plates as a source of outside income for the jail.

Some prison jobs were particularly sought after. Among them was the position of writer. Writers in the divisions or offices were afforded more freedom and trust, and also performed more interesting work. The writers organised clerical activities and provided general assistance as required. But probably the most prestigious job was that of disc jockey for A, B or D Division. The DJs played musical requests and sent messages – particularly related to prison procedures – throughout the jail, to which the inmate could listen via the headphones in his cell. The privileges attached to this position included being permitted to have a television set in his cell. The DJs' small 'studios' had links to the Governors' residences, to security, and to the chief prison officers' rooms.

An outdoor occupation that kept a sizeable group of prisoners employed was the tending of the vegetable beds at the eastern end of the prison. This large farm area made a considerable contribution to the prison's food supply. And the drabness of the prison buildings was relieved by the gardens adorning its buildings and walls. Regularly maintained by various prisoner groups, they were a joy to behold.

Whatever their employment, Pentridge prisoners in the early 1970s worked a 35-hour week and earned 50¢ a day, which was kept in trust for them and paid on release. This daily employment provided some relief from the loneliness of the prison cell, but at weekends the inmates had to devise their own entertainment. Their main pastime was gambling, just as it was in the remand section.

In the early 1970s there were three SP bookmakers operating in the jail – one in each of A, B and D Divisions. Although officially illegal, their activities were unofficially sanctioned, as they were seen as an outlet for prisoner tension and a means by which the prisoner could deal with the issue of 'doing his time' – especially for the long-term inmate.

The bookmakers would accept bets on the horses, dogs, football, the fights – anything at all. The currency used was occasionally cash, but most commonly tobacco or chocolate. But throughout the prison the main form of betting was on card games, the most popular by far being Red Aces, where up to seven players could participate simultaneously, and Rickety Kate. The SP had to be a man who could control others and look after himself, particularly when it came to unpaid debts.

Each week, the prisoner filled out a canteen slip, from which he could purchase items such as chocolate or tobacco using his prison earnings. These commodities formed the basic gambling currency, and – as is the punter's way – an inmate would frequently lose a week's supply of tobacco over the weekend.

Concert evenings in the prison were a welcome relief

from the daily monotony of prison life. Big-name artists such as Johnny O'Keefe, Johnny Farnham and Ernie Sigley were among those who performed at Pentridge. The inmates of A Division also had sports nights, where sports stars – including international cricketers, footballers, horse trainers and jockeys – visited the prison to address enthusiastic audiences.

But the built-up tension of prison life – and the soul-destroying prospect of spending many more years in Pentridge – was an ever-present problem confronting long-term inmates. Some simply couldn't cope. There were quite a lot of suicides, and reports that a prisoner had launched into a 'slash-up', cutting his wrists or mutilating himself, weren't uncommon. The most common methods of suicide were by hanging – usually in a cell at night – or by leaping from the top tier of the cell block. Hunger strikes were also a popular form of protest.

Life in Pentridge revolved around aggression, and if an inmate wasn't aggressive by nature, he soon learnt to be in order to survive. The threat of physical violence was ever present, and the problem was heightened by the shortage of staff to supervise many areas of the prison. There was a constant risk of assault in the prison's showers. Male-on-male violence was a major problem throughout the prison, and sexual violence was not unknown, especially in the dormitory areas of J Division.

Victims rarely reported these assaults for fear of reprisals. Sometimes they were warned that if they broke the 'code of silence' they wouldn't live to give evidence about what had happened to them. This code demanded that the prisoner didn't 'give anybody up' – not even a prison officer. The lowest form of life among all prisoners was the informer – known throughout the jail as a 'dog'. Such inmates were ostracised, and were the scorned targets of other prisoners. Adherence to this code was also what made it possible for the guards of H Division to abuse their authority for as long as they did.

Trouble in the prison was always just around the corner; prisoners frequently assaulted one another – and prison officers. When inmates were charged with offences committed within the prison itself, the charges were heard at what was known as Governor's Court. A visiting justice would attend to hear the charges, which were usually presented by the prison governor. The complainant – such as a prison officer – could give evidence, but the accused prisoner couldn't have this evidence tested by cross-examination. At the conclusion of the hearing, the visiting justice would hand down his decision and, if the charge was proven, impose a penalty such as some loss of remission or, frequently, a term in H Division.

In the view of most prisoners, these hearings were nothing more than kangaroo courts. When a prison officer made an allegation against an inmate, the prison officer's word was, almost without exception, accepted over the prisoner's. To compound his problem, the accused prisoner didn't have access to legal representation. It was only after an inquiry in the mid-1970s that prisoner disciplinary charges began to be heard in open court with the accused entitled to legal counsel.

Daily life in Pentridge for the majority of its 1200 inmates was very harsh. Gloom surrounded the prison, and for much of the year it was bitterly cold. Even in summer it took some time to warm its buildings, which then became oppressively hot. Its harshness, regimentation and monotonous routine broke both body and spirit. Almost all of its inmates experienced depression, loneliness and frustration.

Throughout the jail, prisoners of all kinds were herded together. First offenders, fine and maintenance defaulters, murderers, rapists, standover men, armed robbers and wrong-doers of all kinds were often housed together, regardless of age or criminal experience. Disturbingly, first-time offenders were often locked away with hardened criminals, and men convicted of minor offences were incarcerated with habitual criminals, murderers, child molesters and armed robbers – which hardly seemed conducive to rehabilitation.

This prison was no place for offenders to make new lives for themselves. For most, that was just a pipe dream; at least three-quarters of Pentridge's population were habitual criminals. For many of its inhabitants, prison was a way of life, a home away from home. Having spent so much of their lives there, they were lost without regimentation and routine. This 'institutionalisation' meant that many couldn't adjust to life on the outside. On release, each prisoner had to face the problem of re-establishing himself in the community, and few managed to do so. Prisoners were immediately discriminated against because of their convictions. Faced with being unable to obtain work, many chose the obvious alternative of returning to crime, and so the cycle went on.

CHAPTER 3
H DIVISION

The physical and psychological brutality of H Division ...
turned bike thieves into murderers.
                    Pentridge chaplain Father John Brosnan

Pentridge had always contained a special punishment area
for prisoners who infringed within its walls. From the 'Crystal
Palace' of the 1850s to the rock-breaking yards built in the
1890s, the prison relied on physical punishment to deal with
escapees and repeat offenders. From the late 1950s, this
disciplinary mantle fell to what was known as H Division,
which took on the hopeless task of 'rehabilitating the
incorrigibles' by a combination of psychological manipulation
and physical force.

After the repeated escapes of the 1950s – especially the two
involving O'Meally and Taylor, which exposed embarrassing
lapses in prison security – the penal authorities proposed
that the rock-breaking section at the rear of A Division be
restructured into a sealed and heavily fortified maximum-
security area. In 1957, the eastern end of the T-shaped A
Division was walled off to create a fortress-like punishment
division. The new H Division opened in 1958 under Chief
Prison Officer Clark and operated until 1994, though in its
last years its extreme security measures were used less for
punishment than to protect prisoners who were in danger
from other inmates.

As a punishment section, it was one of the worst – if

43

not *the* worst – in Australian penal history. It incorporated both physical and psychological brutality. In its heyday, it demonstrated that the harshness of nineteenth-century punishment was alive and well in the twentieth century. Variously known in the prison system as 'the slot', 'Hell Division', 'the punch factory' and 'the bottom', H Division was a universal object of dread.

For almost half of the division's existence, its operations were shrouded in secrecy. There were tales of ill-treatment and brutality, but the official line was that they were myths. Prisoners who had been detained in H Division, the authorities said, 'had made a reputation for themselves by providing exaggerated tales of the treatment they had received, in order to impress others that they had survived it all'. The stories were overstatements and outright lies. During the 1970s, however, it became apparent that there was substance to the inmates' claims.

THE SHAPE OF H DIVISION

To reach H Division, you had to go through a large grille gate known among prisoners as 'the entrance to Hell'. Immediately inside the gate was the cell block, which was about eighteen metres long by five metres wide and contained two tiers of cells. In total, there were 39 cells, five of which were observation cells.

One of H Division's first inhabitants was William O'Meally, who saw the division at its inception. He said the cells were bare and had no beds – just five blankets on a bare floor. Later, each cell would have a bed, a wooden stool, a wooden stand with drawers, an aluminium wash bowl and a toilet. Each also contained a broom and cleaning cloths. No light could penetrate the wood-and-steel door or the opaque window. The door held a 'trap' and a spyhole through which the prisoner could be watched. Along the floor ran a thin strip of matting with a painted cross. This marked the place where the prisoner had to stand at attention whenever an officer entered.

On the ground floor of the cell block sat the 'hot box' where the prisoner obtained his meals, and at the end lay the office of the chief prison officer. Outside his office was a small reception area where new prisoners were 'welcomed' to the division.

Immediately east of this area, accessed by a few steps, was a corridor known as 'the tunnel', which led to the labour yards. Work in the yards was originally confined to rock-breaking, but the range of activities diversified during the 1960s. By the 1970s, there were two exercise yards on the right of the corridor, in one of which the prisoners showered, and on the left were two industry yards – a button shop and a brush shop.

Further along the corridor were the remaining labour yards – six on each side – where prisoners smashed bluestone into fingernail-sized pieces. The yards were unroofed, covered by thick steel bars and wire mesh. Hanging on one wall were what inmates called the 'instruments of torture' – one long- and one short-handled hammer used to break the rock – and along one side lay a bed to break it on, which was about 1.5 metres long by 60 cm wide. In the wall opposite the entrance were two metal trapdoors. From one of these, the prisoner would take the large bluestone rocks he had to break down, and through the other he'd pass the crushed rock back in buckets at the end of the week. The only other furniture in the yard was a small wooden stool and a steel bucket that served as a toilet. Outside each yard, a white cross was painted on the floor, where the prisoner stood to attention until a prison officer let him in.

Above the corridor ran a gallery known as the 'tower', which was accessed by a ladder running up from the reception area. Situated at about the same level as the wire mesh

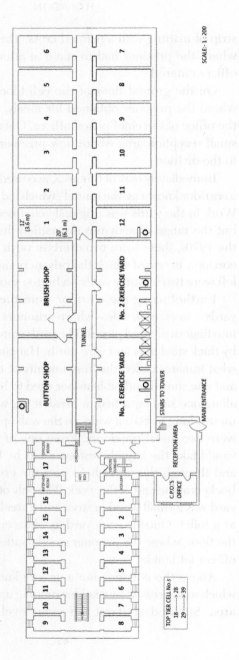

'H' DIVISION

SCALE - 1:200

BRUSH SHOP

BUTTON SHOP

No. 1 EXERCISE YARD

No. 2 EXERCISE YARD

TUNNEL

STAIRS TO TOWER

MAIN ENTRANCE

RECEPTION AREA

C.P.O's OFFICE

OFFICERS ROOM

TELEPHONE ROOM

INTERVIEW ROOM

SOLICITOR

HOT PEN

12'
(3.6 m)

20'
(6.1 m)

6   7

5   8

4   9

3   10

2   11

1   12

17

16   1

15   2

14   3

13   4

12   5

11   6

10   7

9   8

CELLS 9, 10, 15, 16, 17 OBSERVATION CELLS (10' x 6') (3 x 1.8 m)

TOP TIER CELL No.5
18 ——> 28
29 ——> 39

covering the yards, the gallery was manned by a guard who had an uninterrupted view into each yard and could lock or unlock the yard doors. The gallery also had a fire hose, which the tower guard could use to spray a powerful stream of water into any of the labour yards below.

From the outset, prisoners in H Division were subjected to rigid discipline. O'Meally reports that the prisoners had to run everywhere, including up and down the stairs. By 1962, this had been replaced by a requirement that prisoners go everywhere at a quick march – 'arms reaching to shoulder height, hands clenched, thumbs pointing horizontally in the direction of the march', as former inmate Doug Robinson described it in his book *H: The Division From Hell*.

This was one of the innumerable rules imposed on the hapless prisoners. They were also forbidden to look officers in the face and instructed always to address them as 'Sir'. Inmates had to salute the guards in a particular way: 'extending the right arm at a 90° angle to the body, then bending the elbow and touching the side of the forehead with the middle finger. Then the hand was withdrawn to the side with a vertical motion.'

Another odd regulation was that when a prisoner passed the 'hot box' that contained the meals, he had to salute the chief prison officer, even if he wasn't there, as he was present 'in spirit'. And an even stranger custom – though unwritten – was that prisoners should salute the division's black cat. Rules like this were part of the 'mind games' played by the guards, who would order an inmate to get down on his hands and knees, and 'bark like a dog', 'howl like a hyena', 'cackle like a hen', 'flap wings like a bird', and similar humiliation.

The inmate had to keep his cell spotless and even fold his bedding in a precise manner. Ex-inmate Edwin Eastwood, in his book *Focus on Faraday and Beyond*, records that the folding had to be in military style, with 'hospital corners' leaving no edges visible. The cells were inspected daily, and if guards found the tiniest speck of dust, an inmate could be charged, physically assaulted or both.

Throughout the prison system, H Division was seen as the ultimate deterrent for recalcitrant prisoners. A fair percentage of its inmates were escapees from various prisons around Victoria. Every escape was an embarrassment to the prison system, and those who perpetrated the offence had to be severely punished. As well as the escapees, many of the division's inmates were 'incorrigibles' – prisoners who refused to conform to prison regulations – or had been sentenced to a term in H Division for misconduct within the prison. Some had been involved in crimes of violence, but many hadn't.

H Division had a reputation for turning non-violent prisoners convicted of relatively minor offences into hardened, embittered men who later took revenge on society. Inmates recorded it as a place marked by a reciprocal hatred between guardian and prisoner, a site for physical violence and psychological intimidation. Many prisoners in the Victorian prison system called the guards the 'real criminals of Pentridge'. Deep within the dungeons of H Division, guards tormented prisoners with unpredictable physical violence, psychological torture and cruel mind games. Here, out of sight and away from any sort of interference, the H Division guard could inculcate fear from the moment a prisoner set foot in the division until the time he left – and this fear would linger long after release.

THE RECEPTION BIFF

The 'reception biff' remained a constant for almost the entire lifetime of H Division. In order to instil fear and enforce obedience, each newly arrived prisoner was subjected to an intrusive and humiliating strip-search, which was accompanied by gross physical violence. This was the newcomer's introduction to H Division.

The prisoner would be taken to the reception area, where he was quickly joined by several of the division's guards and ordered to remove his clothing. Hopelessly outnumbered, he'd then be set upon by the guards, using fists, boots and batons. There were no witnesses, and medical attention was virtually non-existent. As William O'Meally recorded in his autobiography, *The Man They Couldn't Break*, 'There is no such thing as medical treatment in the punishment section. If you complain to the doctor about your illness or injury you are charged with maliciously inflicting bodily injury to yourself, and with making a false statement.' The more the prisoner resisted or protested, the more mental and physical abuse he'd suffer.

Just how long this thrashing lasted depended on the whim of the guards or the resistance put up by the prisoner, but it was usually for a considerable time. The physical assault was accompanied by much personal and psychological abuse. The terrified newcomer was learning that the 'myth' of H Division was no myth at all.

He'd then be made to stand at attention, still naked, on a painted cross, and ordered to touch his toes for an 'inspection'. William O'Meally provided a graphic account of being strip-searched at reception. 'Probing fingers search your body. Every orifice is explored.' Then half-a-dozen guards begin striking him with spring steel batons. They order him to run. 'The air is filled with screams of pain, anguish, horror,' he writes. 'You suddenly realise the screams are yours.' He then receives a kicking and is tossed into a cell.

Similarly, a later inquiry into H Division recorded Raymond Chanter's experience:

When Chanter entered the reception area of H Division he was picked up by the neck by Prison Officer Ackland and shaken about. He was then punched in the face, throat and chest by Ackland. He was then punched on the upper body by Prison Officer Dickson. He was then repeatedly punched in the face and upper body by P.O. Chanter [no relation]. His feet slipped in his own blood from his nose, and a prison officer threatened that he would be charged with making a mess on the floor.

Mental, as well as physical, abuse was the stock-in-trade of the H Division guard. The verbal abuse was just as severe as the physical, and a program of dehumanisation, humiliation and debasement was the norm. From the outset, fear was the prisoner's constant companion. Everything was based on fear. Fear of the guards; fear of the punishments meted out for the slightest infringement; and fear of the unknown horrors awaiting the prisoner next day. All were designed to destroy the prisoner's will – to break him mentally and physically.

By the time the newcomer was given his H Division uniform, his worst fears seemed to have been realised – but this was only the beginning. The uniform consisted of a greyish-white-striped shirt, blue denim trousers with a thick white stripe down the sides, a thick woollen jacket, to be buttoned to the neck, thick grey woollen socks, heavy black shoes, and a floppy hat with a wide brim. He could hardly fail to see the vital-spot target circles painted on the front and back of his shirt, or the prominent one on his hat. These were to guide the prison guards' shots if an inmate attempted to escape.

The newcomer was now bullied into moving at the 'quick march' all around the cell block – including up the stairway and along the top tier – being roared at and swiped with batons as he went, saluting officers and trying to avoid their blows. The bellowing and verbal insults were non-stop, as were the baton blows from his tormentors.

Finally, the prisoner reached his cell on the top tier of the block. There he was ordered to remove his shoes, enter the cell, and stand at attention on the cross painted on the mat. Woe betide him if he didn't salute the officers who entered his cell or if he looked either of them in the face. Any minor infringement would be used as an excuse for an assault, and the newcomer would spend that night – and many more to come – recovering from his injuries.

LIVING BY THE RULES

As soon as he could, the newcomer would familiarise himself with the standing orders of the division, a copy of which was in every cell. Inmates were expected to know the rules by heart, though the newcomer would already have learnt some of them the hard way.

After familiarising himself with the 'standing orders', the sick and sorry inmate was probably unconscious by 'lights out' at 8:30 pm. However, a night's sleep in H Division was no certainty. O'Meally described nights there as 'terror-filled'. He wrote, 'You cannot sleep as the light is continually flicked on and off, and the steel door is kicked repeatedly. When morning comes you are in a state of shocked numbness.'

Bright and early next morning, the prisoner would be found assiduously cleaning his cell – ensuring there wasn't a speck of dust, that the toilet, washbowl and floor shone and that the blankets on his bed were folded as the regulations demanded. Breakfast was passed through the trap in the cell door at about 7 am. Then a little before 8 am, he'd stand to attention on the cross in his cell to await its inspection – being ever-fearful of the physical and verbal abuse to follow.

When the newcomer's turn arrived, the senior prison officer – together with another officer, the 'locker' – entered his cell for inspection. Conscious of not looking either of them in the face, the prisoner saluted and awaited the order to leave his cell, don his shoes and stand at attention on the cross outside, where he'd wait in fear that his cell hadn't passed inspection. On command, the prisoner again saluted the guards and stated his name as they left his cell. Then he'd be told of any breach of cell requirements.

These cell inspections were often sheer farce. If a cell wasn't absolutely immaculate – and often even though it was – it afforded the 'inspectors' an opportunity to assault its occupant or lay a charge for 'failing to obey a lawful order'. Any charge would be heard internally, and it would invariably result in an extension of the prisoner's confinement in the division. And it was a simple matter for the guards to enter a cell and disturb it – particularly by interfering with the blankets – thereby providing the 'evidence' for a charge.

According to Doug Robinson in *H: The Division from Hell*, one of the tricks the inspectors used to charge a prisoner was to enter a cell smoking and flick the butt into the toilet bowl. They could then charge the inmate with 'having disobeyed a lawful order', or being in possession of contraband, as smoking was strictly prohibited. In fact, both charges were likely to be laid.

After the cell inspection, it was time for the morning 'run-out', when inmates were escorted to work. On command – and at the 'quick march' – the prisoner would make his precarious way downstairs to the ground floor. There, amid bellowed orders and swipes from batons – still at the 'quick march' – he'd pass the 'hot box', salute the CPO whether present or not, and enter the end cell for a shave with an electric razor. (No blades were allowed in H Division.)

To constant roars from the guards, the newcomer then made his way to the small flight of steps that led to the division's notorious 'tunnel'. He saluted the guard at the entrance – known as the 'casual officer' – and received his command, then descended the steps, still at the 'quick march', negotiating the tunnel as best he could. William O'Meally remembered the fear the tunnel inspired: 'You feel yourself falling down the steps, feel the cruel blows smash into your body, feel you are going to die as the boots sink in'. Similarly, Gregory Roberts, who spent time in H Division, wrote of the tunnel in his novel *Shantaram*: 'Those guards had made us run their gauntlet down a long, narrow corridor, leading to the tiny exercise yards. And as we ran they'd swing their batons and kick us, all the way to the steel door at the end of the line.'

Only after the prisoner was in the tunnel would the next prisoner be taken from his cell to continue the 'run-out'. This system meant that no prisoner assigned to the labour yards would see another prisoner or witness any of the 'treatment' that had been so freely dished out to his predecessors.

Once he was through the 'tunnel', the newcomer knew which yard he was assigned to for the day by the officer – known as the 'overseer' – outside it. The prisoner would then stand at attention on the cross at the entrance to his yard and salute the overseer; if he forgot and looked the 'overseer' in the face, a blow from fist, boot or baton would be sure to follow. Once the prisoner had stated his name, the overseer would order the 'tower guard' above to release the mechanism that opened the door, and the prisoner then entered his yard.

Inside the yard, the prisoner again stopped, saluted the tower guard, stated his name and awaited the order to commence his work. In an enclosed space about twice the size of his cell, he picked up his instruments of torture – the heavy hammer and the lighter one – and commenced a morning's continual hammering of rock until lunch at approximately 11 am.

The prisoner's hard labour was just that – and it was non-stop. As William O'Meally recalled, 'Soon your arms are aching and your hands are blistered, but you must go on.' One of the first lessons the newcomer would learn was that if he decided to stop for a rest, he'd receive the full force of a jet of water from the fire hose above until he began hammering again. There was also an ever-present danger that the 'overseer' or the 'casual' would flog him for this breach of work requirements. The only break that was permitted was when he used his toilet bucket, which he had to do under the watchful eye of the tower guard.

The 'run-in' for lunch commenced at about 11 am, when the morning's 'run-out' procedures were reversed. Always at the 'quick march', the prisoner required great dexterity to salute, collect his plate and balance its contents as he negotiated the stairs to his cell – making sure he didn't drop any food, as a charge would certainly follow. Back in his cell, he had to eat lunch smartly, as the 'run-out' began again at 11.30.

Back in the labour yard, the prisoner smashed rock until 3 pm, when the 'run-in' was conducted again. This time, if he was quick enough, the prisoner could try to get some relief from the monotony of his sixteen hours lock-up by grabbing a book or magazine from the 'library' – a small bookshelf in the corridor that held a few books of little interest. No other recreation was afforded the labour-yard prisoner.

Having reached his cell – being roared at and belted all the way – and removed his shoes, the prisoner would invariably find the cell in total disorder. The task of the 'locker' of the day was to enter each cell and search it, tossing its contents everywhere. The prisoner had to stand at attention, salute his guards and undergo the ritual strip search for contraband before being allowed back into his cell for the evening meal, which was probably stone cold by now.

Shortly after he'd eaten, a muster was conducted. The senior prison officer and two others walked past each cell. As they approached, a guard opened the trap, and the prisoner had to state his name with his hand on the trap. By the time the muster was over, it was around 5 pm and time for another prison officer to take over the division.

The nights were long and lonely, with no radio, television, heating or cooling. The prisoner's only sustenance was to drink water from the tap in his cell. Whether he could sleep depended on the mercy of his guard and his own level of physical exhaustion. Even so, solitary confinement while it lasted was a blissful respite from the brutality of his guards.

This routine only varied at weekends, when the labour-yard prisoner had to thoroughly clean his yard of rock and dust. Each Saturday, more large bluestone rocks were delivered by a group of prisoners. At much the same time, they'd take away the crushed rock that the inmate passed through in buckets. He was supplied with a small brush and shovel to clean the yard, and like his cell, it had to be spotless.

After this task was completed, the prisoner spent the rest of his day walking the yard – eight or so strides one way and eight or so the other – all at the quick march. If he stopped, he was charged with disobeying a lawful order, hosed from above, or given a sustained hiding by his guards. Apart from an extension to his sentence, the most likely punishment for 'disobeying a lawful order' was a period spent in an observation cell, which was little more than a torture chamber. The prisoner had to strip down to his underpants before entering the observation cell, which was practically bare, with just a toilet on a wooden floor. There, in total isolation – and chained to the grille, or wearing a straitjacket – he awaited whatever his guards had planned for him.

One of the most distressing features of life in H Division was that prisoners constantly heard others being bashed or distressed by psychological abuse. All the former prisoners who have written accounts of the division relate the anguish they felt. O'Meally wrote, 'The guards took great delight in knocking down the inmates outside my cell door. The ensuing screams were horrifying.' He said the constant cries of anguish went close to sending him insane. Similarly, Edwin Eastwood emphasised his sense of helplessness at other prisoners' pain:

> One of the hardest things to deal with while in H Division was listening to the officers assaulting the younger prisoners. The screams of pain and the sounds of the violence, while locked in a cell or in a separate yard, will stay with me for the rest of my life. Unable to help, all we could do was to yell out, 'Leave him alone!' Eventually the screams ceased – when the prisoner became unconscious.

Many H Division inmates would contemplate suicide, and some managed to carry it through. There was regular self-mutilation, and some prisoners swallowed anything they could get down to try to escape the rigors of their captivity. The longer a prisoner stayed there, the more he became consumed by hate – an emotion that would become the most enduring of his coping skills.

FROM LABOUR YARDS TO INDUSTRY YARDS

By the mid-1960s, H Division had two 'industry yards' – the brush shop and the button shop – to employ its longer-serving prisoners. These 'veteran' inmates included O'Meally, who had served six years in the labour yards. Unlike the labour-yard prisoners, who were kept in isolation, those in the industry yards worked together at much lighter labours. They were also housed on the bottom tier of the cell block and could enjoy 'luxuries' such as radio headphones, access to a 'canteen' buy, the raising of their wages from 15 cents to 35 cents a day, and having the weekends off, mainly playing cards.

On the whole, the long-term H Division prisoners gained relief from the systematic beatings from the guards, but they were still subject to manipulation. There were conflicts, for example, over the prisoners' participation in was what was known as 'doing buttons' – assembling small electrical components in their cells of an evening. This wasn't a popular activity, as the inmates believed the prison officers were using it to make money on the side. Veteran inmates reported to a later inquiry that they were struck, denied canteen privileges and had their food rations cut if they refused to 'do buttons' or worked too slowly.

In conversation with his new friends, the industry yard prisoner would soon learn the 'official' nicknames given to the guards – though his own would probably be far worse. O'Meally reported that the Chief Prison Officer was known as 'The Black Prince' and his offsiders included 'The Beast', 'The Psycho', 'The Animal', 'The Bastard', 'The Marquis De Sade' and 'The Sadist'. Collectively, they were known as 'The Dirty Dozen'.

Apart from being permitted one letter per week, and a possible fortnightly visit, the H Division prisoner of this time had virtually no contact with the outside world. According to Doug Robinson, one letter a week meant just that. If a prisoner received more than one, a guard would shuffle them up, pick one out and throw the rest away.

Another unsettling factor to contend with was that H Division inmates were never sure when they'd be released from the division, as incarceration there was usually for an unspecified time. Those classified as incorrigible had to resign themselves to very lengthy stays. O'Meally, who had already spent a total of about two years in the rock-breaking yards before the escape that helped bring about the construction of H Division, served twelve consecutive years there, thus qualifying as one of the most punished prisoners in

Australian history. Peter Walker spent six years in H Division after his escape with Ronald Ryan at the beginning of 1966. This uncertainty, in combination with the guards' mind games, constituted a large part of the H Division prisoner's psychological punishment. Furthermore, once a prisoner had been sent to H Division, it was extremely difficult to get out. Even veterans of the division fell foul of its harsh disciplines and constantly changing 'standing orders', leading to charges that would inevitably extend their incarceration there.

REBELLION

For more than a decade after its inception in 1958, H Division's operations went unchallenged and unobserved. Few but its staff and inmates had any knowledge of what transpired there, and the code of silence among prisoners prevented criticism from leaking out.

In 1968, Chris Flannery was sent to the punishment section for assaulting another prisoner and insulting a prison officer while on remand. At reception, he was given a verbal and physical thrashing, and he subsequently received several other brutal beatings from prison guards in H Division. A couple of years later, news of this reached the ears of his half-brother Edward, a lawyer, who began to mobilise support from outside pressure groups, including the Council for Civil Liberties.

There was also trouble building inside the prison. In 1970, two significant events created much unrest among B Division prisoners in particular. In May 1970, after more than twelve years in the punishment section, William O'Meally was re-classified to B Division, where the effects of the treatment he'd received became palpably obvious. Then, in October of that year, Archie Butterly, a B Division prisoner who'd been sent to the punishment section, was so severely bashed that Prison Governor Grindlay reported the incident to police.

Butterly was hastily transferred back to B Division, but the incident caused much unrest among his fellow inmates, several of whom were in turn sent to the punishment section. The already tense B Division – the hard core of the prison, whose inmates constantly lived under the threat of a term in H Division – began to simmer. Butterly himself sought damages against three H Division officers, though he later dropped the action.

Criticism of H Division began to appear in the press. A B Division prisoner who didn't want to be named told the *Age* newspaper that he'd been hit over the head with a fire extinguisher in H Division, and on another occasion had lost teeth when he was punched by one of its guards. He also told the newspaper he'd been sent to an observation cell, stripped naked and placed in a straitjacket. He was so helpless that when his dinner was shoved along the floor to him, he had to lie on the floor and put his mouth against the plate in order to eat. In a comment that reflected the attitude of many H Division inmates, he said, 'The only thing that kept me sane was the thought of the gruesome revenge I would have one day.'

The situation in the prison reached crisis point in the summer of 1971–72. Some prisoners in H Division defied the order to break rocks, and revolt was suddenly in the air. Chris Flannery deliberately had himself sent back to H Division, aiming to break the system by challenging the other prisoners there to 'jack up' on their guards, refuse to break rocks, and generally reject mistreatment. He'd organised backup from some other prisoners but didn't receive it until a week later. Meanwhile, he went on a hunger strike.

There was a serious outbreak of prisoner unrest. On 13 January 1972, Flannery's mate Laurie Prendergast deliberately organised a fight between himself, Dennis Kane and three other prisoners so that they'd be sent to the punishment section. There they engaged in various acts of rebellion and incited others to join them.

Kane was heard to yell, 'This is 1972 – we don't have to break rocks any more.' He reminded the other inmates, 'There is no I Division – so this is the end of the line. If we stick together, they can't do a thing to us. If they like, we'll help pull it down for them.'

After so many years when the deeds of the guards had gone unopposed, these young, rebellious and spirited prisoners were audaciously challenging the legitimacy of H Division's operations. Suddenly, its iron hold was loosened and many other prisoners began to indulge in a campaign of disobedience.

That night, Governor Grindlay visited H Division and heard a loud commotion coming from the cells. When he entered, most of the tumult died away, but the rebels on the top tier kept going. He climbed the stairs and warned them to quieten down. But the din continued, and some of the rebels were charged with making unnecessary noise.

The rebels gained support from mainstream prisoners. Flannery urged fellow inmates to break the prisoners' code of silence and dob in the guards for subjecting them to ill-treatment. These acts of rebellion from within the prison were assisted by outside pressure groups. A public campaign to 'Ban the Bash' put considerable pressure on the State government. In what could have been construed as a retaliatory threat, the Minister for Social Welfare, Mr Smith, told State Parliament that the government was considering extending H Division. Later, the government declared it intended to tighten security there. Mr Smith declared, 'I do not believe allegations of brutality by warders. I have been very strict on brutality in H Division. I can't accept that it exists because I have no proof of it.'

Meanwhile, inmates of other divisions at Pentridge were

supporting the defiance within H Division. The prison was now in turmoil, and the 'Ban the Bash' campaign was gaining momentum.

As a consequence of the rebellion, prisoners in H Division reported that unlawful violence against them was somewhat curtailed. Then Governor Grindlay made some major concessions to H Division inmates as a peace offering. The concessions included the abolition of shoulder-length arm swinging, the wearing of hats, 'doing buttons' in the cells, and saluting prison officers. In addition, H Division prisoners wouldn't have to seek permission to write one letter per week; they were also granted a five-day working week, with two clean shirts a week and daily showers. Medical treatment and tablets would be administered by a hospital attendant when required, and the governor would attend one 'run-in' or 'run-out' per day.

The prison officers responded by holding stop-work meetings at which they branded Governor Grindlay 'weak'. But the public campaign was now out of the prison officers' hands. When it became known that prison officers had mounted a baton charge against several inmates of D Division, the Chief Secretary, Rupert Hamer, decided to act.

THE JENKINSON INQUIRY

On 15 May 1972, the State Government announced that it would appoint a 'Board of Inquiry into Allegations of Brutality and Ill-Treatment of Prisoners at H.M. Prison Pentridge' in order to restore peace and general order to the prison.

The inquiry was conducted at the County Court between June and December 1972 by a prominent barrister, Kenneth Jenkinson QC. The terms of reference of the Jenkinson Inquiry, as it was known, were deliberately restrictive. It could only inquire into events from 22 May 1970 to 22 May 1972. Its terms of reference included some general matters pertaining to prison disciplines and procedures, but its main focus was on weighing up individual prisoner complaints of ill-treatment.

Nevertheless, in spite of these limitations, there was cautious approval of Jenkinson's inquiry into H Division. The punishment section was at last being brought under some sort of public scrutiny, and many hoped that its veil of secrecy would be disturbed.

The inquiry heard evidence from both prisoners and prison authorities, but its terms of reference virtually restricted the complaints it could hear to those by prisoners currently housed in the division or recently released. It was a very brave inmate who would lay a complaint against the officers of the prison where he was currently incarcerated, knowing he would face reprisals from those against whom he'd complained. If this was a deliberate ploy to reduce the number and detail of these complaints, it was successful to a degree. The focus on individual complaints over a restricted time also prohibited any wider appreciation of the conduct of the division since its beginnings.

Yet, for all these limitations, 82 prisoners laid written complaints of unlawful assault by prison officers during the period of the terms of reference, and 40 gave evidence in person. Their complaints alleged multiple unprovoked assaults, as well as systematic verbal and physical abuse.

But the prison officers employed in H Division claimed to have seen nothing of this. To a man, they swore on oath that they'd never, ever participated in unlawful violence or seen any other prison officer do so. Some conceded that 'on occasion' it was necessary to use 'lawful force' with rebellious prisoners. One officer went as far as to say, 'Only a clout behind the backside will get the desired result.' A senior prison officer described the prisoner evidence as 'a pack of lies'.

The lines of division became obvious at the commencement of the inquiry, when representatives spoke on behalf of prison officers and prisoners. Mr Lennon, appearing for prison officers, described the prisoners' evidence as 'the result of a criminal conspiracy on the part of some prospective witnesses to perjure themselves at this inquiry'. Mr David Ross of the Council for Civil Liberties thought otherwise. He described the deputy governor of Pentridge, Mr Vodden, as 'the managing director of brutality in H Division' who had 'directed a system of violence'. He went on to describe H Division as 'a concentration camp of the most vicious type, staffed by savage, brutal, and sadistic prison officers, some of whom were giants specially selected for that purpose'.

But Prison Governor Ian Grindlay told the inquiry that officers in H Division were simply the best available. Under oath, he said, 'I have never seen any signs of brutality at H Division, never at any time. I have heard from prisoners and from other people that any provocation was greeted with perhaps a slap to the tail with a baton, perhaps a back-hander or an open hand, and to my mind this is what went on in H Division over the years.'

After several months of evidence, the inquiry closed in December 1972, and Jenkinson presented his findings to State Parliament in 1973. One of his first observations on H Division contained a classic understatement: 'H Division is generally regarded by prisoners as the least desirable place of confinement'. He described the division as prison authorities would have done: its physical layout, the class of prisoner housed there, its organisation and procedures, and its military disciplines. But he then posed the problem: many prisoners have asserted that this description 'has omitted reference to a carnival of violence by prison officers' that was 'systematic, gratuitous and unlawful'. These allegations in turn were denied on oath by prison officers, most of whom asserted that force was rarely used against H Division prisoners. Jenkinson said he believed this was correct.

To explain the division's 'H for Hell' reputation, Jenkinson offered the prison officers' version of the 'myth':

> On release from H Division, [prisoners] magnified their own hardiness – and their reputations – by telling tall tales about the rigours of H Division, and the brutality of its more celebrated warders, and by boasting of their capacity to withstand the physical punishment they falsely claimed to have suffered. Thus grew and flourished among prisoners the myth that gross violence was perpetrated upon prisoners in H Division. In that way, prison officers reconciled, in evidence before the Board, the existence of the myth and its falsity. Because the myth conduced to good order and discipline, no proclamation of its falsity was essayed in Pentridge. The more timid prisoners resolved to keep out of H Division by behaving themselves. Those who were relegated there for the first time entered the Division in a state of mind which facilitated their acceptance of its discipline. The whole system worked on bluff.

Jenkinson demanded a high standard of proof before accepting prisoners' evidence against prison officers. He wouldn't accept allegations without independent evidence. But this was always going to present difficulties, as much of the alleged violence occurred when prisoners were alone with the guards in the reception area, during the 'run-out' and 'run-in' procedures and in the labour yards. He also checked every allegation against official records to ensure the accused officer was on duty at the time of the alleged assault. This stipulation required the complainant to have a remarkable memory for dates, as there were no clues to be found in the Governor's

Request Book, which didn't refer to any prisoner complaints of ill-treatment from 22 May 1970 until 23 December 1971.

Even where there was supporting evidence, Jenkinson compared different prisoners' statements to ensure they hadn't put their heads together. He believed that the rebels 'exerted great influence' and may have induced other prisoners to claim ill treatment by prison officers. He was sceptical of prisoners' truthfulness:

> Many of the prisoners who volunteered complaints of such ill treatment seemed ... unlikely to let regard for the truth embarrass them in their adherence to so attractive a cause as the public discrediting of H Division prison officers.

In dismissing one complaint, Jenkinson said that although the prisoner was 'a persuasive witness', his evidence against a prison officer couldn't be relied on because of 'his long dedication to crime, and his family connection with a prisoner who was prominent in the rebellion against H Division discipline'.

He took into account each prisoner's criminal, psychological and prison record. 'Hard-core' prisoners stood little chance of having their evidence accepted. In one case, an H Division inmate of long standing, Stanley Taylor, alleged that on 28 April 1971 he heard prisoner Terrence Vallance crying in his cell. When Taylor called out to him, Vallance explained that a prison officer had tipped his toilet bucket over his head in the labour yard and had refused to let him wash himself. Vallance was found hanged in his cell the following morning.

In dismissing Taylor's claims, Jenkinson said he'd found no supportive evidence from other prisoners or the prison officer on night watch, who would have taken preventative action to ensure Vallance didn't suicide. Also, letters Vallance had written that night indicated that he'd intended to suicide before his transfer to H Division. Jenkinson added, 'If the prisoner had been befouled by excrement, the Board is convinced that he'd have been showered and reclothed before the division closed for the night, for the standard of cleanliness is high in H Division.'

In spite of his scepticism, Jenkinson named five individual prisoners – Raymond Chanter, Michael Godfrey, Colin O'Toole, Garry Mayne and Peter Robertson – who had convinced him of the truth of their evidence. He explained he'd been deterred from accepting several witnesses' evidence out of concern that there may have been a conspiracy. One of his reasons for accepting the evidence of these five men was their 'disassociation from such a conspiracy'.

Jenkinson found that each of these prisoners had been repeatedly struck by prison officers in various areas of H Division. Godfrey had witnessed Chanter's beating and was also struck himself. Seventeen-year-old O'Toole was struck several times in reception and on his way to his cell, and again on many of the succeeding days. After a prison officer threatened him and knocked him out in a labour yard, O'Toole had slashed his wrists in his cell with a broken cup.

Mayne's evidence echoed that of many other prisoners:

He was struck about the body by two prison officers in the reception area during the strip-search while an officer sat in the glass office near by. He marched around the cell block naked, being struck on the back and legs with fist and baton; and ... on the following morning he was repeatedly punched about the body for failing to observe the rules applicable to the morning run-out procedure.

Mayne was also the target of mind games by Ackland, who would sometimes be friendly and cheerful, then turn unpredictably violent for no reason. Jenkinson described Mayne as a 'convincing' witness. He was also persuaded that Robertson was telling the truth when he gave evidence that he'd been struck without cause. Jenkinson found:

> that Robertson was repeatedly struck by a number of prison officers in H Division during the first ten days of his confinement there; that PO Chanter was one of these officers; that Robertson was struck with open hand, closed fist and baton and he was kicked; that he urinated blood and his nose bled in consequence of blows struck by Chanter; that none of the violence done to him was justified and all of it constituted ill-treatment of him.

In summary, Jenkinson found that there was a 'distinctive pattern of unconcealed, frequent and unlawful violence by prison officers against quite passive and inoffensive prisoners', which had occurred in the corridor, the reception area and the main cell block. Virtually no complaints were received from prisoners in company, in the industry or exercise yards. Nor was this violence confined to the five 'proven' cases. Jenkinson found that ill-treatment of prisoners in H Division was frequent during 1970 and 1971, and that 'there was a convincing and consistent picture of this ill-treatment', which was intended 'to terrify and, by fear, to inculcate a determination not to return to the Division'.

Yet Jenkinson referred to the violence as 'moderate' rather than 'gross'. He didn't spell out his definitions or illuminate the differences. Considering that the proven cases involved prisoners being driven to attempt suicide, urinating blood and slipping in their own blood, it is difficult to imagine how much worse 'gross violence' could have been.

Jenkinson also noted an unusual pattern of activity in H Division after Archie Butterly was bashed in October 1970.

He observed that for the rest of that month and through November, 'hardly a day passed without a visit to H Division by an officer of the rank of Governor, usually at the time of a run-out or run-in of prisoners'. Jenkinson believed that these visits were intended to convey, 'plainly but not offensively, a warning by the Governor to the H Division officers that he disapproved of unnecessary violence to prisoners'. The point was that, having referred Butterly's complaint to the police, Grindlay couldn't investigate it further himself, but could only hope to deflect similar complaints. One is left to wonder how Grindlay was able to claim in sworn evidence to the inquiry that he had 'never ever seen any signs of brutality at H Division, never at any time'.

Jenkinson didn't consider Butterly's complaint, which was then the subject of a civil action, but this still left Grindlay's official denial threadbare. While praising many of Grindlay's qualities, Jenkinson said he 'was greatly mistaken in his belief that nothing worse than "a back-hander, or an open hand ... a clip and a smack on the tail with a baton" occurred in the Division'.

The prison officers Jenkinson named as being directly involved in prisoner ill-treatment or having witnessed it without reporting it were CPO Carrolan, SPOs Lindgren and Gardiner, and POs Ackland, Chanter and Dickson. He observed that there may have been others: 'Prison officers not named may have committed more acts of ill-treatment than those named'. But he emphasised that it would be 'quite erroneous' to believe 'that prisoners in H Division were subjected to unremitting brutality by prison officers, and were kept in constant fear of violence for no reason except the gratification which may be derived from the infliction of pain'.

Jenkinson concluded that the aim of the prisoners' rebellion wasn't to 'stop the bash' but to achieve, 'if not the abolition of the Division, at least a very great relaxation of the lawfully prescribed procedures of the Division so that life there would be as little different from life elsewhere in Pentridge as possible'. Although he was critical of the rebels, he did give them some credit when he concluded:

> The rebellion has so far achieved little for those who led it. But they may find consolation in the knowledge that their efforts have saved, and, it is hoped, will save their fellow prisoners from the painful and terrifying experiences which Chanter, Godfrey, O'Toole, Mayne, Robertson and many others suffered in H Division.

One extraordinary omission in Jenkinson's report was that it didn't recommend that rock-breaking be abolished as a barbaric and useless punishment. But at least the prison authorities could no longer credibly claim ignorance of the brutality surrounding H Division.

LIFE AFTER JENKINSON

When the Jenkinson Inquiry's report was released, most prisoners in Pentridge were dissatisfied with its findings, which they claimed didn't reveal the true brutality of H Division. Many declared the inquiry a whitewash and argued that only a Royal Commission could uncover the extent of maltreatment there.

One of the inquiry's most strident critics was Ray Mooney, who had been a prisoner in Pentridge and later became a playwright and author. After Mooney was released from Pentridge, he wrote a play depicting the physical and psychological brutality of H Division. Entitled *Everynight ... Everynight* and later made into a film, the play focused on the experiences of a character named Dale, whose treatment mirrored that dished out to Christopher Dale Flannery.

On reception to the division, Dale is set upon by the guards, who bash him repeatedly with fists, boots and batons before leaving him semi-conscious in his cell. After further relentless bashings, he refuses to observe the division's rules and regulations. He incites other inmates to report the guards' ill-treatment, thus breaking the code of silence and becoming a 'dog'.

Mooney himself had been sentenced to time in H Division for representing the interests of A Division prisoners during a riot. Of his stay in the division, he said, 'I could see, ultimately, that if I was going to survive H Division and get through it without ending up a raving ratbag, or ending up a dead-set crim, that I would have to find a way of getting them back for what they had done. Because that's the way it is inside. It's part of the culture.'

When it was first performed, *Everynight ... Everynight* was greeted with much scepticism, and Mooney was accused of giving a misleading account of H Division's operations. He retorted that if the prison officers had written the play, 'the brutality would not have existed. It would have been a figment of the imaginations of the prisoners, which is exactly what [the guards] said when they went to the Jenkinson Inquiry. Now, I lived through it, so I don't see any value in writing a play which pretends that it was anything other than what it was.' The play had a surprisingly positive effect on life in H Division. Though rock-breaking was supposed to have ceased in 1976, it was actually still going on two years later. The Minister for Social Welfare discovered this during a performance of *Everynight* and ordered it to stop forthwith. So, as a direct result of Mooney's work, rock-breaking was finally abolished.

Other improvements in H Division could be directly traced to Jenkinson's recommendations. Prisoners classified to the punishment section were now given official reasons for the decision and could challenge it if they believed they had a strong case. The authorities also implemented Jenkinson's recommendation that disciplinary charges against prisoners be heard in open court, with the prisoner entitled to legal representation. This substantially weakened the iron grip the guards had once exercised over the prisoners' fate.

In general, with some of the more 'celebrated' guards no longer employed in H Division, life there became a little more relaxed. In his book *Focus on Faraday and Beyond*, Edwin Eastwood wrote that the assaults in the tunnel 'had abated somewhat as a direct result of the Jenkinson Inquiry'. However, he also reported that the reception 'biff' survived, as had the use of strict military discipline and prisoner manipulation. H Division still had many of the qualities that led William O'Meally to describe it as 'the lowest hell earth had to offer'.

In 1978, a New South Wales Royal Commission strongly criticised the running of H Division's interstate counterparts – the maximum-security section of Grafton Gaol and the Katingal Special Security Unit in Long Bay Gaol, which the Royal Commission slated for closure. The 'disciplines' in Grafton were eerily familiar – the 'reception biff', the violent strip-search, the quick march, even the method of making one's bed. All these practices had prevailed in Grafton for fifteen years before H Division was even established.

As had happened in Victoria, the prison authorities argued that exaggerated stories of bashings were merely part of a useful myth about Grafton that kept other prisoners in line. But the head of the Royal Commission, Justice Nagle, would have none of it. He expressed astonishment that the penal authorities were 'unwilling or unable to discover' what was patently obvious: that their staff had employed practices 'utterly opposed to normal standards of decent human conduct'. He ridiculed the authorities' claim that prison officers in Grafton had to be 'robust and tactful' to perform the 'arduous duties' required of them. According to Nagle:

> The arduous duties required of these officers largely consisted of inflicting brutal, savage and sometimes sadistic physical violence on the hapless group of intractables that were sent to Grafton.

Nagle described what had occurred at Grafton as 'one of the most sordid and shameful episodes in New South Wales penal history' – a description equally applicable to its Victorian counterpart.

When news of this report broke, H Division was already on edge, with a spate of complaints about inmates being placed in solitary confinement and arbitrarily deprived of privileges. On the weekend of 15–16 April 1978, there was an outbreak of violence in H Division, with prisoners breaking up their metal beds and using the pieces to damage the doors of their cells. But in spite of this renewed unrest, there would be no Royal Commission into Victorian prisons. Instead, the Director-General of Social Welfare asked the State Ombudsman, John Dillon, to investigate the 'trouble' in H Division. Dillon visited Pentridge and interviewed prisoners immediately after the riot, and produced a report by 20 April. In his report, Dillon said he'd always believed that H Division was 'essential for the proper administration of the prison system in the State'. He accepted the prison authorities' assurances that incarceration there was intended to provide security, not punishment, and said that he didn't believe that conditions were 'harsh, unjust or inhumane'.

But it was becoming obvious that the notorious 'H for Hell' Division was past its heyday. Security there was increasingly lax. There were accounts of knife-fights between prisoners and the formation of prisoner gangs. Prisoners were seen 'bombed out of their minds', and hypodermic syringes and needles were found. Seven prisoners held in the division had sliced off all or part of their ears. When the school kidnapper Edwin Eastwood was caught sawing through the bars of his cell, he was found to be in possession of a small pair of bolt cutters, a grappling iron and a keyhole saw. There was even an escape, when three prisoners got out through the roof and made their way onto the roof of A Division.

One source of dissension in 1978 had been the government's delay in building a promised new security wing that would provide prisoners with far more modern accommodation than the 114-year-old cell blocks of H Division. This new wing, called Jika Jika, finally opened in 1980. It replaced the disciplinary system of H Division, which set out to achieve prisoner control through brutality and fear, with a regime of isolation and surveillance. In Jika Jika, prisoners and prison officers were separated, and prisoners were constantly monitored by video cameras. Doors, heating and lighting were all controlled electronically by the guards.

Meanwhile, H Division continued to operate. The discipline there was more relaxed, but violence was still used at reception to gain prisoner control. Father Peter Norden, who was prison chaplain during the 1980s, wrote in an article for *Right Now*, an online human rights site:

The reception biff was the regular practice for any inmates received into H Division. The heavy metal door to the Division was closed, the newly arrived inmate was told to strip off all his clothes and he was surrounded by several burly prison guards who proceeded to belt him with batons, fists and even boots until he fell to the floor and stopped any resistance to their brutal assault. There were no witnesses, and it remained an accepted practice until the prison closed in 1996.

Norden visited H Division each Wednesday morning, when he'd see the battered faces of the prisoners who'd recently been 'welcomed' to the division and hear the usual excuses from the guards – that the prisoner had fallen over, or had attempted to attack a prison officer. H Division, Norden said, was 'a world within a world, and the staff were the hard men of the prison service'.

While Jika Jika was operating, H Division was increasingly used to house prisoners who needed protection from other inmates. But the Jika Jika experiment only lasted until 1987. The unit was closed after a fire lit in protest claimed the lives of five prisoners.

After the closure of Jika Jika, the hard cases were returned to H Division, but the old controls and military disciplines were gone. In fact, violence perpetrated in H Division now was more likely to be prisoner-on-prisoner, sometimes as part of a long-running vendetta. In July 1988, for example, H Division prisoner Craig Minogue murdered fellow inmate Alex Tsakmakis in an industry yard by hitting him over the head with a pillowcase containing six kilograms of gym weights. Some years before, Tsakmakis had murdered an H Division 'graduate', Barry Quinn, in Jika Jika. Tsakmakis threw industrial glue over Quinn and then flicked lit matches at him until one ignited the glue. As Quinn was burning, Tsakmakis reportedly sang, 'Come on baby, light my fire.' After Quinn died in hospital from massive burns, a death notice was placed in Melbourne newspapers: 'Barry we always stuck together – Alex.' Tsakmakis had received an additional ten years imprisonment for this murder. Few in Pentridge mourned his passing when his turn came.

* * *

It is difficult to comprehend why prison authorities couldn't see, or chose to ignore, that by taking the non-conformists of the prison system and housing them in places like H Division, they were creating a greater problem when embittered, resentful and dangerous prisoners were eventually released into the community as 'loose cannons'.

The H Division 'graduates' who became conspicuously violent criminals included Chris Flannery, who hadn't previously displayed homicidal tendencies but on release became a contract killer, reputed to have murdered up to a dozen people. Another was Stanley Taylor, also previously non-homicidal, who was convicted for masterminding the 1986 car-bomb attack on Russell Street Police Headquarters, where Constable Angela Taylor died and more than twenty others were injured. This is to name but a couple of the many whose later violent activities shocked the community.

While the secrecy surrounding H Division created some doubt as to the extent of the violence, there is no doubt that prisoners there were subjected to nineteenth-century punishments at best. The mental torture of total isolation and sensory deprivation, combined with the physical and psychological punishment of breaking rocks in the labour yards showed no advance in the treatment of 'intractables' since the 1850s. Their management was totally counterproductive to the better interests of the community.

William O'Meally was flogged and spent twelve years confined in H Division. Would the reputedly cruel Samuel Barrow or the tyrannical John Price have overseen the punishment countenanced by their supposedly more humanitarian counterparts a hundred years later? In truth, no person who oversaw the operations of H Division was a humanitarian. Its guards thoroughly terrorised a generation of victims, who never knew when, where or how they'd be attacked. As Greg Roberts wrote, 'No beatings I'd ever suffered were as savage as those inflicted by the uniformed men who were paid to keep the peace, the prison guards.' These cowards were never brought to account – not one of them. Several were named in the Jenkinson report, but the authorities didn't see fit to lay charges against them, even though they'd compounded their crimes by failing to be truthful at the inquiry.

In the dreadful dungeons that formed this house of horrors, they'd painted their crosses, gathered their tools of torture, committed heinous crimes against defenceless men – and escaped scot-free. These monsters, and those who gave them a licence to commit their crimes unwitnessed, unaccounted for and unpunished, could well be called the 'real criminals of Pentridge'.

CHAPTER 4
AN EDUCATION OFFICER

It seemed everybody in Pentridge was some sort of officer, apart from the clergy and the prisoners. There were prison officers, senior prison officers and chief prison officers, as well as governors and deputy governors of various grades. Even the teachers were known as education officers. In early 1970, I became an education officer at Pentridge.

My first impression was that an education officer wasn't exactly welcomed – far from it. In fact, the prison officers exuded an air of aggression, mistrust and hostility. I soon discovered that there had recently been a confrontation. My colleagues in the A Division education office informed me that the previous chief education officer, a man of many years experience in Pentridge, had been dismissed for 'trafficking' – being found in possession of contraband. This was a rule never to broken around the prison.

One of the A Division writers, a young prisoner named Norm who was dressed in the white overalls that designated a 'trusty', jumped in and declared that the sacking was a setup. The former chief education officer would never have engaged in trafficking. He was too experienced in prison ways. At the same time, Norm warned us that some people around the jail might try to plant contraband on us and report it to security; then, before you realised what was happening, you'd be found in possession of items you'd never seen before. I decided there and then that I'd never attempt to leave the prison without first checking the contents of my bag.

I discovered that there were often rumours around the prison that a particular chaplain or education officer was involved in trafficking. Being aware of that – together with the ever-present fear of a 'plant' – kept you on guard at all times, regularly checking your bag and personal belongings.

'Security' was a special group of prison officers who could search you at any time for possession of contraband. Of course, the ones most concerned about security were the inmates, who regularly had their cells raided – a process referred to throughout the prison as a 'ramp'. Oddly, though I was issued with a prison pass later in the day, I was never asked to produce it, nor was I ever personally searched when entering or leaving the prison grounds.

I was assigned to work in B Division's chapel, which was used as the division's daily classroom. I soon made the acquaintance of the prison chaplain, Father John Brosnan. Knowing he was a font of knowledge on all things Pentridge, I decided to ask him about my impression of hostility from the prison officers.

The priest smiled and said he was surprised I'd noticed so quickly. He explained, 'Their attitude is: "Why should these men get a free education for doing the wrong thing and being in prison? I can't get one – why should they?" I've always experienced the same attitude towards me,' Father Brosnan added. 'Most, if not all, of the screws regard me as a "crim's man", because I talk to them and associate with them all the time. It won't take you long to became a crim's man too,' he said, laughing. I'd gain many insights into prison life from John Brosnan and learn many survival skills.

A notable exception among the generally unfriendly prison officers was 'Scotty' Patterson, the guard on regular duty at the gate to the prison officers' mess. A jovial Scotsman, Scotty was a great talker, and it was a work of art to get past him. He had been a key prosecution witness in the trial of Ronald Ryan and Peter Walker, having fired a shot during their attempted escape. He was always a bright and cheerful conversation source – if you could understand his accent. Actually, most of the prison officers seemed to have recently arrived from Britain.

It didn't pay to be running late around the prison, because tower guards often engaged in petty displays of power. When you arrived at an internal gate, if the guard who controlled the gate was so minded – and most of them were – he'd go for a stroll along his walkway and make out that he hadn't seen you below. You'd stand there waiting while the guard looked in the opposite direction. Usually, the only way to proceed was to shake the gate violently until the 'unobservant' guard condescended to release it. This didn't help the relations between civilians and prison officers. To be fair, though, the prison officers had to deal with some violent, cunning, disturbed and evil inmates, who often verbally abused them.

At any gathering in the officers' mess, the civilian staff sat at one table and prison officers at the others. Prisoners prepared the meals, which always seemed of good quality, but the young A Division writer cautioned me not to dine there, claiming that the cooks added extra ingredients. 'Ya know what they do there, don't ya?' he said. 'The cooks spit in the food, piss in the gravy and get all the cockroaches and stuff, grind 'em up and put 'em over the top – and youse eat it.' I think that was about when I stopped going to the mess.

It wasn't easy to adapt to Pentridge's archaic conditions. This was a nineteenth-century penal establishment in full working order. Entering its precincts was like going back in time. This grim, soul-destroying institution was the ultimate in prisoner deprivation. Most of its buildings weren't fit for human habitation – particularly C Division, where the smell was sometimes overpowering. Actually, all the prison buildings had a strong musty smell that lingered long after you left the gates. When I talked to the more approachable prison officers, they reported that they could never wash that smell from their uniforms.

SCHOOL IN THE CHAPEL

Pentridge was full of tension, heartbreak and human tragedy – nowhere more so than in B Division, where the atmosphere was always tense. The regimentation and long lock-up time were constant sources of conflict, and B Division prisoners knew they were just one false step away from the dreaded H Division. The fear of being sent to the punishment section was always in the back of the inmates' minds.

In the chapel up on the second tier of the cell block, about ten volunteer prisoners would shuffle in each morning and sit in the pews used for religious services on Sundays. There were no desks to write on; the prisoners could only take notes by balancing the paper on their knees, or by combining forces to turn the pew in front of them around and form a makeshift writing bench.

At the end of the room was a table on a raised dais, where I sat to supervise and assist the inmates. It was an awkward arrangement. To approach me for help with their written work, the prisoners had to walk over, step onto the dais and hand the material over.

I soon realised that I wasn't only expected to assist them with their studies, but also to become their counsellor and confidant. It was quite surprising the matters they'd want to discuss. Many of the prisoners in B Division had nobody to relate to other than their fellow inmates, and they were eager to talk to someone from outside the prison walls. They'd raise personal topics such as their marital relationships, which were mostly in a state of conflict because of the length of their sentences. Then there were those who wanted to 'try you on' – to find out if you would do them a favour by taking out a letter or, most commonly, providing a cigarette. Father Brosnan had advised me to give a firm knockback to the first request of this kind so as to spread the word that I wasn't a soft touch. This was another survival skill I learnt from John Brosnan.

The facilities for education at Pentridge were quite limited. It wasn't until the mid-1970s that portable classrooms were placed near A Division, and also on the old site of C Division in the Square, at last making it possible to offer better prisoner education in more appropriate situations.

When I worked at Pentridge, most of the prisoners were doing correspondence courses, usually through the Royal Melbourne Institute of Technology. The most popular course in B Division was a boiler attendant's certificate. It was a rare prisoner in that division who tackled anything more demanding. Inmates of A Division were more likely to study for matriculation, or even enter higher education. Ray Mooney managed to complete university studies from A Division. While he was at Pentridge, he became the first Australian prisoner to start and finish a university degree from prison – a bachelor's degree in social science. This was a great achievement at the best of times, but even more so given that he'd been in Pentridge through a period of unrest that was a constant source of distractions.

In B Division, though, I had the feeling that the prisoners were just going through the motions. I was always walking a tightrope, because I knew that if I tried to make any great demands of the prisoners, they would simply leave.

Also, correspondence courses were of no use unless prisoners were already literate, yet quite a few prisoners could barely read or write. Illiterate prisoners got around this problem by seeking out others to write their letters and written requests for them, but there weren't enough specialist teachers to tackle the root cause of the problem. As a result, those who would have most benefited from the educational classes didn't take part.

In fact, there were disincentives to attending the educational classes. Those who opted for classes earned less than prisoners in the work gangs. They were usually also denied remission on their sentences. The overseers on the work gangs usually recommended that prisoners' sentences be remitted by three days for each month served, but there was no comparable remission for study. We fought to have this discrimination rectified, but without success. As a result, prisoners were discouraged from studies that would have helped them find work after they were released.

Many inmates had quite amazing talents, which they displayed in their art and craft work. It was quite astonishing what they could create with such materials as matchsticks, wood and leather. It wasn't unusual for a prisoner to invite me into his cell to view some of his leisure-time handiwork. In this way, some of the prisoners tried to make their cells a little more homely. Most, however, remained bare – drab and lifeless places of confinement for many hours of the day.

Part of my job as education officer was to run weekly film nights for the A Division prisoners. One evening, my wife accompanied me to a showing. As I was packing the projector away afterwards, an inmate – himself doing time for murder – leaned across and said quietly to her, 'What's it feel like to be in a room full of murderers?' He seemed disappointed when he didn't get a reaction.

For B Division prisoners, there were no film nights and little else in the way of entertainment. Occasionally, a big-name entertainer would perform in the chapel. One of the Melbourne newspapers ran a photo showing the audience at a concert by Johnny O'Keefe, with Bill O'Meally raising his arms in joy. Mostly, though, the prisoners were interested in betting, particularly on the horses. I kept up to date with the racing, as it was always a good talking point. A prisoner would sidle up to me and ask, 'Who are you backing in the third at Flemington on Saturday?' or give me a tip about something he had on good authority from 'outside'.

You rarely heard laughter in B Division, but one morning I was involved in an incident that caused much amusement among the inmates. I was leaving the chapel after the morning class, walking along the top tier of the cell block, when a commotion broke out somewhere below. I soon realised that the sounds were catcalls coming from several of the cells.

As I continued along the walkway, I noticed a prisoner heading towards me, shaped – and walking – more like a woman than a man. The catcalls stopped as she wiggled by me, but then a low, blood-curdling wolf whistle echoed through the division. To my horror, I realised that she was whistling at me!

As I reached the top step of the staircase, a voice resonated throughout the building, 'She fancies the schoolteacher!' This caused an uproar. I'm not sure how I managed to descend the stairs to the 'circle' below, but I got out of the division in record time.

The following morning, as I was on my way to the chapel, the familiar voice of the B Division writer came from the office, 'Hey, Mr Osborne. That sheila that went through yesterday – I can give you her cell number if you want it.' The offer was followed by raucous laughter. Transvestism and homosexuality were simply part of prison life.

PRISON CONVERSATIONS

The prisoners generally were quite easy to get along with, provided you heeded some basic rules of encounter. One of the first of these I learnt was never to gawk at a prisoner, as they were extremely sensitive about anyone who they felt was staring at them. I'd warn people of this whenever I took visitors into the prison. But there was always a temptation to go and have a 'gawk' at the more notorious prisoners. One in particular that I went out of my way to see was the killer paedophile Derek Percy. Percy had been found not guilty of murdering a schoolgirl on the grounds of insanity, and was consequently serving time at the Governor's pleasure in G Division, the psychiatric hospital section. I knew that he'd been made the writer of G Division, so there was no problem in locating him there. Percy was quite young, about 23, and he had two unforgettable features – his eyes, which were like those of a dead fish, and an unusually gruff and guttural voice. I asked him if I was in F Division, well knowing I wasn't, and received the reply, 'No, this is G.' His eyes looked straight through me as though I wasn't there. As I left, I was certain that I had just looked into the face of pure evil.

I never asked a prisoner what he was 'in' for, and conversely prisoners rarely volunteered information about their crimes. Though prisoner files were always available for perusal, after some experience I decided it was easier to maintain open personal contact if I didn't know the details of a prisoner's past.

Appearances were deceptive; it was often surprising to learn what a prisoner was 'in' for. Some brutal criminals appeared quite harmless, and simply talking with them gave few clues as to how callous they could be. An example of this occurred one evening when I was assigned to take a representative of the Ryder-Cheshire charitable foundation to the industry area of the prison. His purpose in visiting the jail was to pass on the organisation's gratitude to the prisoners in the printing shop, who had produced various printed items for sale that had raised a considerable amount of money for the foundation.

While he was there, the rep chatted freely with several

prisoners – one in particular, Wally Willgoss, with whom he spent quite some time. Later, as we walked toward the main gate, the rep kept telling me how surprised he was that the prisoners were so normal and friendly – particularly Wally, who he said was 'an absolutely charming fellow'.

I was hoping that he wouldn't, but in the very next breath he asked me what Wally was in for. To his obvious horror, I replied, 'Murder.' With that, he took his leave and headed off in shock through the main gate.

As I walked back to A Division, I wondered what his expression would have been like had I told him that the 'absolutely charming' Wally had shot a 72-year-old farmer three times in the head before shoving his body down a well during a foiled robbery at a property in Lara.

It is a common belief on the outside that everyone is innocent in jail, but the inmates I spoke to rarely said, 'I'm in here for something I didn't do.' During the years I was in Pentridge, I only heard that on the odd occasion. On the other hand, almost all the prisoners would speak about the police practice of 'verballing' – fabricating a confession and attributing it to a suspect. According to the prisoners, this practice had come to be used regularly and had generally replaced 'physical persuasion' as a means of obtaining a confession. The most reticent prisoners were easy to get going on this topic – particularly in B Division, where the hardliners took particular exception when it was done to them.

The B Division prisoners were generally suspicious. If you did something to assist a prisoner, the immediate reaction would be: 'What's he helping me for? What's in it for him?' You constantly had to cope with this attitude when dealing with career criminals who were institutionalised and set in their ways.

It was always a relief to go from a morning in B Division to an afternoon in A Division, where the inmates were far more receptive toward those who were there to assist them. There were some very decent inmates in that section, but the B Division prisoners I worked with each day were habitual criminals with little regard for others. They knew nothing but a life of crime and were no sooner released than they'd be back again.

THE SHADOW OF H

During the early part of my time in Pentridge, I wondered whether to accept the official line that prisoner accounts of what took place in H Division were greatly exaggerated, or to accept the prisoners' version that it was a place where the 'bash' prevailed. Strangely enough, it wasn't easy to find prisoners who had been in H Division to confirm one version or the other. Once a prisoner had been sent there, it took a long time, sometimes years, for him to rejoin the mainstream prisoners. Through observation, I soon distinguished the H Division guards from the regular prison officers. Most of the H Division guards were huge. I regularly followed them out the main gate of an afternoon, and was always taken by the size of them.

Soon after I began working at the prison, I had an opportunity to visit the punishment section when I was asked to deliver a parcel of correspondence work to an inmate who had recently been sent there. I immediately thought I might learn more about H Division, but the writers quickly informed me that I wouldn't get past first base.

H Division was part of the same bluestone building as A Division, but was sealed off from it. A pathway along the side of A Division led to a bluestone wall containing a steel door, over which was a sign: 'H Division'. I approached the entrance and made my presence known. A disembodied voice came from inside the 'trap' on the steel door, asking me my purpose there. After explaining, I was permitted entry into a dark, eerie foyer containing a small counter enclosed by wire mesh. I placed the parcel on the counter, and the same voice told me I could leave now. Apart from that voice, there was no sign of life, just total silence. That first encounter didn't tell me much about H Division, but I'd soon learn much more.

In May 1970, after twelve years in the punishment section, William O'Meally was finally reclassified to B Division. He'd been the prison's most publicised inmate in the 1950s, when he was reputed to be the toughest man 'inside', but he'd fallen out of view during his many years of isolation in H Division.

One of the first things he did on arriving in B Division was to ask to see the education officer, as he'd been writing for some years and wanted his work appraised. After arranging for O'Meally to be sent up from the boot shop, where he was working, I awaited his arrival with keen anticipation.

A short time later, there was a commotion on the landing outside the chapel. I heard a voice say 'Yes sir', 'No sir', and then a small, thin old man appeared at the entrance. He stood at attention for some seconds and saluted in my direction. That was the first shock. The second came when I beckoned him in. He goose-stepped rapidly toward me, like a child's clockwork soldier that had been fully wound up and placed on the floor. I'd seen H Division prisoners quick marching before, but this was more than quick marching. His head, arms and legs were going in all directions. He tried to stand to attention when he reached my table, but his body kept twitching and contorting.

He was carrying a folder, the contents of which were soon all over the floor. As he attempted to co-ordinate himself to pick them up, he loudly stuttered, 'Good morning, Mr Osborne, sir! I'm Bill O'Meally, sir!'

Everything about this man indicated maltreatment. His sallow skin and emaciated body – mere skin and bone – told much of what he'd endured in the punishment section. When speaking, he used the title 'Sir' so many times that it was difficult to follow what he was talking about.

Overcome with feelings of horror and pity, I asked him what he'd done to become the target of such obvious retribution.

He explained that he was in prison for a crime that he hadn't committed, and because he had no way of proving his innocence while in jail, he'd engaged in unruly and rebellious behaviour through sheer frustration in the early stages of his imprisonment. His attempts at escape were intended to publicly highlight his plight, he said, and his flogging, combined with the many years he'd spent in H Division, were revenge for the embarrassment he'd caused the authorities.

Perhaps indiscreetly, I asked him about his flogging. He had no hesitation in talking about it. He said that after his mate Jack Taylor had been flogged and cut down from the triangle, O'Meally was told to expect a 'special'. When he was whipped, the tails of the 'cat' went around his sides and ribs. He quickly raised his shirt and there, wrapped around his ribcage, were rolls of skin that he said were the welts from the 'cat'. I have since read accounts claiming that Taylor took his flogging 'like a man' and was seen out in the yard that afternoon, but the cowardly O'Meally was heard all over the prison with his screams of protest, and took days to reappear. If my eyes didn't deceive me, he may well have received a far more severe flogging than his mate.

O'Meally suddenly became even more agitated, explaining that he'd been ordered to be back at the boot shop without delay. Then, just as dramatically as he'd arrived, he turned and goose-stepped his way out of the chapel.

The prison governor didn't approve O'Meally's attendance at my class, and the education office soon received a message to say that he wasn't to attend again. We fought this directive on the grounds that it was discriminatory. Now that he was a B Division prisoner, we argued, he was entitled to use the educational facilities. But hostility toward him still ran deep. Although the governor's directive was amended, it was only to the extent that he was allowed to come for whatever educational need he had, then promptly return to his work gang, as he was 'a special prisoner, and a security risk'. The governor didn't explain how a man who goose-stepped his way around the prison could possibly constitute a 'security risk'.

O'Meally attended the chapel for quite some time, and I got to know him well. He was never the hard man he was reputed to be. This wasn't just my judgement, but that of long-serving prison personnel such as Father Brosnan and senior guards. O'Meally's obvious suffering during his many years in H Division gave me an insight into the extreme punishments practised there, and the fortitude he possessed to have survived there for so long. By any measure, it was an extraordinary feat of endurance on his part, and an indictment on the authorities that allowed his incarceration to go on for all those years.

I marvelled that he'd come out with his spirit intact. I once asked him how he'd managed to survive, and he replied that it was hate that kept him going – hate for those who put him there and kept him there, as well as for those who were punishing him. He'd also retained control of his mind, which helped him cope with the physical brutality and psychological torture he'd received over so many years.

In the early stages of his imprisonment, O'Meally was deemed to be incorrigible and violent. I never saw any signs of that in him, but he had gained this reputation before he was sent to H Division. I asked Father Brosnan what the pre-H Division O'Meally was like.

Father Brosnan laughed. 'Well, he was never the standover man of the prison that the *Truth* newspaper would have had you believe. He was very vain, though – actually quite narcissistic. He'd sit around the exercise yard of a weekend, constantly combing his hair and looking at himself in a mirror.'

I made many attempts to get O'Meally to relax, to stop quick marching, to stop calling me 'Sir' every few words, even to look at me. It was many months before he showed signs of overcoming the reflexive behaviours forced on him in H Division. In his autobiography, O'Meally wrote that he had trouble learning to relax after his years 'living like an animal, always alert to danger, sleeping fretfully with one eye open'. I can certainly attest to that. I did my best for him with his writing, but not much from a narrower educational standpoint. Over the time I spent with him, he made considerable progress, both mentally and physically.

In conversation with O'Meally, I was careful not to raise the subject of H Division, as I could tell by his expression that the very mention of the place provoked flashbacks. When the Jenkinson Inquiry was announced in 1972, it seemed suspicious that its terms of reference covered the period beginning 22 May 1970, a matter of weeks after O'Meally was released from H Division. It was a travesty of justice that he was denied the opportunity of officially reporting the abuses he'd suffered.

Whether he'd have given evidence is another matter, though. The title of his autobiography, *The Man They Couldn't Break*, was a misnomer. He was broken and totally servile by the time he left H Division, and I'm told he remained that way until his eventual release from Pentridge. In his book, he claimed to have been a leader of the B Division rebellion against 'H', but I doubt it. He would have been well aware that any such action would put him back in the punishment section again.

O'Meally wasn't the thug's thug depicted by the media in the extraordinary publicity they gave him. In one newspaper article of the 1950s, a prison officer who was retiring after many years experience at Pentridge told the reporter that if he was ever asked his occupation he'd always reply that he was a public servant. If he said he was a prison officer, he was invariably asked, 'What is O'Meally really like?' This was a sign of the enormous amount of publicity he was receiving.

One morning, I asked O'Meally whether he ever had visitors in prison. He cheerily replied, 'Oh, yes. I must have more underwear in my cell than what you would find in Myers.' He went on to explain that he had some friends who regularly visited him and brought him underwear each time. He encouraged me to meet these people – a man and his wife who were licensees of a Brunswick hotel. As I was living in Brunswick, I took my wife to the hotel for dinner one evening and introduced myself. During a very cordial conversation, the couple told me that they'd applied to correspond with a prisoner, and to their horror, received notice that their correspondent would be none other than the notorious Bill O'Meally. Their concern, however, soon turned to a very warm affection for the much-maligned prisoner, whom they now regarded as a friend.

I feared for O'Meally's safety within the jail, as there is no-one more likely to incur the wrath of other inmates than a troublemaker whose actions threaten their privileges. The fact that O'Meally had been responsible for the creation of H Division heightened my concern. I also worried that some young up-and-comer might seek to advance his reputation by cleaning O'Meally up. Bill was now a shadow of his former self, so he'd have presented an easy target. In fact, none of these possibilities eventuated. O'Meally's fellow prisoners largely left him alone.

To encourage him with his writings and to assist in the presentation of them, my wife suggested that a typewriter would be an asset to him. Much to my surprise, the prison governor gave permission for me to bring one into Pentridge, together with typing paper and a book of instruction on typing. A pleasant morning ensued in the chapel when Bill was presented with these items. Some time later, he gave me a couple of his typed-out poems for my wife as tokens of appreciation.

One morning toward the end of my time at Pentridge, I sent a message through the B Division writer calling Bill up to the chapel, but he didn't arrive. Puzzled, I asked the writer what had happened, and he said that Bill hadn't wanted to come. I remembered one of John Brosnan's wise warnings: 'Once you've lost a crim, forget about it – you'll never get him back.' Reluctantly, I decided to follow his advice.

The next time I saw Bill O'Meally was on television, where he was being interviewed on the *Don Lane Show* after his release from Pentridge in 1979. Throughout the interview I wondered how people could possibly comprehend what had happened to O'Meally and the punishment he'd endured.

The print media used to bestow the title 'King of Pentridge' on the inmate who was supposedly running the prison. In the early and mid-1950s, the *Truth* newspaper referred to O'Meally as the 'king'. But another inmate of B Division, the escape artist Maxwell Skinner, disagreed. In a newspaper interview given on his release in 1955, Skinner said that O'Meally's fellow inmates despised him and had 'nothing to do with him'. This dislike was almost certainly a result of O'Meally's rebellious behaviour, which had resulted in other prisoners losing privileges they'd formerly enjoyed.

Yet I was still asked a surprising number of times on the outside, 'Is O'Meally still the King of Pentridge?' Actually, the 'king' during my time there was undoubtedly an A Division inmate I shall call Pat A.* Pat had the total respect of both

---

* I have referred to A Division prisoners, who were first offenders, by their first names and last initials only.

prisoners and prison officers. Even the toughest of the jail's standover men would back off if he confronted them. He had exceptionally large hands and strong arms, and exuded a 'don't mess with me' attitude that all in Pentridge appeared to respect. He was far and away the most powerful prisoner in the jail at this time. Ray Mooney told me that Pat even had his own shower in the communal washing area, and no other prisoner was game to use it. If there was a tougher man in Pentridge than Pat, I never saw him.

FAMILY MATTERS

One of the more disturbing aspects of Pentridge was the number of young, impressionable prisoners who weren't receiving any real help to change their lives for the better after they'd served their sentences. I saw a clear example of this in my experience with two young prisoners I got to know well – the writer in A Division, Norm D, and the soon to become quite notorious Laurie Prendergast, housed in B Division, who attended the educational classes. The two were similar in age and outlook, but one had family support and the other didn't.

Laurie was always clean-cut and presentable, unlike most others in B Division. Certainly he wasn't easily angered, unlike most inmates of the division, and I had no trouble with him. He successfully completed his course and appeared to be pretty much of average intelligence.

Prendergast was a virtual unknown in criminal circles at this time, but was later to gain notoriety over a couple of highly publicised crimes. He had little or no outside support, and his criminal associates were the only influences he had. Pentridge afforded him a first-class education in crime, a one-way ticket into the criminal world.

Laurie's classification to B Division made this almost inevitable. Housing young prisoners with the career criminals of B Division could only further their criminal activity. The Classification Committee had decided to place two eighteen-year-olds, Chris Flannery and Laurie Prendergast, among hardened prisoners who knew no other way of life. Both were subsequently further embittered by spending time in H Division. It came as no real surprise when they later became involved in major crimes.

Prendergast was initially given a lengthy sentence on a charge of rape, which had been hotly contested on the grounds of consent. He often said to me, 'Fair enough, I'm no angel and done wrong things, but I never raped nobody.' From this time onwards, he took the attitude that society owed him, and there was no other path to follow than that which led to a life of crime.

His counterpart in A Division was writer Norm D. Norm was the same age as Laurie, but he had family support and also received assistance from his fellow writer, Alan C. Norm's brother, a successful businessman, sold his business in order to take Norm out of Victoria and make a fresh start. As far as I know, he succeeded.

Laurie had no such support. He may not have been beyond redemption when he entered Pentridge, but he almost certainly was when he left. After his 'graduation', he led a life of crime until he mysteriously disappeared in 1985.

At one level, you could argue that the system had failed both Laurie and Norm. Pentridge was no place for young, impressionable prisoners. To make matters worse, both of them served time in H Division. The difference was that in Norm's case, his brother was prepared to make an unusual sacrifice to counter the damage Pentridge had done.

* * *

Pentridge was a soul-destroying institution, a disgraceful place for human confinement. Had animals been held in such conditions, they'd have come to the attention of the RSPCA, but no such protection was afforded the Pentridge prisoner.

If the penal authorities had wanted to devise a place to breed, nurture and hone the skills of criminals, it is difficult to imagine a better facility than the exercise yards of D Division. If they'd set out to degrade and debase a human being, the conditions experienced in C Division would surely have had no peer. And if they wished to turn men into beasts by tearing every strip of humanity from them, the creation of H Division achieved that aim in spades. And, finally, if they wanted to fit more than a thousand people at a time in a place that would destroy both body and soul, Pentridge fitted the bill perfectly.

Pentridge's musty, soulless divisions with their overcrowded and unsanitary cell blocks had to be seen to be appreciated. Its archaic nineteenth-century buildings were a blight on the Social Welfare Department in particular and the community in general. Those who believed that prisons were 'easy' on their inmates had never been in Pentridge.

It took all types from all walks of life to make up the Pentridge jungle. For most, the jail was a home away from home. To many it was the only way of life they could cope with, and release into the outside world was to be dreaded. There were also some very decent human beings who should never have been behind those walls, but who made my Pentridge experience worthwhile. Nobody left Pentridge the same as he was when he entered. The challenge was to leave without feeling frustration and despair about what you had seen inside. But that was something I could never do.

CHAPTER 5
ESCAPES

Pentridge experienced many sensational jailbreaks over its long history. Although escape was never easy, more than a hundred prisoners managed it, belying the prison's fortress-like appearance. For more than a century, the large farm area on the eastern side of the prison was the prime objective for would-be escapees. Reaching the farm almost guaranteed an escape, as the wall around it was only two metres high and often unmanned. It was so low that children had been known to scale it to retrieve a wayward ball.

The land around the wall was also unkempt, with hollows and discarded equipment providing ideal spots for outsiders to plant items of escape for their friends inside. Hacksaw blades, guns, ammunition and homemade ladders were often concealed there for the farm workers to gather and distribute around the prison. It wasn't until the 1950s, after a spate of escapes, that authorities excised a large portion of the farm and its low wall from Pentridge, enhancing security and challenging the ingenuity of the would-be escapee.

Of the various methods of escape, tunnelling wasn't actually worth consideration, though many tried to do it. No prisoner ever seems to have succeeded in digging his way out of Pentridge. All were eventually foiled by the walls. Most of the successful escapes were more ingenious, involving elements of deception, nerves of steel and often well-placed assistance from outside.

If escaping required a good deal of enterprise and a large slice of luck, staying out was even harder. The successful escapee had virtually no chance of avoiding recapture. It was just a matter of time. Escapees usually returned to the places they knew, narrowing the authorities' search and allowing the police and media to mobilise thousands of wary public eyes to assist them. Few fugitives had the means to finance a successful escape, let alone the support required to stay out of jail. In all the prison's history, it is generally accepted that only one escapee ever remained free: John Henry Sparks, who escaped in 1901.

Some escapes ended in farce, some in tragedy, but almost all in abject failure. On recapture, most escapees found their reward in the punishment section, either in the labour yards or later in H Division. But in spite of all these obstacles, many desperate men still plotted to achieve liberty, often enduring extremes of physical hardship in the process.

An Early Fatality: Pentridge's history of violent escapes began in August 1851, when eleven men were flogged over a single escape attempt. About thirty prisoners had broken free from the stockade, including five who had been in irons but had managed to chisel their way out of their chains. One escapee, Robert Taylor, was shot dead as he ran through the bush to the north of the stockade. All but three of the escapees were quickly recaptured by Aboriginal troopers with the help of local residents. The remaining three enjoyed a year's freedom before they were caught.

Edward Ryder: A particularly daring escape was that of Edward Ryder, who escaped in 1854 under the tyrannical rule of Inspector-General John Price. Sentenced to seven years for horse stealing, Ryder had been assigned as a servant to Price's wife. Early in December 1854, he donned some of

Mrs Price's clothing, strolled out the main gate undetected and disappeared.

Further Fatalities: In January 1859, another escape attempt was met with fatal consequences. Nine convicts made a rush and leapt the wall at the north end of the stockade, hotly chased by several armed warders. The warders fired on the escaping prisoners, who scattered in all directions, and one of them, Charles Willmott, was shot fatally in the head. In less than an hour, the rest of the prisoners were recaptured. They were later sentenced to an additional two years imprisonment, one to be spent in chains.

Another fatality occurred in 1884 when three men working at the quarries made a run to the southern wall. Equipped with a light ladder and rope, they reached the base of the wall just as warders arrived and fired warning shots in their direction. Undeterred, the prisoners quickly planted the ladder against the wall, and one of them, 21-year-old Thomas Kelly, began climbing it. Just as he placed his hands on the top of the wall, a warder took careful aim and fired. Kelly fell to the ground, mortally wounded. For their part in the escape, his two companions were placed in solitary confinement. This was the last fatality of that century, but more were to come in the next.

Pierre Douar: In February 1890, there was a daring, cleverly contrived escape from C Division. Pierre Douar, a skilled metalworker, had been sentenced to eight years for manufacturing fake coins and being found in possession of 300 skeleton keys. While he was working at the prison forge, he used a piece of sheet iron to make a skeleton key that would open the padlock that held the bolt on his cell door. Despite several searches, Douar managed to hide a boring tool, a pair of pliers and a knife in his cell by hollowing out a space in a piece of furniture and slipping them inside. He also had a piece of parchment that was similar in colour to his cell door.

Late one wild and windy night, when the lone warder on duty was out of sight, Douar used his pliers to remove the metal sheathing of his door, then bored several holes close together under the padlock. Using his knife as a saw, he cut between the holes until he had sawn an opening big enough to put his hand through.

After triumphantly opening the door, he stuck the parchment over the hole, shut the door, scaled the C Division wall and headed for the prison quarries. There he took off his prison uniform and donned some clothes a friend had hidden for him. His friend had also planted some rope and a hook, which Douar threw over the prison wall. The hook caught, and over he climbed. He met up with his accomplice, and the two walked to Melbourne.

Douar said he spent the first night wandering around Fitzroy Gardens, sleeping occasionally on park benches. The next night, his friend had arranged lodgings for them at the Melbourne Coffee Palace in Bourke Street. Unfortunately for Douar, two detectives who were canvassing the hotels and coffee palaces in that part of Melbourne discovered the strangers' presence. Douar was quickly recaptured, but his accomplice got away with cash and clothing stolen from another guest at the coffee palace. For his escape, Douar was given an additional two years imprisonment in irons and was placed in the area that would become known as B Division, where he had to serve his sentence in solitary confinement.

A despondent Douar found life in his new surrounds particularly harsh. He was only permitted to exercise for one hour each day, and he detested wearing irons. He was unable to communicate with others, and was constantly searched.

Douar begged the authorities to allow him to work in his

cell during the day, promising to behave himself if his request was granted. Eventually, he was put to work making straw hats, but he became increasingly depressed.

On 16 July 1890, Douar was found dead in his cell. He'd wrapped a towel around a cleaning brush and wedged it through the opening of his cell window, tied the strap of his irons to the towel and made a running noose with the buckle. He put this over his neck and threw himself at the floor. Unfortunately, the strap broke, but the noose – still attached to his neck – eventually strangled him. He was buried in a pauper's grave at Pentridge on unconsecrated ground.

John Sparks and John O'Connor: There was a successful escape from the prison on 3 July 1901, when convicted armed robbers John Henry Sparks and John O'Connor got over the farm wall on a morning when thick fog hung over Coburg. Sparks and O'Connor weren't missed until the midday muster, and even then the warders believed they were hiding somewhere inside the prison. Searches were conducted, but to no avail. It wasn't until about 3 pm that police were notified of the escape. Sparks, 27 years old at the time, was serving ten years for the robbery under arms of a Rutherglen mine manager, and was working as a tinsmith in the fitter's shop. His mate, 32-year-old John O'Connor, was serving twelve years for robbery under arms at Albert Park, and was working in the prison's lumber yard.

On the morning of their escape, Sparks left the tinsmith's bench unobserved and joined O'Connor in the timber yard. They managed to open a gate that led from the yard to the outer prison grounds. Under cover of the thick fog, they scaled the outer prison wall to gain their freedom.

Later, two men answering the escapees' descriptions held up three woodcutters making their way home to Greensborough along the Bundoora road. The woodcutters had previously noticed the two men loitering suspiciously on the roadway, and they'd taken the precaution of putting all their money in a horse's nosebag. This foiled the would-be robbers, who left in the opposite direction.

The government offered a large reward for the men's arrest, but nothing further was seen of the two escapees. Not long after they vanished, bank notes of the numbers Sparks had stolen at Rutherglen turned up in circulation almost simultaneously at widely separated places.

Early in September, a man who answered to the name John Hastings was arrested in Sydney on suspicion of being a deserter from the Royal Australian Artillery. He fired a revolver at a constable trying to affect the arrest before he was overpowered and taken away. The man soon admitted that he was John O'Connor.

He told authorities that he and Sparks had separated in Melbourne, and that Sparks had intended to go to America. For his escape from legal custody, O'Connor was sentenced to an additional three years in jail.

There was a suspicion that at least one warder had contributed to the escape's success by failing to supervise Sparks and O'Connor. As a result, three warders were charged with neglect of duty. The results were mixed: one was dismissed from his position, one had his annual salary reduced, and the third warder's charge was not proven.

In 1914, a rabbit trapper from Omeo known as Ted O'Neil was identified as John Sparks by a police inspector who had been on the Rutherglen robbery case. O'Neil was duly charged, but the case was dismissed after three other detectives stated that O'Neil was definitely not the escapee. Sparks was never heard of again, though it was rumoured that he had been murdered in South Africa.

William Evans: William Harold Digby Evans made an audacious escape using a disguise in July 1921. Evans had recently
been sentenced to nine months imprisonment for larceny, and
had been put to work as a servant to the deputy governor, a
post that gave him greater freedom than his fellow inmates.

One afternoon, a tower guard observed Evans going about
his normal duties in his prison uniform, but shortly afterwards,
he was reported missing. A quick search revealed his prison
clothes in the deputy governor's residence, where one of
that officer's suits had disappeared. Taking full advantage of
his position, Evans had swapped his prison garb for the suit,
walked to the outer wall, scaled it and calmly walked away.

He fled to Adelaide, where he was soon in trouble with
the law again under his real name, William Digby, being
arrested and jailed on larceny charges. During the next four
years, Digby managed to escape from custody on three more
occasions. On his fifth escape, however, he was shot dead by
a policeman while running through a street in Port Lincoln.

John Monson: On the morning of 6 July 1926, John Kelvin
Monson, aged 22, escaped from the Metropolitan Gaol at
Pentridge. Monson, also known as Richard Morenci, was on
remand waiting to be sentenced on a larceny charge.

The escape required great agility, as Monson had to climb
two very high walls. It also required him to have nerves of
steel. Challenged by a guard at the main gate, Monson quickly
replied that he was an electrician repairing some wiring in
the prison. As a remand prisoner, he was dressed in civilian
clothes, and this helped to fool the guard. Monson then
climbed to the top of the outer wall, dropped to the ground
and made good his escape. By the time he was found to be
missing, he had a head start on his pursuers.

Enquiries revealed that Monson, who came from Perth,
already had several convictions, beginning when he was

only fourteen. This also wasn't his first escape. He'd already absconded twice from custody in Perth. In criminal circles, he was known as 'The Kid'.

As well as possessing considerable daring and presence of mind, Monson had a sense of humour. After breaking into a safe at the Apollo Inn – the source of his latest conviction – Monson posted to the licensee a note to explain that he was returning some receipts. He signed himself 'Theo, the Thief'.

Seven weeks after his escape, Monson turned up in Fremantle, Western Australia, where he'd arrived as a stowaway on a ship from Port Melbourne, bound for London. He was recognised by a policeman and arrested in a barber's shop. He was escorted back by train to Melbourne, where he was given a further three months in Pentridge.

Reginald Barker: The first escape of the twentieth century to end with fatal results occurred in February 1932, when a seventeen-year-old youth, Reginald James Barker, on remand in the Metropolitan Gaol for having shot at a policeman and stolen a motorcycle, attempted an escape that cost him his life.

In the early afternoon of Saturday 27 February, Barker was in the exercise yard with several other remand prisoners, all dressed in civilian clothes. Unobserved, he climbed the wire fence and used an old iron ladder to reach the watchtower, where a warder named Arthur Bennett was stationed. Barker climbed into the tower and took Bennett completely by surprise. Snatching Bennett's rifle, Barker used it to knock the guard unconscious with a sickening blow to his head. He then climbed on to the top of the remand yard wall and ran along it, carrying the warder's rifle, until he reached the inner wall, which was separated from the outer wall by a strip of turf.

Another armed warder named Thomas O'Dowd, having noticed Barker's progress along the wall, ran along the grass strip until he was almost directly under the young inmate. Barker spotted O'Dowd and took a flying shot at him, but missed. The guard returned fire but he too was off target. Then Barker fired a second shot, which went straight through O'Dowd's stomach.

By now several other warders had raced to the scene and, after a volley of shots, Barker was hit in the forehead. He toppled from the wall and fell to the ground. Warders carried the young prisoner to the jail hospital, but he was already dead. There were no other fatal casualties of this ill-starred escape attempt. Though O'Dowd was rushed to hospital in a critical condition, he recovered after an operation.

Police later described Barker as one of the most desperate young criminals they'd encountered. Had he lived, they said he'd have been charged with another murder. They'd connected him with the death of a man who was shot after surprising a burglar at his Clifton Hill home.

Barker's body was buried at Springvale Cemetery, and a later coroner's hearing found that his killing was justified.

Kenneth Jones: In early December 1940, 20-year-old house-breaker Kenneth Raymond Jones, known as the 'Lone Wolf', executed an audacious plan to escape from the prison farm, where he'd been working that day.

Jones returned to B Division with his work gang at 4.20 pm. When the prisoners were sent to their cells, he quickly assembled a dummy by stuffing blankets down the legs of a pair of pants and attaching boots to the bottom. He placed it inside the door of his cell, where only its legs were visible through the trap. Before the warder arrived to lock his cell, Jones slipped out, shut the door and managed to leave the division unnoticed. He made his way back to the farm, where he hid in a shed for a while, then scaled the farm wall with the help of a wool bale he'd placed there during the day.

Meanwhile, the warder on lock-up had seen the legs inside Cell 6 and assumed they were Jones's, so he'd locked the cell and moved on. Jones wasn't missed until 9.35 pm, when the night-shift warder shone his torch into Cell 6 and, to his great surprise, saw a dummy sitting there. By now, Jones was some distance away from the prison.

About a fortnight later, he was recaptured in Sydney, where he'd been a guest for several days at Milson's Point Hotel. He was arrested for stealing goods from the hotel, but once the police had him in custody, they realised he was wanted for escaping from Pentridge.

At his hearing on the escape charge, Jones told the judge he'd only wanted to contribute to the war effort by joining his brother in the army. Despite the originality of his plea, he was sentenced to an extra twelve months imprisonment. The judge noted that Jones had form, having escaped from a boys' home four years earlier.

Nine months later, Jones tried again, even though he'd been placed in an observation cell. He somehow managed to smuggle in a couple of pieces of hacksaw, which he used to saw through one of the bars on his cell door. He squeezed through the gap and levered back a bolt to get out into the corridor. But he must have used up all his luck on the previous escape. This time, he was challenged by the warder on duty. Jones turned and struck him heavily across the head with the cell bar, but the warder drew his revolver and forced Jones back into his cell.

This was to be Jones's final escape attempt. In March 1945, he was involved in an altercation with another prisoner. During the wild brawl that followed, he was struck a hefty blow and fell to the ground, where he hit his head on the concrete and fractured his skull. He died in the prison hospital later that night.

George Howard: In the early hours of the morning on 18 April 1949, habitual criminal George Thomas Howard cut his way out of his second-tier cell in C Division, scaled two prison walls and disappeared.

Howard prised up the floorboards in his cell with a table knife and lowered himself into the kitchen, using a rope he'd made from blankets cut into strips. He got out of the kitchen by taking the door off its hinges.

He eluded the sentry on patrol along the inner perimeter wall, which he scaled by standing on a wheelbarrow, then jumped down and ran to the prison farm. He again used his blanket rope, weighted with a stone as a grapple, to pull himself up to a metal ladder on the unmanned outer wall, from which he dropped into Gaffney Street.

This was his second jail escape in two years. Along with seven other prisoners, he'd earlier escaped from Beechworth Prison. Two of his mates had overpowered a warder, locked him in a cell and used his keys to release the other six. Then, using tables and chairs as a ladder, they scaled a five-metre wall and escaped, only to be recaptured shortly after.

Howard's escape from Pentridge only lasted two days. He was arrested drinking in a Northcote hotel, where he was found to be in possession of two sticks of gelignite and a box of detonators. He'd broken into the Merri Creek quarry office the previous night and stolen stamps, cash and a quantity of detonators.

Howard had a long list of convictions dating back 33 years. This time, he received an extra five years jail – two years for escaping legal custody and three more for breaking and stealing. It would be quite some time before he'd be having another drink at the pub.

Victor Franz: One of the most ingenious escapes from Pentridge occurred in July 1951, when 26-year-old Victor Franz cut his way out of his C Division cell.

Franz, already a notorious house-breaker, had carefully planned his escape. A couple of months earlier, he'd taken the lid of a metal mess tin and gradually fashioned it into a key by watching closely every time a guard locked or opened the cell door. When Franz was satisfied that his key would serve its purpose, he acquired a boring bit from another prisoner for the price of a week's ration of tobacco. From the prison boot shop, he obtained strips of leather, which he made into a couple of ladders.

For six nights before his escape, Franz bored holes in the plating of his cell door, then covered his work each night by filling the holes with soap. Eventually, he created a square panel that he could prise open and put his hand through, then use his key to open the door. He locked the door after he left his cell and then, using the leather ladders and a grappling hook, scaled two high walls to gain his freedom.

For all his patience and ingenuity, his freedom didn't last long. Fifteen hours after his escape, he was arrested in a Port Melbourne street. The arresting police had questioned him for acting suspiciously, and didn't realise at first that he was an escapee. A Port Melbourne man called Maurice Gleeson, who had previously worked in the boot shop at Pentridge with Franz, was later charged with having harboured him. A slippery customer himself, Gleeson escaped a month later from the Carlton watch-house, along with two others under arrest for car theft.

Franz, who was serving a three-year term for house-breaking and stealing, was given another six months imprisonment on the escape charge – time for him to rue the cost of a mere fifteen hours of freedom.

Maxwell Skinner: Victoria's most prolific escapee was Maxwell Carl Skinner. During a life of crime that spanned almost twenty years, Skinner claimed to have escaped from fourteen jails or reformatories. He described himself as a 'national champion escapologist'. For his efforts, he was nicknamed 'Houdini', after the great escape artist.

At the tender age of sixteen, Skinner made his first escape when he got out of Castlemaine Reformatory with four other prisoners. He was recaptured and put in Pentridge, where he spent the first two months of an eighteen-month sentence in the labour yards. He was then sent to French Island to complete his sentence. Over the next several years, Skinner proved difficult to contain anywhere, escaping at various times from the watch-houses in central Melbourne, Fitzroy and Richmond.

In November 1951, after declaring no jail could hold him, Skinner escaped from the remand section of Pentridge in full view of armed prison officers. From the exercise yard of D Division, he noticed that the warder in the tower above the main outer wall had his attention elsewhere. At this, Skinner quickly made his move. Dressed in his civilian clothes, he ran from the exercise yard and scaled the five-metre wall, getting two other prisoners to bunk him up. He then ran across a section of the prison farm, dodging a fusillade of bullets, scaled the outer wall beside an unoccupied sentry box and dropped to the ground.

Surprised witnesses watched as Skinner ran past some tennis courts, joking with the players and local residents as he passed, before stealing a bicycle and riding it to a tram stop in Nicholson Street. He boarded a tram there and took a seat in the rear driver's cabin. When police boarded the tram and approached him, he quickly alighted in Carlton and disappeared into the Melbourne General Cemetery.

He then ran through the streets of Carlton until he reached

Fitzroy, where some friends took him in. He remained free for a little over a month, but was then recaptured in a Fitzroy hotel. He'd dyed his hair and eyebrows and grown a moustache, but police quickly recognised him.

For this escape, the 23-year-old was given a further nine months imprisonment. At his hearing at the City Court, authorities took no chances with him: a constable held him in the dock, and other police were on guard at all exits. He was returned to Pentridge, where he spent time in the labour yards on half rations and in solitary confinement.

Escape was always on Skinner's mind, though, and in mid-April 1952 he teamed up with convicted murderer Kevin 'Hoppy' Joiner in making a daring escape bid from the heavily guarded B Division. Nine other prisoners were supposed to be involved in what was planned to be a mass breakout, but the others pulled out at the last moment.

The two prisoners, armed with a dummy pistol, fled the division through a gate that was normally locked and bolted, but which authorities later suggested had been opened for them by a trusted inmate. In fact, another prisoner who was supposed to be in the breakout scaled the fence and broke the lock on the gate with a crowbar. Skinner and Joiner raced to the outer wall of the prison, where they found a ladder that belonged to a firm building a new prison boiler. Joiner went first, climbing the ladder to the top of the outer prison wall near No. 1 tower. When he reached the tower, he poked the dummy gun into the guard's midriff and took his rifle from him.

Then the sentry on No. 2 tower caught sight of Joiner jumping from the wall, armed with the rifle. The guard fired a couple of warning shots, but Joiner ignored them and ran towards the nearby St Paul's Church. The sentry now took careful aim and fired directly at Joiner. Joiner was hit, but staggered on into the grounds of the church. By this time,

Skinner had reached the top of the wall, but as he did so, the warder in the tower emerged and knocked him off. The would-be escapee fell to the ground, breaking his ankle as he landed. As he lay in pain, Skinner defiantly yelled, 'I'll really do it yet. I'll get away and no-one will ever get me again.'

His accomplice, however, was beyond words. Warders found Kevin Joiner dead, lying in a bed of lilies at the back of the church. They carried his body back to the prison.

It was to be Skinner's last attempt at escape. Influenced by a prison chaplain, he decided to change his ways and serve out the rest of his sentence quietly, declaring that he was a reformed character and wanted 'to shake hands with society'. In 1954, however, he narrowly avoided being shot by another prisoner, Robert Walker, as I'll outline in chapter 7. Skinner was released in 1955, leaving the bluestone walls legally at last. He vowed to 'go straight' and changed his name. 'Maxwell Carl Skinner is dead – thank God,' he declared.

Kathleen Allwood and Margaret Burke: During the 1880s, a woman named Anna Minerva Davis, who was on a life sentence for attempted murder, successfully escaped from the prison governor's residence at Melbourne Gaol in the city, but the only women ever to escape from Pentridge were 23-year-old Kathleen Allwood and 18-year-old Margaret Burke, who fled F Division in late May 1954 while their matron's back was turned. They reached the farm area and attempted to scale the low outer wall, but discovered they couldn't manage it with their shoes on. They removed their shoes, then Allwood climbed on Burke's back and reached the top of the 3.6-metre wall. A strong girl, she reached down and hauled Burke up after her. They later told police they sat on top of the wall in broad daylight for about twenty minutes, giggling, before jumping to their freedom on the other side.

Freedom was short-lived for them, though. The next day,

a patrol car discovered them, barefoot, in an Albert Park street. After a short chase, they were captured and charged with absconding from legal custody. Later, they were each sentenced to an extra month's imprisonment for the escape.

It was difficult to understand why Allwood had wanted to escape, as she was due for release less than a fortnight later. She was quite erratic, however. She had previously attempted escape a year earlier, in the company of two other prisoners. The three of them locked a female warder in a cell, but they were discovered hiding in a prison building before they could effect their escape.

William Davies: In February 1955, 37-year-old William Joseph Davies, awaiting trial on charges of shop-breaking and stealing, managed a unique escape from the remand section, using materials he'd smuggled into the jail.

With his bed as a ladder, Davies reached a window 2.4 metres above the floor of his cell, where he heated the thick glass with a blazing kerosene-soaked singlet, then doused the window with a container of cold water. The glass cracked, exposing the 4-cm thick iron bars on the cell window. Davies then used a hacksaw blade to saw through a bar, enabling him to squeeze through the gap and slide down a drainpipe to the ground. Under cover of darkness, he ran to the prison farm, where he used a guard's ladder to scale the wall, leapt down and disappeared into the night.

When Davies rang his wife after his daring escape, she didn't believe it was him on the other end of the line. She threatened to call the police, then hung up. She only learnt that it was indeed her husband when police later called at her house.

Davies headed for Sydney and enjoyed two years of freedom before being recaptured and returned to Pentridge. His escape was one of several, which officials blamed on the fact that the prison authorities were trying to introduce modern methods of detention in buildings that were over eighty years old.

Gary Oak, William Kelly and Graeme Wilson: One of the most sensational Pentridge escape attempts occurred on Sunday, 6 November 1955, when three seventeen-year-old prisoners from A Division – Gary Oak, William Kelly and Graeme Wilson – managed to slip away unnoticed from the shower area after lunchtime muster. They scaled a low wall near the printer's shop and got into the prison farm, where they climbed a ladder leading to the unmanned No. 7 post. From there, they jumped to the grass in Gaffney Street and ran off into Murray Road.

Prison authorities first heard of the escape when a passer-by called out to two off-duty warders playing tennis outside the main gate, 'Do you know three of your blokes have hopped the wall back there?' The warders quickly dropped their racquets and ran. One went to the main gate to pass on the news while the other ran to his car and drove it to the front gate. Other armed warders jumped in, and they took off in pursuit.

Meanwhile, the escapees were attempting to hijack nearby vehicles. They eventually succeeded in commandeering an old-model car and had just taken off when the warders approached and began firing on the car, with at least half-a-dozen bullets striking the back of it. Undeterred, the escapees gunned the car down the road and zigzagged through several Coburg streets, hotly pursued by the warders. The car chase came to an end in West Preston, where the escapees raced across Gilbert Road, lost control of their vehicle and mounted the footpath before crashing outside a milk bar, showering nearby children with broken glass.

Shocked onlookers saw the escapees abandon the car and

race down May Street where one of them, Kelly, jumped a fence into the backyard of a house. The other two, Oak and Wilson, ran down a nearby lane in opposite directions, pursued by the warders, who fired two warning shots before twice hitting Oak in the back. Oak fell to the ground, critically wounded. Wilson and Kelly quickly surrendered and were returned to Pentridge, while Oak was rushed to the Royal Melbourne Hospital where he eventually recovered from his wounds.

Following this escape – which happened soon after the mass escape from the football oval discussed in chapter 1 – embarrassed prison authorities moved to eliminate the low farm wall that provided such an easily scaled exit from the prison grounds. But the excision of the farm area in 1958 didn't deter would-be escapees. It simply made the challenge greater.

John Gill: In November 1956, 29-year-old John Noel Gill, who was serving a term for 'illegally using cars' and 'breaking, entering and stealing', planned an escape via a hospital visit with the help of his wife. Gill swallowed a comb in his cell and was taken to the Royal Melbourne Hospital.

On his release from the hospital, an armed warder and a hospital sister escorted him to the casualty entrance, where a woman was standing. Gill told the warder that he knew the woman and asked if he could get a cigarette from her. The woman handed Gill a packet of cigarettes, and when he returned them, she handed him a pistol. Gill waved the weapon at his guard and ran off. Dressed in pyjamas and dressing gown, he dashed into the grounds of Melbourne University.

Luck wasn't on Gill's side, though. A couple of police had observed what was happening and chased him. They fired at him, wounding him in the hand, and captured him. He was charged with escaping from custody, being a felon in possession of a pistol, and having an unregistered firearm. His eighteen-year-old wife – and mother of his two children – was charged with 'carrying a pistol without a permit', and 'being in possession of an unregistered pistol'. On her arrest, Mrs Gill told detectives, 'I should have kept the gun. I could have handled it better than he did.'

Gill himself received fifteen months jail for his escape from custody, but he spoke in support of his wife when she appeared in court. He pleaded with the judge for leniency, telling him she was just a kid who had been influenced by 'undesirables' – including himself. She was given a month's jail, which the judge told her was an extremely lenient sentence.

James Gribble: The safety precautions introduced in the late 1950s to reduce the frequency of escapes included the distribution of twelve new high-powered rifles to warders on wall duty. These new rifles were put to the test with fatal results six months later, when fourteen-year-old James Ronald Gribble lost his life attempting to scale the outer wall. Gribble, an introvert who lived in a dream world, was serving an indeterminate sentence for the murder of his seventeen-year-old sister Margaret, whom he'd stabbed 48 times with a knife.

On the day of his fatal attempt, 20 September 1957, Gribble had been working with a group of other prisoners in the printing shop. In mid-afternoon, he walked away and climbed a wire security fence inside the outer bluestone wall. He then attempted to climb a grille-gate set in the wall, but was observed by warders, who immediately fired warning shots in his direction, blew whistles and called on him to stand. Gribble ignored them and kept climbing. When he was almost at the top of the wall, he was struck by a bullet in the upper body and fell to the ground. He was carried back into the prison on a stretcher, but died there half an hour later.

The boy's heartbroken parents claimed he'd been treated like a hardened criminal, but Whatmore, the director of penal services, said the boy had been afforded special care, frustrating every attempt to rehabilitate him. Whatmore repeatedly referred to the boy as being fourteen-and-a-half, and claimed that 'the new security arrangements had worked perfectly'. Many questioned why a fourteen-year-old boy was being held in Pentridge in the first place.

Richard Horsley: Perhaps the most farcical escape from Pentridge, and certainly one of the most embarrassing for prison authorities, occurred in December 1958, when 20-year-old Richard George Horsley absconded. Horsley was serving a twelve-month sentence for illegal use of a motor car. He escaped one night by scaling a wall, and his disappearance went unnoticed. He had walked out of his cell, closed the door, slid the bolt back in place and dropped back the top catch, leaving the impression that everything was as it should be.

After he escaped, however, things quickly went wrong for Horsley. When he leapt from the prison wall, he severely injured a leg. He spent seven hours hobbling around Coburg back streets, barefoot and in prison garb, before he decided enough was enough. Finding a public phone booth, he rang police and asked them to come and get him. When they arrived at 4 am, a barefoot, dejected and defeated Horsley greeted them with the words, 'I've had it. I got out of the Pen. I've hurt my leg and I'm lost.'

When police rang Pentridge to ascertain whether a prisoner named Horsley was indeed missing, it was the first authorities knew of his escape. Charged with escaping from legal custody, a remorseful Horsley told the court, 'I ended up getting lost. I realised I could not get home with my leg hurt, so I rang the police.' He received little sympathy from the judge, however, and was soon back in Pentridge with extra jail time.

Rex Elston: There were few escapes from G Division, the psychiatric section of the jail, but in February 1962, eighteen-year-old Rex William Elston got out and terrorised communities in northern Victoria before being recaptured. Charged with murdering his mother, whom he'd shot at their home in the Gippsland town of Sale, Elston had been found not guilty on the grounds of insanity and had been committed to Pentridge at the Governor's pleasure.

Elston used a carpenter's clamp, which had been supplied to him for woodwork, to bend two bars of his cell together, creating a space through which he managed to squeeze out. He scaled the outer prison wall and headed north, eventually reaching the Seymour area, where he broke into a homestead and stole a rifle. He then began terrorising residents in the area, waving the rifle around and revealing his identity to them, saying he had nothing to lose.

Eventually, he broke into a farmhouse at Landscape and entered the bedroom of Alfred and Valda Sharp. The couple worked together to overcome Elston, with Alfred overpowering him and Valda wresting his loaded rifle away. The kindly Mrs Sharp then fed Elston, gave him coffee and aspirin and put him to bed before seeking police assistance.

She later received the British Empire Medal for her gallantry in disarming Elston. Before receiving the award, the diminutive Mrs Sharp – 1.6 metres tall and weighing 63 kg – said, 'I'm not afraid of man or beast and very few women.' She also remarked, 'I don't know whether to laugh or cry. I don't like getting the honour for some kid's misfortune.'

Elston was sent to Ararat Mental Home, but three months

later he escaped again. His escape caused anxiety in the Ararat district, where a large-scale search was organised. Barefoot, he fled the area and boarded a freight train to Port Pirie in South Australia, but two off-duty policemen recognised him, and he was quickly recaptured. 'I suppose I'll have to go back to that rat-house,' he told police. This time, however, the authorities weren't so considerate. He was sent back to Pentridge and placed in H Division, working in the labour yards – an extraordinary placement for an unconvicted young man detained at the Governor's pleasure. Fortunately for Elston, a sympathetic judge later ordered that he be placed on probation and given an opportunity to reform.

Keith Sims, Frederick Shea and Ronald McCaul: On 20 July 1963, three prisoners executed one of the best-planned escapes ever made from D Division. Keith Sims, 29, serving three years for breaking and entering, Frederick Shea, 29, serving seven years for manslaughter, and Ronald Colin McCaul, 32, serving eight years for armed robbery, were all in the remand section awaiting appeals against their convictions.

During the early hours of the morning, the men rolled up their blankets, left them in their beds as dummies, and hacksawed through the bar on the window of the top-tier cell they shared. Some time later, they forced the bar back and crawled through the gap. Under cover of darkness, they dropped onto the tin roof of the prison building, leapt into the exercise yard, and scaled the inner wall. They crawled along the wall until they reached the north wall, from where they managed to reach the unmanned No. 5 post – a distance of about 400 metres. They used torn-up knotted sheets to lower themselves to the ground, then fled.

The prisoners were missed the following morning – and so were four hacksaw blades, which had been taken from a Public Works Department toolkit being used by workmen at the prison. Police raided several properties in the Gippsland area before rounding up Sims and Shea. McCaul was arrested six months later in a flat in Sydney where he was found to be in possession of a stick of gelignite and three detonators. He told arresting detectives he'd intended to rob a safe and steal enough money to leave the country.

Harold Peckman: In early 1973, 33-year-old Harold Peckman contrived a clever plan of escape that involved his work in the prison tailors shop. Peckman was serving a 50-year sentence for murdering Kathleen and Albert Taylor, a young couple he beat to death with a tomahawk as they lay in bed. It was said that the couple had sabotaged Peckman's car, and he'd murdered them in reprisal. Twelve months after the murders, their mutilated bodies were found in a shallow grave off the Princes Highway near Traralgon.

An inmate of B Division, Peckman spent weeks secretly making a pair of trousers, knitting a red cap and making a red shirt from material stolen from the hobby group. He also wove pieces of teased string into some elastic, creating a bushy false beard that he dyed so that it looked natural.

On 1 February 1973, Peckman put his plan into action. During the morning, he reported in sick and lined up to see the prison doctor. When the queue neared the doctor's office, Peckman moved out of sight of prying eyes, rid himself of his prison clothes, donned his new outfit and false beard, and made his way to the administration block, where some electricians had left an extension ladder. He placed the ladder against the wall and climbed onto the roof.

When the guard on No. 1 tower challenged him, Peckman called back, 'Public Works electrician. Tell B Division the power will be turned off in a few minutes.' Satisfied, the guard moved further along the catwalk to convey the message.

Peckman crossed the roof to the side facing Champ Street,

where he secured a long rope to one of the turrets and slid quickly to the ground below, waving to a tower guard as he went. When the guard waved back, Peckman knew his plan had worked perfectly. A witness later said that Peckman had 'sauntered across the street as though he was out for a Sunday stroll'.

His freedom, however, lasted just thirty hours before he was recaptured in a block of flats in Flemington. Peckman was soon back in Pentridge, this time in the dreaded H Division.

Donald Marshall: In March 1975, Donald James Marshall, a convicted armed robber, made a farcical attempt to escape Pentridge. Having been placed in D Division due to overcrowding in the prison, Marshall used a hacksaw blade he'd hidden in his shoe to saw through a window bar of his cell. It took him five-and-a-half hours, but when he tried to squeeze through the gap, he could only get his head and part of his upper body through. He wriggled and pushed, but all he achieved was to get himself thoroughly wedged between the bars.

In desperation, he asked the prisoner in the next cell for help, but the prison officers overheard him. They tried to free him but failed. Despite their most vigorous efforts, the guards couldn't budge him. Finally, two medical officers were called and managed to get him loose by pouring oil all over him.

Originally, the hapless Marshall was sentenced to three months extra imprisonment, but on appeal his sentence was reduced to two months. By that time, he'd already spent three-and-a-half months in H Division for his attempted escape.

Gregory Smith and Trevor Jolly: On 22 July 1980, Gregory Smith and Trevor Jolly pulled off a remarkable escape in broad daylight, going over the front wall near the main gate of the prison.

Trevor Raymond Jolly, 24, had been convicted of the contract murder of Paolo Leone of Thornbury in April 1977. Leone's wife and her lover had taken out a $5000 contract on Leone's life, and Jolly had accepted it. Leone was stabbed to death as he got out of his car after returning from work. Later, Jolly told police he was heavily under the influence of heroin at the time of the murder.

Gregory John Peter Smith – aka Gregory Roberts – aged 28, was known as the 'Building Society Bandit'. Smith had been a brilliant student at Melbourne University until his marriage broke up and he began taking drugs. To feed his heroin habit, he took to armed robbery, mainly targeting building societies and using an imitation pistol. He netted about $38,000 from these robberies in the 1970s, acquiring a reputation as a gentleman bandit who wore three-piece suits and often said 'please' and 'thank you' to his targets. At the time of the escape, he was serving a 23-year sentence, with a minimum of 16 years, for 24 armed robberies. While in Pentridge, he had fallen foul of prison authorities and had been placed in H Division, where he claimed he was severely beaten by prison guards.

On the day of their escape, Smith and Jolly were dressed in overalls and had been working unsupervised on some garden maintenance outside B Division. At about 1 pm, they made their way across the Square to the administration building and broke into the office of the governor of security, where renovations were in progress. They climbed up into the ceiling and used a buzz-saw to cut a hole, through which they climbed into the roof. From there, they draped an extension cord over the wall and used it to lower themselves to the ground below. The pair walked calmly to a nearby laneway, where they couldn't be observed. Eventually, they made their way to Sydney Road and disappeared.

The prisoners' timing was good, as the workmen

demolishing the office were at lunch. Also, the place where they scaled the wall was a blind spot for the guards on tower duty. Although a prison officer later told police he'd noticed a power cord dangling over the wall at about 1.30 pm, the men weren't missed until after muster in B Division at 4 pm. By this time, they'd long gone.

Having escaped, Smith and Jolly initially obtained assistance from a bikie club, then they decided to split up. Smith headed for New Zealand. He later claimed that he spent time working as a doctor in an Indian slum and had many adventures in Europe.

After ten years of freedom, in 1990 he was arrested at an airport in Frankfurt, Germany, for attempting to import heroin. Sniffer dogs had detected the drugs in his luggage, and then Interpol matched his fingerprints to those of the 'Building Society Bandit'. He was eventually extradited back to Australia to serve the remainder of his sentence in Pentridge.

His mate Jolly had already been recaptured after only six months, following a shootout with police. He was incarcerated in Jika Jika and was later to play an unintentional role in the only escape ever made from that maximum-security section.

Smith, now calling himself Roberts, served two years in solitary confinement in H Division, where he began writing a novel based on his overseas adventures. Twice his manuscript was torn up by prison officers, but he refused to be discouraged. After he was released back into the mainstream prison, he continued writing for the remainder of his sentence. After he was released from Pentridge in 1997, Roberts had his novel *Shantaram* published, and it became a major success.

Larry Simpson: One escape that had a happy ending occurred in May 1982, when 30-year-old Larry Simpson, serving eight years for two armed robberies, escaped from Pentridge in the company of another prisoner, Kevin Gutsell. The two men had climbed a seven-metre gas pipe wrapped in razor ribbon, cutting their arms and hands so badly that the pipe was covered in blood. After dropping from the wall, they were chased by a prison officer, who fought with them before they commandeered a car and sped off.

Although their escape was short-lived – lasting just 24 hours – as a result, Simpson found his mother. His picture was published in the papers, and when Mrs Betty Lazzaro saw it, she became convinced that he was her son. She'd had an unhappy first marriage, losing her son when he was two because her husband took him away from her.

After Simpson's recapture, Mrs Lazzaro went to see him, and an emotional reunion took place. Simpson tearfully declared that he'd been all over Australia looking for her. Father John Brosnan, who attended their meeting, described it as the most beautiful thing he'd seen in the 28 years he was prison chaplain.

Norman Bloomfield, Peter Morgan, Trevor Bradley and Ross Burleigh: Four dangerous prisoners escaped from the recreation area of J Division one evening in April 1983. Convicted murderer Norman Bloomfield and armed robbers Peter Morgan, Trevor Bradley and Ross Burleigh used hydraulic rams from the prison's workshop to force the bars apart on a vent at the rear of the hall, then climbed into the ceiling and onto the roof before lowering themselves to the ground with an extension cord. From there, they used a homemade ladder and grappling hooks to scale the outer prison wall.

Authorities soon discovered that in order to facilitate their escape, the men had used architectural plans of the prison provided to Morgan as part of an architectural course he'd undertaken in the prison. A total of 31 plans were found under Morgan's bed. The escapees had also used a two-metre hydraulic ram, a crude wooden ladder and two pairs of bolt cutters, which they used to hack through a wire fence. Forensic police later said they believed the escapees had obtained the equipment in the guise of seeking props and building materials for a play they'd been rehearsing.

The escapees made their way to a house in Smith's Gully on the north-east fringe of Melbourne, and forced their way in at knifepoint. There, they held two adults and their two children captive for about thirteen hours before leaving with a .22 Ruger rifle and some cash. The escapees then split up and went their separate ways, but all four had been captured within five days of the escape.

Needless to say, Morgan was never re-issued with plans of the prison, but he was nothing if not a trier. Two months later, he and convicted murderer Barry Robert Quinn attempted to escape from the prison's maximum-security section, Jika Jika. Using broken hacksaw blades, they managed to saw through the 30 x 30 cm metal grille covering the ventilator in the ceiling of their cell. They crawled through the roof cavity to the exercise yard, where they were caught by prison guards as they tried to hack their way through the mesh above the yard. Their term in Jika Jika was about to be extended.

Robert Wright, David McGauley, David Youlton and Timothy Neville: In July 1983, the impossible happened. Four prisoners – Robert Wright, David McGauley, David Youlton and Timothy Neville – escaped from Unit 3 of the 'escape-proof' Jika Jika maximum security unit, severely embarrassing prison authorities.

At the time, the former escapee Trevor Jolly had been engaged in a hobby involving the use of spray paint, which required ventilation, and the guards had allowed corridor locks to be left open to clear the air. On the day of the escape, the four prisoners hid under a workbench, then slipped through the opened doors unnoticed. They next used a bar to prise open a space in the upper covering of the exercise yard. They climbed through, scaled the division's perimeter fence and reached the prison's outer wall. Using blanket strips and a grappling hook fashioned from a notice board, they climbed the wall and gained their freedom.

Police were later to say they believed the escape plan had been hatched well in advance of its execution. The prisoners also gained a head start after duty officers didn't notice their absence at muster. Later, these officers were disciplined over their negligence. The authorities' embarrassment over the escape was prolonged when Wright avoided recapture for five months, though his mates were caught within two. There was a tragic aftermath for two of the escapees, Robert Wright and David McGauley, who later perished in the Jika Jika fire of 1987.

Peter Clune: As a well-behaved prisoner in A Division, Peter Patrick Clune was granted permission to perform in one of the prison theatrical group's productions, *One Flew Over The Cuckoo's Nest*, for which he was given the task of director of sound and lighting.

On the last night of performance in early July 1983, Clune decided to leave – not with his fellow inmates, but with the audience. Decking himself out in a coat and wig, he mingled with the audience as they were departing. When he reached the door, he told the warder on duty that he'd lost his visitor's pass. To Clune's great surprise, the warder handed him a fresh pass. He then had no problems at the main gate: he simply surrendered his pass to the guard, who bid him a cheery 'good evening' and wished him a safe trip home.

Clune eventually made his way to Sydney, where he was

recaptured some seven months later. At his hearing on the escape charge, Clune told the judge that he'd escaped because he believed his life was in danger. He owed $2000 to another prisoner, who had threatened to kill him if he didn't pay up. His defence left the judge unmoved. Clune was sentenced to an additional term on top of the three years he had left to serve of a nine-year sentence for armed robbery.

Dennis Quinn: The last prisoner to escape from Pentridge proper was a 27-year-old B Division prisoner, Dennis Mark Quinn. In mid-November 1987, Quinn sawed through two bars of his cell window, then used a rope to drop to the ground outside and to get over the outer perimeter wall. On the wall of his cell, he'd painted a message to one of the prison warders: 'Merry Christmas, Mr Williams.'

Quinn caught a ship to New Zealand, where his family lived. He later claimed that he'd escaped to see his mother, who was gravely ill. After he was recaptured nineteen days later, a judge ignored Quinn's pleas for leniency and gave him an additional twelve months in prison.

Christopher Binse: Christopher Binse could well be described as a modern-day Maxwell Carl Skinner – the Houdini of Pentridge. During the latter stages of Pentridge's existence, Binse was the last inmate to escape while under sentence at Pentridge.

In September 1992, Binse – or 'Badness', as he liked to call himself – made an extraordinary escape from a high-security ward at St Vincent's Hospital, where he was being treated after being stabbed at Pentridge. Binse got out using a gun that had been smuggled into his ward, but he was soon recaptured after committing an armed robbery in New South Wales. Sent to Parramatta Gaol, he escaped from there as well, having sawn through the metal bars of his cell and climbing onto the roof of a nearby building with the aid of some bed sheets tied together. From there he jumped a four-metre gap onto another building, but fell and broke a wrist.

Binse returned to Victoria and was soon back in Pentridge, having been recaptured holed up in a safe house at Daylesford with 'Jockey' Smith. Placed in H Division, Binse soon made another attempt to gain his freedom. Almost twelve months after his flight from hospital, he and a few others devised a plan for a mass escape from H Division. The plan was to have an inmate overpower the night guard, disarm him, and use his keys to open about thirty of the cells in the division. To bring this about, Binse had cut through the lock on his cell door with a hacksaw blade. He didn't intend to release all the prisoners in the division, though, as he had some of them on a blacklist. One in particular was Hoddle Street killer Julian Knight, who was believed to be an informer. If things went to plan, Knight was marked for death.

Binse's plan allowed for two eventualities – the prisoners could either escape into the main jail and scale the outer prison wall, or use a guard as hostage and escape through the prison's front gate. However, the best-laid plans of mice and men often go awry. During a security crackdown after an attack on a prison officer elsewhere in the jail, authorities discovered Binse's diary in his cell and read of his plot to escape. As a result, the plot was aborted, and we will never know if his master plan would have cracked the fortress that was H Division.

Two years later, he attempted escape again. After sawing his way through the bars of his cell, he was caught within the prison grounds. With his record now showing seven escapes, Binse was considered such a high security risk that prison authorities had him shackled in leg irons for 23 hours of the day and wearing handcuffs and a body belt whenever he left his cell.

CHAPTER 6
EXECUTIONS

Hanging is one of the oldest and most widely used forms of execution worldwide, and has always been the form used in Australia. In the early part of Australia's history, capital punishment by hanging was used for many crimes including theft, arson, sexual offences, manslaughter and murder.

The first execution conducted in Victoria was the hanging of two Tasmanian Aboriginal men, Tunnerminnerwait and Maulboyheenner, who were convicted of murdering two whalers as part of a violent campaign of resistance to white settlement. The two were publicly hanged outside the Melbourne Gaol in 1842. This jail was to be the scene of 133 hangings, the last of which was in 1924. The Metropolitan Gaol – or D Division – at Pentridge then became the site for future Victorian executions. By this time, however, only the most serious crimes resulted in the death penalty, and after World War Two, most death sentences were commuted to life imprisonment. Consequently, only eleven executions took place in Pentridge from 1924 until the abolition of the death penalty in 1975.

Hanging is a relatively humane method of execution, provided the drop is accurately calculated by weighing and measuring the prisoner, and the noose is correctly placed under the left jaw to effect the cervical displacement fracture necessary to cause instantaneous death.

The gallows used for hanging consisted of an overhead beam, together with the rope and noose, and a double trapdoor operated by a lever. The rope was attached to a strong chain, which was fitted to the overhead beam in such a way that it could be raised or lowered, then secured at any desired height to adjust the drop to the height and weight of the prisoner. The noose had several coils, which slid down the rope and delivered a solid blow to the side of the neck. With the knot of the noose positioned under the left jaw, the head was forced backwards and this, in combination with the downward force of the body, snapped the neck and the spinal cord.

At Pentridge, condemned prisoners spent their last hours in a cell on the second tier in the main central corridor of D Division, close to the gallows, which were situated in the middle of a steel catwalk spanning the first-floor galleries of the corridor. Underneath, on the ground floor, were a few cells set aside to house condemned prisoners from the time of sentencing until the execution was imminent.

The condemned cell actually consisted of two cells converted into one. When a prisoner was taken there, he knew that the sheriff or his deputy would soon arrive and knock on the door to escort him to the gallows. His last walk was a short one, just seven or eight paces along the catwalk.

After the hangman had secured the prisoner, pulled the lever to release the trapdoor, and the prisoner had fallen to his doom, a medical officer would ascertain death before the prisoner was cut down. After an autopsy was performed, the body was taken away to a secret site inside the prison, sprinkled with lime, placed in a coffin and buried.

After Melbourne Gaol closed in the 1920s, the gallows beam and trapdoors were moved to Pentridge and installed in D Division by carpenter prisoner David Bennett, who was serving a lengthy sentence over an armed robbery he'd committed in company with Angus Murray. Murray was later involved in the fatal shooting of a Hawthorn bank manager and became the last man executed at the Melbourne Gaol. Much later, Bennett, on release, raped a four-year-old girl; for this offence, ironically, he became the first man hanged at Pentridge, on the gallows he'd installed there. Thus the two mates, Murray and Bennett, entered the history books – Murray as the last to be hanged at Melbourne Gaol, and Bennett as the first to be executed at Pentridge. Bennett was also the last person executed in Australia for a sexual offence.

Details of hangings were recorded in a 'Particulars of Executions' book kept by the sheriff in charge of the execution. This book recorded graphic details for ten of the eleven executions carried out at Pentridge. The exception was the execution of the American serviceman Edward Leonski during World War Two.

These are the crimes for which these prisoners paid the ultimate price.

David Bennett: On Sunday 3 July 1932, a four-year-old girl was returning to her North Carlton home with her six-year-old brother after attending Sunday school. As they were making their way along Drummond Street, they were approached by a man of about sixty named David Bennett, who asked the girl if she'd like him to buy her an ice-cream and some lollies. She readily agreed.

Shortly afterwards, a young man named William Houston noticed Bennett walking down Drummond Street with a little girl and then entering an unoccupied house. Further down the road, he encountered a small boy, obviously distressed, who told him he was looking for his sister. Houston took the boy back to the Sunday school, where he obtained the assistance of another man and three women. Returning to Drummond Street, the party knocked on the door of the house where Houston had seen Bennett take the girl. Bennett opened the door and quickly ran off, hotly pursued by Houston, who caught him in nearby Amess Street and overpowered him. Meanwhile, the little girl was taken to hospital, where it was found that she'd been subjected to sexual abuses and was seriously injured.

The following month, when Bennett faced the Magistrate's Court, he declared, 'I have never seen this little girl in my life until this morning.' However, this wasn't Bennett's first charge. His remarkable record of crime included being sentenced to life imprisonment with nine lashes of the cat-o-nine-tails for a similar offence against a girl in Western Australia. Despite his denials, Bennett was remanded for trial on charges of gross sexual assault.

The newspapers reported that, while in custody awaiting trial, Bennett had given detectives information about the murder of a twelve-year-old girl named Mena Griffiths. This led to the arrest of a man who was later found innocent. Four years later, another man altogether, Arnold Sodeman, confessed to the murder.

Bennett stood trial at the Criminal Court in Melbourne. On oath, he denied having seen the girl that day. He told the court that he had an appointment to show a woman through the house, which he'd recently repaired. The woman had been unable to keep the appointment, and her daughter had been sent to let him know. That was the child he'd been seen to take into the house, he told the court.

The jury took just 40 minutes to consider this account before returning a verdict of guilty. Asked if he had anything to say as to why sentence of death should not be passed on him, the 59-year-old Bennett answered, 'I pleaded not guilty and I am not guilty. I still maintain my innocence. I did not see the child until I was confronted with her by the police.' Sentence of death was then formally pronounced. An ashen-faced Bennett collapsed and had to be assisted from the dock.

While awaiting execution, Bennett wrote several letters to

MPs in which he begged for mercy. As the girl hadn't lost her life, he reasoned, neither should he. He claimed his sentence was unjust, but his pleas were ignored.

On the morning of 26 September 1932, Bennett was taken from the condemned cell at Pentridge and led to the gallows at 10 am for the first execution in the Metropolitan Gaol. All other prisoners incarcerated in the immediate vicinity were relocated into cells away from the drop. Bennett walked from the condemned cell and faced the hangman calmly when he reached the gallows. Asked if he had any last words, Bennett made a statement that lasted nine minutes – the longest ever made by a condemned man in Victoria. He concluded by saying, 'I repeat that I am not guilty, and again ask for forgiveness from those whom I have wronged, as I forgive those that have wronged me. Goodbye.' At 10.09, Bennett dropped 2.3 metres to his death. The Government Medical Officer reported that death was instantaneous.

Arnold Sodeman: When Arnold Karl Sodeman stood trial in the Criminal Court in February 1936 for the murder of a six-year-old girl, he'd already confessed to murdering three other girls over the previous five years. The 35-year-old labourer admitted that he'd held the girls by the throat until they'd become limp and died.

His victims had been Mena Griffiths, aged twelve, murdered at Ormond in November 1930; Hazel Wilson, aged sixteen, murdered at Ormond in January 1931; Ethel Belshaw, aged twelve, murdered at Inverloch in January 1935; and June Rushmer, aged six, murdered at Leongatha in December 1935. It was for this last murder that Sodeman stood trial. He pleaded not guilty on the grounds of insanity.

After playing in a reserve in Leongatha with other children, June had left for home at about 7.15 pm. The next day, her dead body was found in the bush off a lane. She'd been tied up, and her bloomers had been crammed into her mouth. She'd died of shock. The community of Leongatha was terrified by the find, as other girls had recently been murdered in a similar manner.

Sodeman had been seen riding his bicycle along a Leongatha street at about 7 pm on the night of June's murder. Shortly afterwards, a man was seen riding a bicycle with what seemed to be a girl sitting on the handlebars, heading toward the area in which June's body was later found. Witnesses passed this information on to police. When questioned by detectives, Sodeman provided an alibi that was found to be false. After that, he confessed. 'This is not the only one,' he said. 'There are three others, Mena Griffiths, Hazel Wilson and Ethel Belshaw. I was riding my bicycle when I met June Rushmer. She wanted a ride, so I put her on my crossbars.' Sodeman had grabbed June when she got off the bike, and 'she went limp all of a sudden'. He described how he'd bound and gagged her, then ridden away, leaving her in a paddock. 'I then realised I had done a dreadful act and I went round to try and show I was away from the scene.' He concluded his confession by saying, 'The sooner I go through the drop the better.'

Five years previously, Mena Griffiths had been playing with her sisters in a park in South Yarra before she was coaxed away by a man. Her dead body was later found in a deserted house in Ormond, where she'd been tied up, sexually assaulted and suffocated. In his confession, Sodeman said he'd been drinking that day, and that he and Mena had gone from South Yarra to Ormond by public transport. He'd taken her to the empty house and 'grabbed her by the throat'.

A couple of months later, Hazel Wilson was found dead in a paddock near her Ormond home. She'd been tied up and gagged. Sodeman told detectives he'd been drinking that day as well, and on his way home, he'd struck up a conversation with Hazel. They'd started pulling each other about and skylarking, he said, but then an urge overtook him and he grabbed her by the throat. She went limp almost immediately, so he dragged her to a nearby vacant allotment and tied her up before going home.

On New Year's Day 1935, twelve-year-old Ethel Belshaw had been to a carnival at Inverloch when she disappeared. Her body was found next morning in some scrub behind the beach. From the manner in which she'd met her death and the way she'd been tied, detectives knew this was the same killer who had murdered the other girls. At the inquest into her death, Sodeman had actually given evidence that he'd seen Ethel earlier in the evening of her disappearance. Now, he told detectives he'd been drinking again that day. He described how he'd grabbed Ethel by the throat until she'd gone limp, tied her up, and used a stocking to gag her before dumping her body.

In defence of the accused man, Sodeman's counsel put it to the jury that at the time of June's murder his client was insane. The court was told that Sodeman's family had a history of insanity, alcohol abuse and violence. His father had died in a mental hospital, as had his grandfather. Three psychiatrists told the court that he wasn't responsible for his actions. One said that at the time June Rushmer was killed, Sodeman wasn't conscious of what he was doing. He was suffering from obsessional impulse, which was exacerbated by alcohol. Sodeman's counsel submitted that the jury should be instructed to acquit the accused man on the grounds of insanity, but Justice Gavan Duffy declined to do so.

The prosecutor pointed out to the jury that Sodeman had left no gaps in his accounts of what had occurred, and argued that he wouldn't have been able to recall events so well if he were insane. The jury retired for just over two-and-a-half hours before returning with a guilty verdict, and the judge passed the sentence of death.

An appeal to the Victorian Court of Criminal Appeal followed. It was submitted that Sodeman 'was entitled to have it put to the jury that his irresistible impulses were a result of a disease of the mind which prevented him from controlling his actions'. A submission was also made that 'he was sane in the ordinary sense of the word, but at the time he killed he was acting under the influence of an uncontrollable impulse'. The appeal was unsuccessful.

At the time of his execution, Sodeman made no statement and appeared unconcerned as he went to the scaffold. Given a drop of 2.4 metres, the Government Medical Officer recorded that 'the drop given was exactly what was required for instantaneous death', though the right pulse continued for fifteen minutes and the left for eight. Significantly, a post-mortem revealed that Sodeman had leptomeningitis – a disease of the brain that rendered him unaccountable for his actions.

Edward Cornelius: While awaiting execution in Pentridge, Arnold Sodeman had a constant companion – another condemned prisoner, Edward Cornelius. The pair played draughts on Sodeman's last night.

Cornelius had also been sentenced to death for murder. His crime had been discovered on the evening of 12 December 1935, when the vestrymen of St Saviour's Church of England in Fitzroy had arrived at the vicarage in Smith Street. The vicar had arranged a meeting for 8 pm and was always punctual, so they were puzzled to find the place in darkness. Fearing something was wrong, they forced their way into the building, where they came upon a ghastly sight. The vicar, Harold Laceby Cecil, aged 59, lay in a pool of blood in the hallway. All indications were that he'd been savagely attacked in the hall, but there were also bloodstains on the furniture in the study, indicating that there had been two attacks.

Police were quickly summoned. Cecil had suffered seventeen wounds to the head, and his skull had been fractured. The attack had occurred some hours earlier. Robbery was an obvious motive. One of the drawers of a desk in the study had been ransacked, the pocket on the vicar's trousers was torn out, and the wallet in which he carried his banknotes was gone, together with two watches, a distinctive chain and a gold cross, which he always wore. On the table in the study was a notice of marriage dated 12 December 1936 with the signature of one Francis Edward Layne.

The following day, police discovered a bloodstained spanner at the vicarage. Shortly afterwards, a 29-year-old mechanic named Edward Cornelius was charged with the vicar's murder. Police discovered that Cornelius had sold two pieces of gold chain at shops in Richmond two days after the murder, and had also been identified as selling a gold cross and another piece of chain to a jeweller in Prahran. It was also discovered that he had bought the spanner found at the vicarage the day before the murder. Furthermore, he had gone by the name of Frank Layne four years previously, and the handwriting on the marriage card bore striking similarities to his. Cornelius had a record for house-breaking, and had only recently been released from Pentridge.

At trial, Cornelius entered a plea of not guilty. His counsel accused detectives of being 'physically vigorous' in obtaining a confession from him – an allegation that was strongly denied. Evidence was led that Cornelius, who lived in a flat in Gipps Street near the vicarage, had suddenly come into money on 12 December, when he'd given a new pair of shoes to a lady friend and spent up on a new suit, hat and shoes for himself. Investigating police also found human bloodstains on a blue suit he had worn that day, although it had subsequently been washed.

In sworn evidence, Cornelius told the jury that on the day of the murder, he had passed the vicarage carrying some tools he wanted to sell. He remembered having heard that there was money in the vicarage, so he decided to see if he could get in. When he rang the bell, the vicar answered. To justify his visit, Cornelius decided to invent a story about wanting to make arrangements for a wedding under the name of Francis Edward Layne. While in the study, he noticed money on the desk.

After the vicar showed him out of the house, Cornelius quickly returned and entered the study. He was looking through the desk when he was grabbed from behind, he claimed. There was a short struggle, and the vicar reached for his pocket as though he was going to produce a weapon. 'More instinctively than intentionally,' Cornelius said, 'I grabbed the spanner, which was on the desk, and hit him once. He fell to the floor.' Cornelius ran to the door, intending to seek assistance, but noticed blood on his face and realised his position was serious. 'I closed the door, and when I turned, the vicar was in the hallway – it was the most terrifying sight of my life. He grabbed me and I think I lost control of myself, for I cannot give any clear recollection of what happened afterwards,' Cornelius said.

The accused man then added that he'd picked up his tools, taken some money and a couple of watches, and left the vicarage. Asked by his counsel whether he at any time intended to kill the vicar, Cornelius answered, 'No.'

On 26 March 1936, Cornelius was found guilty and sentenced to death. Asked by the judge if he had anything to say, he replied, 'Your Honour, I am not guilty of this offence, and I am afraid the jury have made a grave mistake in bringing in this verdict.'

Cornelius was hanged at Pentridge on 22 June 1936. Though few particulars were given as to his death, it was officially recorded that there were technical problems with the mechanics of the trap.

Thomas Johnson: The Windsor Castle Hotel had stood in the main street of Dunolly since the central Victorian town experienced a gold rush during the 1850s. By October 1938, it no longer had a liquor licence and there were just five male lodgers there. One lodger, 40-year-old labourer Thomas William Johnson, had just taken up lodgings a month before. He had been given a room free of charge on condition that he cleaned the premises, and he had also been given keys to all the rooms.

On the morning of Thursday 6 October, two lodgers – Bill Radley and Fred Douglas – decided to go upstairs and look for fellow boarders Bob Gray and Charlie Bunney, who hadn't been seen out of their rooms for a few days. They knocked on Gray's door, but received no answer, and on trying the doorknob, they found it to be securely locked.

Radley climbed up onto the outside veranda to look through the window into Gray's room. There he saw the bodies of the two friends lying on the floor in pools of blood. Horrified, Radley and Douglas summoned the local policeman, who found the two men horribly battered about the head, lying on their backs with their heads towards the door. A bloodstained axe, which had obviously been used in the murders, lay near a wall in the room. There were bloodstains on the passage walls, the door and the floor. Bunney had suffered four distinct head wounds and Gray two. The police quickly established that all the lodgers were accounted for except Johnson, who had left the day before. They also discovered that Johnson had been out of money the previous Monday but the next day, 4 October, he was all 'cashed up'.

On Friday 7 October, Johnson walked into Dandenong police station and declared, 'I am the man you are looking for in the Dunolly murders'. He then made a signed statement in which he said that he'd become angry because Gray was 'hammering and making a noise in his upstairs room'. 'There was an axe in my room and I took it up and hit Gray on the head with it and he fell to the floor,' Johnson said. 'Another man named Bunney then came into the room. He looked at Gray but did not speak, and then I hit him on the head. I think I hit Bunney twice and Gray twice with the axe. Then I locked Gray's room and went outside and threw the key away. My only excuse is that Gray was making a noise hammering and I did not want Bunney to be a witness. This is why I killed him. I was in a bad temper when I killed Gray. I make this statement of my own free will.'

Tried at the Ballarat Supreme Court in December 1938, Johnson pleaded not guilty on the grounds of insanity to the murders of pensioners Robert McCourt Gray, 73, and Charles Adam Bunney, 61, at Dunolly. Evidence was led that Gray had been in his room when Johnson burst in carrying an axe and demanding that Gray stop making a racket. When Gray told Johnson to 'bugger off', he was struck with the axe, and when he hit the floor, he received a further mortal blow. Bunney, hearing the commotion, came to investigate, but suffered a similar fate to his mate. Johnson then ransacked the room and rummaged through his victims' pockets. He'd stayed in his room for a further two nights, but when he began to notice the smell of the old men's decomposing bodies, he decided it was time to leave.

The court was told that Bunney was a Boer War veteran, a member of the AIF Fifth Battalion at Gallipoli, and had served in France as a stretcher-bearer during World War One. He'd suffered terrible war injuries that had driven him to alcoholism and an attempt on his own life when he returned to Australia. During the Depression, he'd been forced to sell his silver war medals just to get by.

After the prosecution had presented its case, Johnson's counsel entered his plea of insanity, arguing that his client's mental state was such that he wasn't responsible for his actions. In support of this, his sister testified that Johnson had attacked his father and wounded his mother with a knife when he was quite young. In each case, he didn't remember having done anything. She also told the court that other family members were subnormal.

A Collins Street specialist in psychiatry and mental diseases, Dr Raymond Ellery, told the court that after interviewing and examining Johnson at Pentridge, he'd formed the view 'that he was suffering from a hereditary disease which rendered him the victim of periodical insanity leading to outbursts of extreme violence'. The disease, Ellery said, made him aggressive, antisocial and callous, with no clear perception of his acts.

Dr Graham Allan, Government Medical Officer at Coburg, was called by the Crown in rebuttal. He told the court he'd observed Johnson at Pentridge, and was of the opinion that he wasn't insane. Johnson, he said, was typical of a class he saw daily at Pentridge, who were callous and indifferent towards others. He cared little for the lives of others or their property. He also believed Johnson knew he was doing wrong at the time.

In a firm voice, Johnson made a statement to the court. 'I don't know what came over me. These men were my friends. I would never injure them in any way. It is just like a bad dream to me now, but it is coming back bit by bit. When I arrived in Dandenong, I only had the confused idea. Some things I said to the police must have been wrong. I had no intention of robbery and I am sorry for the death of these two old chaps. I leave it in your hands. That is all. When Constable Kirkham says I killed Bunney because he was a witness, I mean Bunney was killed because he happened to be there. That is all I have to say.'

Johnson's defence of insanity failed. After six hours of deliberation, the jury returned a verdict of guilty, and he was sentenced to death.

On Monday 23 January 1939, Johnson was hanged in the Metropolitan Gaol at Pentridge. He hadn't sought the assistance of any clergy during his last days, nor did he on the morning of his execution. He also refused to make a last statement when asked by the sheriff. It was officially recorded that death was instantaneous, but the final recommendation that 'as the man had such a thick muscular neck and shoulders, the length of the drop could have been a few inches longer' tends to indicate that not all was well with this execution.

George Green: Sunday 13 November 1938 was a date Laura Barrett would never forget. At about 10 am, she called in to her sister's Glenroy home on her way to church. Having received no answer when she knocked on the front door, Mrs Barrett went to the rear of the house. Puzzled, she entered the unlocked back door and walked into her niece's room. There she saw Phyllis, her seventeen-year-old niece, lying on the floor with a pair of bloomers tied around her throat. Horrified, Mrs Barrett ran from the room only to discover her sister Annie lying dead on the floor in her bedroom. In panic, Laura rushed from the house screaming for help.

Police quickly arrived. Their impression of the scene was that whoever had entered the house and murdered the two women – Miss Annie Wiseman and her niece Phyllis – had done so with the intention of robbery. In the bathroom, they discovered a handbag and a shopping bag, the contents of which lay on the floor. Further investigation revealed that neighbours had seen a man with a bicycle enter the premises the previous night.

Detectives believed that the murderer was familiar with both the women and the house. He must have known that the back door was left unlocked, as there were no signs of forced entry. Significantly, a portion of a milk bill was found near Miss Wiseman's body, and an address – 118 Collins Street, Thornbury – had been written on the back of it. Detectives believed the killer had dropped it when struggling with Miss Wiseman. Using this clue, detectives took less than a week to charge a 38-year-old chimney sweep named George Green of West Heidelberg with the Glenroy murders. Green had a lengthy criminal record, mainly for theft, under a variety of aliases.

At his trial in the Melbourne Criminal Court, a web of circumstantial evidence was wound around Green, the most important piece being that a woman had given him the milk bill on the Monday before the murders. She'd been supplying the address of a likely customer for his chimney-cleaning work, and quickly came forward to verify it.

Evidence was also given that Green had been to the Wiseman home to clean the chimney, and that he knew the two women lived alone. Also, tracks found around the house corresponded to those made by Green's bicycle, and a footprint found in the garden was of a similar measurement to his boots. As well, spots of blood had been found on Green's clothing, as had some hairs identical in colour and texture with Phyllis Wiseman's. Further, ten days after the murders, a nickel bicycle pump that matched one Green claimed had been stolen from his bicycle was found on the railway line opposite the Wiseman home.

Medical evidence showed that 62-year-old Miss Wiseman had been strangled by direct pressure from bare hands, whereas Phyllis Wiseman had been forced against something hard, perhaps by pressure against the iron bedstead, until she suffocated. An attempted sexual assault had also been made against the unfortunate girl.

The court was told that Green had been drinking in the Sir Henry Barkly Hotel in Heidelberg on the afternoon of the murder and was so intoxicated that he had to be asked to leave. He'd been seen later that day cycling in the direction of Glenroy, and had told a witness he was going to get tools he'd left there. He hadn't returned home until the early hours of the following morning.

Pleading not guilty to the murder charges, Green told the court in sworn evidence that at the time of the murders he was sleeping in a vacant allotment, as he was feeling 'a bit crook' after a heavy day's drinking. He stated that he'd been a chimney sweep for the past five or six years but denied having told two men at Preston that he was going to Glenroy to pick up his gear, as he hadn't been there for months. He agreed that he'd been given a note with the Thornbury address on it, but said that nobody was home when he went there, and he didn't return. On the following day, while working in Alphington, he met a 'couple of sweeps' and gave them the Collins Street address, telling them that if they called there, they might get a job. He hadn't seen them since and didn't know their names. He explained that he'd paid for his board on the Monday after the murders with money he'd left at home on the Saturday for that purpose.

In his address to the jury, Green's counsel warned they should 'regard with caution' the circumstantial evidence against his client. He pointed out that Green's fingerprints hadn't been found in the Wiseman home. There was also no evidence that he was near by on the night of the murders or that he had any extra wealth after 12 November or had in his possession anything that might have come from the Wiseman home. The lawyer described these factors as 'some exceptionally strong links missing from that chain of circumstantial evidence'.

The jury retired at 2.55 pm, and returned a little less than six hours later with a guilty verdict. Asked if he had anything to say before sentence of death was passed, Green replied, 'No. Nothing.'

Green unsuccessfully appealed against his conviction, and was hanged at Pentridge at 8 am on Monday 17 April 1939. When asked if he had any last words, Green said he'd heard that a newspaper had erroneously reported that he'd confessed. 'I did not make any confession,' he declared.

Green wasn't attended by any clergy, and was said to be quite composed on the gallows. It was officially recorded that 'death was instantaneous', but it was also recorded that the knot was not under the left side of the chin and that 'the noose did not tighten on the neck' – requirements necessary for an instantaneous death.

Alfred Bye: When 45-year-old Thomas Edward Walker was found stabbed to death in Melbourne's Treasury Gardens in the early hours of 27 September 1941, detectives were baffled as to the motive for the crime. Walker, a Gallipoli veteran who had re-enlisted in the Home Defence Force, had eleven knife wounds, which had been inflicted with a sheath knife found near the scene of the crime. The deceased soldier was found on a pathway, and his coat lay near by.

Robbery was quickly ruled out as a motive, as money was found in one of the dead man's pockets, and other coins were found where it was thought he was first attacked. Also found in the vicinity were three empty beer bottles, which gave rise to a theory that Walker may have been drinking with another person or persons and that an argument may have broken out between them. Detectives theorised, from marks on the grass, that Walker had crawled or staggered from the place where he was originally attacked to the path where he died and was later discovered.

A woman later made a phone call to police to enquire about Walker's condition and immediately hung up when asked to identify herself. Earlier, a constable on duty near the gardens reported that he'd seen a woman and a soldier enter the gardens about 7 pm, but he couldn't positively identify Walker. At the scene, there was little evidence for detectives to use to discover Walker's killer. However, in a pocket of his army tunic was a notebook containing several names and addresses, and police quickly began questioning these people, among them a Miss Amelia Ogier.

A short time later, 42-year-old Private Alfred Bye, a military transport driver of Railhead Camp, Bacchus Marsh, was arrested and charged with Walker's murder. A small man – 160 cm tall and weighing 45 kg – Bye had no criminal record and had never been in any trouble. He'd enlisted in the AIF in 1917 and had been gassed by the Germans during World War One.

At his trial, it was alleged that jealousy was the motive for Walker's killing. The Crown contended that the story went back to 1930, when Bye had become engaged to Miss Ogier. Although they were happy at first, the engagement was called off a couple of years later, as Bye 'went broke on the racehorses'. Miss Ogier didn't hear from him for several years. During this time she made the acquaintance of Walker, who was living apart from his wife, and they planned to marry as soon as he obtained a divorce. Later, Miss Ogier met Bye on a city street and introduced him to Walker. Bye's affections for Miss Ogier were rekindled, and he urged her to leave Walker and marry him, but she refused.

On the night of the murder, Miss Ogier and Walker had gone to a theatre in the city. They'd gone outside at interval, where they were confronted by Bye, who told Amelia he wanted to discuss arrangements for his military pay with her before going overseas. Walker urged Amelia not to speak to Bye, and an argument broke out between the two men, with Bye throwing a punch. The two soldiers agreed to meet later in the Treasury Gardens to 'sort this out'. Bye initially denied that he was implicated in the tragedy, but later admitted that he'd stabbed Walker as he bent down to fold up his coat.

The key witness for the prosecution, Miss Amelia Florence Ogier, gave most of her evidence from beside Mr Justice Gavan Duffy on the bench, her voice being so low that she couldn't be heard from the witness box. She confirmed the events of the night of the tragedy as given by the prosecutor, and also told the court that she had offered to bank Bye's military pay for him.

Police told the court that Bye had admitted meeting Miss Ogier and a soldier he knew as Tom in the city on the night of the murder. When asked why he'd hit Walker, he claimed it was because Walker wouldn't let her speak to him. He also admitted Walker had said to him, 'I'll see you in an hour's time.' Bye at first claimed he didn't wait for Walker, but after further questioning he admitted being involved in the tragedy, and had made a statement to police.

Bye had pleaded not guilty on the grounds of self-defence. He denied telling police he was jealous of Walker, and said he'd brought a knife to the city that night in order to send it to a friend in Gippsland. But then, when he was talking to Miss Ogier and Walker, Bye thought Walker was going to strike him so he 'got in first'.

Bye had then followed Walker into the gardens, where Walker took his coat off and told Bye to do the same. Bye told the court he then said to Walker, 'I believe you are an old digger. Why should two old soldiers fight?' Bye continued, 'Walker then let fly and hit me on the jaw. Before I could do anything, he made a flying leap at me, knocking me on the broad of my back. He had me by the throat with his hands. His thumbs were pressed into my windpipe and he kept calling out, "You rotten bastard. You rotten bastard." I could not move. I had a knife in my pocket and reached down with my hand to get it out. The knife got Walker in the back as he rolled onto it.'

Bye then claimed they'd fought for the knife and he didn't realise that Walker was seriously wounded. Though Walker was the stronger of the two, Bye also claimed he'd freed himself from Walker's grip, walked away and thrown the knife into the gardens as he went. He'd returned to Bacchus Marsh later that night, he said.

Having listened to the only witness for the defence, the jury left to consider its verdict. Forty-five minutes later, a guilty verdict was announced. Asked by Justice Gavan Duffy if he had anything to say before sentence of death was passed, Bye replied, 'I never intended to murder him. I had to do something to defend myself. When he had me by the throat, I had to make him release his grip.'

While awaiting his execution in one of Pentridge's condemned cells, Bye reflected on the many misfortunes that had come his way. He'd left home and school at a very early age, and could barely read or write. He was hard of hearing, having been kicked in the head by a horse, and later hit by a large stone on the road. He had great difficulty obtaining any sort of permanent employment, going from job to job until he enlisted in the AIF and was sent overseas during World War One. He returned a sick man, having been gassed, and took up a farm on King Island. Fate stepped in when his farmhouse was burnt to the ground, and once again he was looking for work. It was around this time he courted and became engaged to Miss Ogier, but soon found he was also unlucky in love.

Then World War Two broke out. He enlisted but was rejected, so he joined the Home Guard. Again his health failed – but, surprisingly, he was accepted into the Home Defence Force and was passed fit for the AIF. Just before he was to be sent overseas, he once again took ill, and this time he was rejected permanently. He'd never lost his love for Miss Ogier, though, and when he met up with her on that fatal night, he was overcome with jealousy towards his rival, Walker. When they fought, the smaller, ailing Bye was no match for Walker, and he went for his knife. There was now nothing left for Alfred Bye, other than an appointment with the hangman.

He didn't appeal against his conviction or sentence. Despite approaches for clemency from the Howard League for Penal Reform and the Victorian Labor Party, Bye was hanged at Pentridge on 22 December 1941. He didn't go to the gallows with a soldierly bearing. He was a nervous wreck for some days before his execution, and was sedated on the morning of his hanging. He was incapable of standing erect, and had to be placed on a chair above the trap. The hangman released the trapdoor immediately, but there was a slight break in the fall as the chair hit the trapdoor before the body left it. The Government Medical Officer recorded that death was instantaneous, though there was 'some gurgling of air being breathed through the partially compressed trachea'. The pulse beat continued on the right wrist for about twelve minutes and on the left wrist for about eighteen. Heartbeat could be heard by stethoscope for up to 22 minutes. The GMO recorded that death was due to 'fracture of the neck in the region of the lower third and upper fourth cervical vertebrae'.

Edward Joseph Leonski: The hanging of Private Eddie Leonski of the United States Army at Pentridge was a most unusual one, and bizarre stories about the event circulated around Pentridge for many years. I was told that Leonski had been hanged by a couple of American provosts in a cell, which I was shown, but there was nothing concrete to support this theory. His execution was nevertheless enshrouded by mystery.

Leonski's very name filled the female population of Melbourne with terror during World War Two. There had been a succession of murders around Melbourne in the early 1940s by a man who became known as the 'brownout strangler'. Electric power was reduced at night in wartime Melbourne, but the power wasn't completely cut, so what the population faced was not a blackout but a 'brownout'.

The first of the brownout victims was found in Victoria Avenue, Albert Park, at about 7 am on the morning of 3 May 1942. A part-time barman at the nearby Bleak House Hotel, Harold Gibson, noticed an American soldier stooping over something in the doorway of a shop. When the soldier caught sight of Gibson, he quickly walked away and headed towards Beaconsfield Parade.

Gibson decided to take a closer look. Reaching the shop, he struck a match, and to his horror discovered the body of a woman. Her clothing had been torn almost completely from her, and she'd been posed obscenely with her legs apart. It was obvious that she'd been the victim of a vicious attack, as her body was severely bruised. After finding her untouched purse near by, the barman rushed to the nearest telephone and called police.

Investigations revealed that the deceased was Mrs Ivy Violet McLeod, 40, who had been waiting at the shop for an all-night bus to take her back to her East Melbourne home after visiting a friend in Albert Park. Among her numerous injuries was a fractured skull.

Just six days later, a nightwatchman on patrol at about 5.30 am came across the body of a woman who had been brutally attacked on some steps leading to the apartments at 13 Spring Street, Melbourne. Detectives immediately recognised similarities between this murder and the recent Albert Park killing. The victim had been posed in a similar manner, and her clothes had been almost entirely torn from her body. She'd also taken a terrible beating and had been strangled to death.

The victim was 31-year-old Mrs Pauline Thompson, who lived on the top floor of the apartments. She was well known as a radio announcer in Bendigo, and had been working in Melbourne as a switchboard operator at Radio 3AW. Earlier that night, she'd gone to Spencer Street railway station to see off her policeman husband, who was returning to their home in Bendigo. Later, she'd been seen in the Astoria Hotel in the company of an American soldier. They had several drinks, and had been seen leaving the hotel together. Evidently, an American soldier had been involved in both recent killings.

With the city's female population now decidedly on edge and its streets at night practically deserted, the killer struck again a little over a week later. This time, the body of a middle-aged woman was found in parklands off Gatehouse Street in Royal Park, quite close to the Camp Pell army barracks, where many US troops were housed. She was 40-year-old Gladys Hosking, who had last been seen walking home from the University of Melbourne, where she worked in the chemistry department. Her severely bruised body had been discovered lying face down and covered in yellow mud from a nearby trench. Again the victim had been strangled and her clothing torn to shreds.

Soldiers on patrol in the area reported to police that they'd seen a woman, who was identified as Miss Hosking, sheltering under an umbrella in the company of an American soldier. On inspection of the scene, detectives realised they now had a vital clue – there had been a struggle, which left Gladys covered in yellow mud, and it was likely that her killer had been too.

Acting on a tip-off from army personnel at Camp Pell, police went to interview Private Edward Joseph Leonski, 24, of the 52nd Signal Battalion. Yellow mud had been seen on Leonski's uniform, and had also been found in and around his tent. According to detectives – including Fred Adam, who was later to describe himself as a 'specialist in taking murder confessions' – the fair-haired, powerfully built Leonski initially denied involvement in the women's deaths, but then suddenly confessed that he'd indeed murdered them. He offered little in the way of an explanation for the murders, other than to say, 'It was their voices I wanted, so I choked them.'

Leonski was born in 1917 at Kenvil, New Jersey, the sixth child of a Polish mother and a Russian father. His father was drunken and cruel, and his parents separated when he was quite young. His mother later married again, but his new stepfather had similar habits to his father, and his abuse continued unabated.

In early 1941, when he was called up for military service and sent to Australia, Leonski left behind a mentally disturbed mother, two brothers with criminal records, and a third brother in a psychiatric hospital. Eddie Leonski was of medium height and powerfully built, with a boyish appearance and a cheerful demeanour. He displayed his strength by lifting great weights single-handedly and walking around on his hands. Stationed at Camp Pell, he became a massive drinker, often drinking concoctions of beer, whisky, wine, peppers and milk combined, just to show he could handle it. Camp mates described him as 'a good guy when sober, but quite the opposite when drunk'. They told detectives that he often jumped in front of women in the street, whooping, just to frighten them.

After his arrest, there was a battle between Australian

and American authorities as to who should try him for the Melbourne murders. As a goodwill gesture, the local authorities granted the US army's request to conduct a court martial. This was a controversial decision; it was generally felt that as the murders were committed on Australian soil, the cases should be heard in an Australian court.

Actually, had an Australian court heard the charges, the result may have been very different. A panel of eleven US army officers acted as jury at the trial, which was held in a hall in Russell Street, opposite the city watch-house. The court martial began on 10 July 1942, but it was adjourned for a month to have the accused's sanity examined. Leonski entered a plea of not guilty.

The prosecution began by describing the known circumstances surrounding Miss Hosking's slaying. She'd been seen in the company of an American soldier of the general description of the defendant, and the clay found on her body was similar to that on Leonski's person and also on his tent. The court heard that Leonski had been drinking heavily in a Parkville hotel that day, and that he'd also made a written confession to the crime. It was also revealed that Leonski had told a soldier friend that he'd murdered Mrs Thompson, and had confessed in writing to her murder as well as that of Mrs McLeod.

However, witnesses who had seen the mysterious soldier with Mrs Thompson and Miss Hosking were unable to identify Leonski. These witnesses included a barman who had served Mrs Thompson and her friend between eight and twelve drinks, for which the soldier had paid. The barman, when asked to look around the courtroom to see if he could recognise the soldier, was unable to make an identification, although he'd previously identified Mrs Thompson from photographs. He also told the court he'd been taken to a line-up of several soldiers, including Leonski, at a US military camp, but wasn't able to identify the soldier who had been in the hotel lounge with Mrs Thompson.

To confuse matters further, a witness who was a friend of Pauline Thompson and saw her with an American soldier on the night she was murdered similarly failed to identify Leonski when she was asked to look around the courtroom to see if she could recognise the soldier. There was further confusion after an American soldier told the court he'd met Leonski in an Albert Park hotel on the day of the McLeod murder, but another GI rebutted that evidence, saying that he'd seen Leonski in camp that day.

The main piece of evidence against Leonski was the clay on his clothing. The court was told that he'd washed his uniform, which was still damp when detectives inspected it. In fact, there were marks of yellow clay on the inside of the jacket and smeared clay on the outside. The US officer who had inspected them told the court he saw stains of yellow clay on Leonski's bed, and also on the inside of the tent. Significantly, the Government Analyst told the court that the clay found in Leonski's tent was 'similar in colour and constitution' to clay found near Mrs Hosking's body.

Defence counsel then moved for dismissal of all three charges on the grounds that there was insufficient evidence, apart from the confession. Counsel held that it was a recognised principle of law that a person couldn't be convicted of a crime on an unsupported confession. The application, however, wasn't sustained.

Defence counsel next submitted that in a case like this, much depended on the mental state of the accused in respect of the alleged confession. The defence argued that all the evidence indicated that Leonski was a good bloke – and soldier – when sober, but the reverse when he'd been drinking. The court was told how Leonski had suddenly become a very heavy drinker when stationed in Melbourne, and his family had a history of chronic alcoholism and mental instability. An Australian psychiatrist said that he agreed with the medical board assessment that Leonski had a psychopathic personality and would behave abnormally under the influence of alcohol.

The accused man didn't give evidence or make a statement. It took less than an hour's deliberation for a guilty verdict to be returned and the death sentence pronounced. Leonski entered the history books as the only citizen of another country to be tried and sentenced to death in Australia under the law of his own country.

As there was no right of appeal for the condemned man, it was left to General Douglas MacArthur, the head of the US armed forces in the Pacific, to decide whether there should be a reprieve. Leonski himself didn't want a reprieve; he said he didn't want to spend the rest of his life behind bars. So the sentence stood.

The enigmatic Leonski was kept in Cell 6 at the city watch-house from his arrest to his execution. For some time he corresponded with a local woman who gave him a copy of Oscar Wilde's 'The Ballad of Reading Gaol', which he learnt off by heart. His guards at the watch-house found him to be a model prisoner, easy to get along with, and enjoyed playing games such as handball with him.

For a man who was charged with three vicious and frenzied attacks on defenceless women resulting in their deaths, Leonski managed to charm most who came in contact with him. A psychiatrist described him as 'a charming, intelligent, handsome individual, and a man of great physical strength who had the rest of his Company terrorised because of his prowess'.

Leonski was even well regarded by detectives handling the case. Detective Sergeant McGuffie described him as an 'apparently average, decent young American. He had a pleasant manner which, during the investigations, alternated between worry and bravado. He had a ready open smile and clear bright eyes full of good humour. It was easy to enjoy talking with him.' During his trial, the accused man even went so far as to smile, wave and wink to detectives and had a ready smile for all the officers of the tribunal, even though his friendliness wasn't returned.

What drove this pleasant young man to tear apart three women on Melbourne streets – or did he? It has been speculated that Leonski, the great show-off, chose death as the fulfilment of an overwhelming desire for notoriety. Detective Sergeant McGuffie later said, 'Throughout the trial he wanted to jump to his feet and plead guilty. He wanted to be the star of the show.' Others said that Leonski had confessed in the belief that he'd get his picture in the paper.

His defence counsel said:

Leonski was extremely susceptible to suggestion. He was perfectly capable of doing anything, including confessing to something he hadn't done, to attract attention to himself. He couldn't be restrained from discussing his defence with the soldiers guarding him. He repeatedly talked to them about getting in the headlines, and asked their advice as to what he could say that was sensational.

He thought that Leonski was 'as mad as hell, and lived in a world of fantasy'.

Statements attributed to Leonski during his incarceration provided an insight into his personality. When telling a psychiatrist he couldn't remember strangling the third woman, he said, 'After two I suppose you lose count.' When asked about how he'd face his impending execution, he said, 'I am a soldier. I came over here to fight and possibly lose my life. So what does it matter where or how I lose it?' Immediately after the trial, Leonski stamped out a half-smoked cigarette and said, 'I've decided to give up smoking – it's bad for your health.' After his trial, seeing the gloomy looks on his guards' faces, he said, 'What's up? I'm the one who's going to get his neck pulled – not you.' To the US army officers who read the confirmation of the death sentence to him in his cell, he said, 'Say, why don't you hang around? We're going to have a swing party.'

Did Leonski get a fair trial? Almost everyone in Melbourne had already judged him guilty before the trial, and the US army probably had too. There was a growing feeling of rivalry and hostility toward the Americans by Australian men, and the Americans didn't want the situation to worsen. An American soldier being held responsible for murders of Australian women was an explosive situation that they wished to resolve quickly. Was it a case of 'get someone – anyone'? During his trial, probably the biggest blunder the defence made was that they failed to put Leonski in the witness box. The onus was on them to prove that he wasn't sane, and he probably would have done a good job of displaying that on his own.

It seemed that Leonski was looking forward to his execution. Toward the end, he said to one of his guards without the slightest sign of emotion, 'Well, they've measured me and weighed me. It won't be long now.' His apparent indifference to death shocked his keepers. By now, the Americans had been offered the use of the facilities at Pentridge to assist in the conduct of his execution.

Leonski spent his last days quietly singing in his cell. The night before his execution, his guard heard him singing a popular tune, 'It's a lovely day tomorrow, tomorrow is a lovely day'. He was said to be singing it the following morning at 5.20 when some American provosts took him from his watch-house cell to Pentridge. As he was leaving, he thanked his guards for looking after him.

There is no official record of Leonski's execution in Pentridge, though the name Leonski has been pencilled into the book of 'Particulars of Executions'. The only official confirmation came from American authorities, who issued a statement that the death sentence had been carried out.

In his well-researched book, *Private Eddie Leonski: The Brownout Strangler*, author Ivan Chapman wrote that he could find no evidence of any autopsy having been performed on Leonski. He described Leonski as having been hanged on the Pentridge gallows after being attended by two Catholic priests. He also said that the Americans wouldn't reveal how they'd obtained a hangman at such short notice, though some authorities claimed he'd come from Adelaide while others said he was a Western Australian. Chapman further reported that Leonski was cut down after the execution and given an injection. It was his belief that Leonski had died quickly and painlessly, although everything was done for expediency, and the normal formalities of an autopsy were dispensed with.

Newspapers of the day told their readers Leonski was taken to Pentridge at 5.20 am and executed there at 6 am by a civil hangman. They stated that 'apart from the hangman, no Australian official had anything whatever to do with the execution', and that 'all arrangements had been made by US Army authorities'. Other reports claimed that it was an American Provost Marshal who performed the hanging.

The body of Private Edward Joseph Leonski was removed by ambulance from the prison and eventually taken to Springvale Cemetery, where it was buried in the 'isolated section'. Later, his body was exhumed and buried in an all-American part of the cemetery. In 1945, the body was exhumed again, taken to Queensland and buried at Ipswich for two-and-a-half years in order to bring all American soldiers who had died in Australia together. Leonski found his final burial spot when he was exhumed once again and taken to

Honolulu, where he was permanently interred in Plot 9 Row 11 at Schofield Barracks Post Cemetery.

In the novel *Leonski: The Brown-out Murders*, author Andrew Mallon depicts Leonski as a murderer with a split personality. There is Eddie the 'good guy' and his alter ego, Buddy. When he is sober, Eddie is the dominant character, but when he is drunk the archly evil Buddy takes over and wreaks carnage. Perhaps this was the way it was, but one thing seems beyond dispute – Leonski was the most enigmatic character in Australian criminal history.

The doubts about Leonski's guilt were strengthened by an event that occurred on 15 July 1942, during the early stages of his court martial, when the naked body of Mary Agnes Earls, 42, was found in the grounds of St Vincent's Hospital, East Melbourne. She'd been strangled, and had scratches on her face and chest. Although this murder was considered by detectives to be unrelated to the three for which Leonski was standing trial, it had a few striking similarities: the victim was middle-aged; she'd been violently attacked and strangled; her clothing had been taken from her; the murder was seemingly without motive; and – like the other three – no sound of the murder was heard. Newspapers referred to it as 'yet another Melbourne brownout murder', and claimed that she was 'the latest victim of Melbourne's brownout crimes'. There was one other similarity to the other murders – she'd been seen that night leaving a nearby hotel with a soldier. To this day, the murder remains unsolved.

Jean Lee, Robert Clayton and Norman Andrews: Jean Lee was the last woman to be hanged in Australia when she was carried to the gallows in Pentridge's D Division on the morning of 19 February 1951. The 31-year-old Lee was hanged at 8 am, and her two associates in crime, Robert Clayton and Norman Andrews, were executed two hours later. All three needed sedation to meet their fate. The crime for which they paid with their lives was the murder of 73-year-old William 'Pop' Kent.

Jean Lee was born Marjorie Jean Maude Wright in 1919 at Dubbo, New South Wales. A bright girl at school, she later took on several jobs, none of which she was able to hold for long. In 1938, at age eighteen, she married Raymond Brees, and the following year she gave birth to a daughter. The marriage, however, soon ended in divorce, and Jean's mother took over the care of her granddaughter.

Jean turned to petty crime and prostitution, using several aliases – among them Jean Lee. In 1946, she met a professional criminal, Robert Clayton, who began using her in his criminal activities. One of their favourites was known as the 'badger game'. This involved Lee picking up a man and taking him to a secluded place, where they'd get into a compromising position, only to have Clayton appear as the outraged husband. He'd demand money, and if it wasn't forthcoming, the victim would be bashed and robbed.

In 1949, Lee and Clayton headed for Melbourne, where they were joined by an old prison mate of Clayton's, Norman Andrews. During the afternoon of 7 November, the three went to the University Hotel in Carlton. They persuaded a local SP bookmaker, Bill Kent, to join them for a few drinks, which eventually became several. A barman was later to say that Kent 'flashed' a fairly large roll of money while drinking with them.

When the hotel ceased trading at 6 pm, Lee persuaded Kent to take her back to the lodging house he ran in Dorrit Street. She sat on his knee and attempted to pick his pockets, but Kent was too wily, and she was unsuccessful. Another lodger in the boarding house was later to say that he heard a woman leave Kent's front room and go to the back of the house. She returned a few minutes later with two men. As they passed, one of the men opened the curtain near the lodger's doorway and looked into his room before walking on to Kent's room.

What happened next is unclear, as each of the three later gave differing versions as to who did what to the inebriated old man. However, Kent was systematically bashed, kicked and tortured for quite some time in an effort to extort money from him. The lodgers heard groans and the sound of furniture being moved about in Kent's room. A woman went to investigate, but when she knocked on the door, a female told her to go away and not to annoy them. A short time later, a woman from across the road – who often enjoyed a drink with Kent of an evening – also knocked at the door, but was escorted away by Andrews.

Inside the room, the tough old bookmaker resisted his attackers as best he could, but his hands were tied behind his back and his thumbs tied together with his shoelaces. Repeatedly stabbed with a knife and a broken beer bottle, Kent was finally manually strangled.

When a couple of the lodgers heard the three visitors leave, they knocked at Kent's door, which they found to be locked. Having received no answer, and by now quite alarmed, they called the police. When police broke in they found furniture and drawers lying everywhere, and Kent's badly battered body lying face downward in a corner of the room, his wrists tied together with a knotted sheet. The hunt for Kent's killers was quickly underway.

Detectives traced the murderers to the Great Southern Hotel in Spencer Street. Lee, Clayton and Andrews were arrested there next morning and taken to Russell Street Police Headquarters. Each denied participating in the torture and eventual killing of Kent, and told conflicting stories. Lee refused to answer questions until she was told that Clayton had made a statement. She then said that she did her block and hit the old man and tied him up. She didn't rob him, but he was dead before they left, she said. In his statement, Clayton admitted to drinking with Kent in the hotel and at his house, but said he'd left and gone to a café when Jean said she was going 'to get his roll'. Later, he met up with Lee and Andrews, who told him there had been a bad 'blue'. Clayton claimed to detectives that he was 'completely innocent of the attack on the old man.' When Andrews was confronted with Clayton's statement, he maintained that he didn't touch Kent, but that Lee and Clayton had taken his money.

At their trial in March 1950, the court heard that Kent's head was severely battered and that his nose had been broken – consistent with having been hit with a piece of wood. He'd died from strangulation, and marks similar to fingernail marks had been found on his throat. All three accused denied having robbed and murdered him. Lee claimed she'd made her statement 'when she was hysterical'. They'd gone to Kent's, she said, but left soon after, calling goodnight to him.

Clayton told the court he'd made a statement because he'd been drinking and wasn't in a reasonable state, and provided a similar story to Lee's. Andrews also denied having robbed Kent, or in any way harmed him. Throughout their trial, the three accused were very obviously held in contempt by the judge, prosecution and defence counsel alike. Even Clayton's lawyer displayed no respect for him, addressing him by his surname when questioning him during his evidence-in-chief.

The jury deliberated for two-and-a-half hours. When they announced a verdict of guilty, Lee collapsed in the dock. There followed some of the most sensational scenes ever witnessed in court. Asked if she had anything to say, Lee, who was crying hysterically, yelled, 'I didn't do it! I didn't do it.' When Clayton was asked the same question, he replied, 'What I could say would fill a book.' He then turned to the jury and yelled, 'You idiots. May your next feed choke you, you swine.'

When Mr Justice Gavan Duffy passed sentence of death on the three prisoners, Clayton pointed towards police witnesses and shouted, 'Why not hang those lying swine?' He then spat at the jurymen closest to him.

In May, the three condemned prisoners appealed their convictions on the grounds that their alleged confessions were inadmissible, as they'd been unfairly obtained. In a majority decision, the Court of Appeal upheld their appeal and ordered a retrial. Clayton received this verdict in a far different manner than he did the one given at his trial – turning and kissing Jean Lee for so long that two prison warders had to separate them. Their joy was short-lived, however, as a month later the Crown successfully appealed this decision to the High Court, which overturned the Court of Appeal, reinstating the convictions and sentences.

One last chance remained for them. They sought leave to appeal to the Privy Council and asked for financial aid from the Victorian government. The judicial committee of the Privy Council agreed to hear their application, but it quickly decided to dismiss the appeal. Their executions were then set for 19 February 1951.

While awaiting their fate, Andrews – whose real name was Anthes – wrote a letter to the Inspector-General of Prisons in which he attempted to explain his role in the crime. He probably gave an accurate account of Kent's death, though his purpose was self-serving. He explained that at one stage of the night he was pouring drinks while Lee was attempting to relieve Kent of his money. Kent grabbed her by the arm and she cried out to Clayton, who responded by punching Kent several times in the face. Andrews claimed that he then suggested they tie Kent up and leave quietly. As he took a sheet from the bed and tore some strips off it for that purpose, there was a knock at the door. It was a woman from across the road wanting 'to see Bill', but Andrews walked her back out into the street, explaining to her that she couldn't come in as there was a party going on. He walked her down the road, and when he got back, Kent was lying on the floor with Lee kneeling beside him, crying. When he asked what had happened, Clayton responded that Kent had tried to attract the visitor's attention, so he had to grab him by the throat – probably too firmly. On examination, Andrews discovered that Kent was dead, and told Clayton that he'd killed him. Clayton replied that it was accidental, as he only wanted to stop him calling out.

In the few days preceding the executions, Jean Lee became more irrational and distressed. She'd totally absolved herself of blame for the murder and told her keepers that she hadn't done it, as she simply didn't have the strength to choke anyone. None of them meant to kill the old man, she claimed.

It was decided that Lee should be the first hanged, and the time was set for 8 am. Some hours before the execution was due, she was sedated by a doctor. She'd been given a mild sleeping draught the night before, but her condition at the time of execution suggested she was either still drugged, or had collapsed and passed into a state of coma. Newspapers reported that three hours before Lee was hanged, Anglican nuns and clergymen came to visit her in her cell, but they couldn't wake her. Later, the hangman and his assistant – both heavily disguised – entered the condemned cell. There, Lee lay unconscious while the death warrant was read out to her as required by law. The hangman and his assistant strapped her ankles together, put the white hood on her head and carried her to the gallows. There, they placed her on a chair and adjusted the noose. From a balcony surrounding the scaffold, jail officials directed the hangman to proceed. He swiftly adjusted the rope, stood back and released the trapdoor seconds after she'd been carried in. Both Lee and her chair fell from the trap but parted company, and Lee was suspended normally. Death was said to be instantaneous. Her later autopsy report stated that 'death was due to dislocation between the first and second cervical vertebrae caused by hanging'.

To witnesses of the hanging, Jean appeared to be comatose when carried from the cell and placed on the chair. For many years, it was rumoured that she was so terrified of being hanged that she died of fright before the execution. Officially, Jean's death was 'instantaneous and no movements occurred'. It was also recorded that 'at 8.05 am, a few weak pulsations were felt in the right wrist' and that 'no heart sounds were heard'.

Meanwhile, Lee's fellow condemned, Clayton and Andrews, were waiting calmly in their cells. There had been a marked change in their demeanour in the last few days. From constantly arguing with one another, they'd now resumed friendly relations. On the night before their executions, the pair stayed awake and talked with their guards throughout the night. They'd been separated towards the end, and at 10 am they were led from opposite cells adjoining the scaffold. Both seemed calm, having also received sedation. Their heads were covered, and they were handcuffed behind. Both stood quietly on the trap while their ankles were bound together with leather straps. Neither had anything to say, but a few seconds before they fell to their deaths, Clayton called out, 'Goodbye, Charlie,' and Andrews responded, 'Goodbye, Robert.'

The lever was pulled, and with a loud bang from the trap – followed by the thuds of ropes – the two men fell together into eternity. Andrews' death was instantaneous, but Clayton wasn't so fortunate. He'd probably fallen with the knot of the noose under his chin instead of under the left ear, so he strangled at the end of the rope for some minutes. It was ironic that Clayton, who was more than likely the one who had strangled 'Pop' Kent, had himself died by strangulation. A later autopsy performed on Clayton by Dr Whiteside stated that 'death was due to cerebral contusion, shock and asphyxia caused by hanging'. The *Truth* newspaper later reported that Clayton didn't co-operate with the hangman on the trapdoor, which might well have led to an incorrect placement of the noose. After the completion of their autopsies, the three bodies were taken away to a place within the prison, sprinkled with quicklime and placed in coffins for burial.

Long after her two associates in crime have been forgotten, Jean Lee will be remembered as the last woman to be hanged in Australia. She was the fifth female to die this way, but the only one in the twentieth century – the previous one having been executed in 1895.

Ronald Ryan: By the time Ronald Ryan received the death penalty, sixteen years had passed since the last executions, and some 35 murderers had had their death sentences commuted in Victoria alone, as well as many others nationwide. His hanging became a focus for opposition to the death penalty, compounded by controversy as to whether Ryan was guilty of the offence for which he was hanged. The campaign eventually led to the abolition of capital punishment throughout Australia.

Ryan was an unlikely character to ultimately face the hangman. He was of above-average intelligence, had a non-violent criminal record, and those who knew him – including prison authorities – described him as a very likeable person. Probably his greatest downfall was that he was an inveterate gambler. The gamble he took when he decided to escape from Pentridge was his last – and would cost him his life.

Born in Carlton in 1925, Ryan was raised by alcoholic parents in great poverty. He and his three siblings were made wards of the state at an early age, but when he turned fourteen, Ryan absconded and headed for Balranald in New

South Wales where he obtained work as a railway sleeper cutter. By the age of twenty, he'd saved enough money to support his mother and three sisters.

A few years later, he met – and later married – Dorothy George. Together they had three daughters, but by this time Ryan had taken to gambling, and they soon fell into debt. In 1956, Ryan began passing bad cheques around Dandenong and Warrnambool, and for these offences he was put on a bond.

By the early 1960s, Ryan had become a professional criminal, breaking into shops and factories. He faced eight charges of breaking and stealing, and was given eight years imprisonment. He commenced this sentence at Pentridge, but was reclassified to Bendigo prison, where he was regarded as a model prisoner. There, he entered the education classes, obtaining the Leaving Certificate and almost completing his studies for matriculation.

Released on parole, Ryan took up a position as a clerk, but he didn't last long. He was also robbing shops and using explosives to blow their safes. In November 1964, he received an eight-year sentence for breaking and entering, with an extra five years for breach of parole.

Placed in B Division at Pentridge, Ryan soon received news that his wife was getting a divorce. Faced with this news and the prospect of a long sentence, Ryan weighed up his options and decided that escape was the only solution. He chose Sunday 19 December as the date to make his break. It was the day of the prison officers' Christmas party, and there would only be a skeleton staff on duty. He sounded out fellow prisoner Peter John Walker, who agreed to go along with him.

Early in the afternoon, inmates watched as Ryan and Walker climbed the wall of the B Division exercise yard, leapt to the ground and scaled the outer prison wall, then ran along it until they reached No. 1 post. The sleepy warder there,

Helmut Lange, got the shock of his life when he saw Ryan on the catwalk in front of him, holding a piece of water pipe in his raised hand. Before he could do anything, Ryan grabbed Lange's loaded rifle from its rack and pointed it at him. Then Lange saw Walker hidden behind the safety railing on top of the tower.

The two prisoners ordered Lange to come with them down the stairs. The door at the bottom of the staircase was locked, so Ryan took Lange back up the stairs to operate the lever to open the exit door. Backing down the stairs – and still pointing his rifle at Lange – Ryan again reached Walker, and together they ran to a nearby car park. Here, they encountered the Salvation Army prison chaplain, Brigadier Hewitt, and attempted to obtain his car keys. When Hewitt said he hadn't brought his car, Ryan struck the chaplain over the head with the rifle.

The escapees then ran towards Sydney Road, pursued by an unarmed warder, George Hodson, who had just come from the party in the officer's mess and had responded to Lange's alarm. While they were attempting to hijack a passing car, Walker noticed Hodson and called out a warning to Ryan, who turned and pointed his rifle at the guard. A shot was heard and Hodson fell to the ground, mortally wounded. At much the same time, Prison Officer 'Scotty' Patterson, who had Ryan in his sights, fired a shot. He later claimed he'd shot in the air because someone got in his line of fire. At Ryan's trial, nineteen witnesses to the shooting all agreed that only one shot was fired, but no cartridge case was ever found near where Ryan was standing at the time.

Ryan and Walker left the scene, taking over a vehicle and making their way to a 'safe house' in Elwood. A huge manhunt was now underway, but this didn't deter the escapees from holding up the Ormond Branch of the ANZ bank and stealing $4000. Shortly after, the State Government announced a reward of $5000 for information leading to the arrest of the wanted pair.

On Christmas Eve, a party was held at the 'safe house'. There, tow-truck driver Arthur Henderson recognised Ryan, and told Walker that he 'was going to turn Ryan in and cop the five grand'. Walker then arranged with Henderson for them to go and get more beer for the party. Some time later, Walker returned alone. He'd cold-bloodedly shot Henderson in a public toilet block in Albert Park. The body was found early on Christmas morning.

The escapees then headed for Sydney, where Walker made contact with an ex-girlfriend, and arranged a double date with her and a woman she knew. They were to meet at the Concorde Repatriation Hospital, but – unbeknown to the escapees – the police were tipped off. On arriving at the hospital, the escapees were quickly recaptured. Just nineteen days after their break from Pentridge, they found themselves back there, and in the dreaded H Division.

At the subsequent murder trial, Ryan claimed that he couldn't have killed Hodson because he hadn't fired the rifle he was carrying during the escape. Prosecution witnesses stated that they'd seen Ryan fire a shot – though their statements all varied in detail, as most usually do. Four of them placed Ryan to Hodson's left, which was inconsistent with his wound.

Defence counsel suggested that another warder had shot Hodson accidentally when firing upon the escapees. The bullet that killed Hodson had entered his body in a downward direction, which indicated that this might well have happened. Unfortunately, the bullet passed straight through Hodson's body and was never found (so couldn't be tested), and nor was the rifle Ryan had taken from Lange. Ryan's counsel, Phillip Opas QC, enlisted the aid of a leading mathematician to support his claim that Hodson had died from a shot fired from a prison tower. The professor said that from his calculations, the 1.77-metre tall Ryan would have had to be 2.55 metres tall to have fired at the angle of the fatal shot.

Despite the best efforts of his counsel, Ryan was found guilty of murder and sentenced to death. Incredibly, at a separate trial, Walker was found not guilty of the murder of Henderson, but guilty of manslaughter. For this, he was sentenced to twelve years imprisonment, to be served cumulatively with the twelve years he received over the escape – plus the ten years he was already serving on a robbery charge.

Since Jean Lee and her two accomplices had met their fate on the Pentridge gallows, all subsequent death sentences had been commuted to life imprisonment, and the same outcome was generally expected in this case. However, the Victorian Premier, Henry Bolte, was determined that Ryan would hang.

With all appeals having failed, the execution was scheduled for 3 February 1967, and despite massive protests – including thousands who gathered outside the prison walls – the hanging went ahead. It was reported that Ryan met his fate calmly – his last words to the hangman being 'God bless you. Make it quick.' Prison psychiatrist A. A. Bartholomew, who signed the particulars of this execution, recorded that 'as he fell one heard his neck break', and that, 'after the fall there were no movements. The heart beat for 3 to 4 minutes.'

A postscript to this execution was that another warder involved in the escape, Helmut Lange, was to lose his life as a result of it. Lange used his rifle to commit suicide in J Division a little over twelve months after Ryan's execution.

The question remains – was an innocent man sent to the gallows? To his dying day, Ryan's counsel, Phillip Opas QC, fervently believed Ryan was a victim of circumstances, and that Hodson was killed by 'friendly' fire.

✿ ✿ ✿

When capital punishment was abolished in Victoria in 1975, the Pentridge hanging equipment was taken down and put into storage. Later, in 1996, the Supreme Court sheriff loaned this equipment to the National Trust for re-installation in its original place at the Old Melbourne Gaol. However, a problem arose when the trapdoor, which had been modified to suit the catwalk area at Pentridge, couldn't be repositioned, necessitating the installation of a new trapdoor in the original position.

The sheriff also lent the Trust the 'Particulars of Executions' book and the executioner's box containing the hanging equipment, which included leathered ropes, restraining straps, hoods and weights, all of which are displayed at the Old Melbourne Gaol museum.

A few years after the Melbourne Gaol closed and was mostly demolished, part of the site was used in building the Working Men's College, which later became RMIT University. In April 1929, the remains of several prisoners were discovered in what had been a labour yard of the jail. As rubble was being lifted, the name 'E Kelly' and an arrow became visible on a wall. Shortly after, several other coffins were unearthed. The remains found in them were in good condition and were placed in sacks around the workplace. These were the remains of some prisoners who had been executed at Melbourne Gaol.

It was decided to engage a professional undertaker to oversee proper exhumation of the remaining bodies and have the remains taken to Pentridge. Some had already gone the previous week in wooden boxes originally used to hold industrial goods such as axe handles and kerosene tins. With the engagement of the undertaker, remains were placed in individual coffins before being taken to Pentridge. In all, some thirty remains dating back to 1880 were recovered at the site. Four more bodies were located in the grounds of the prison hospital in 1937, and these were also relocated to Pentridge. An archaeological team discovered another set of remains there in 2002.

After his execution in 1967, Ronald Ryan was buried in a small triangular area adjacent to the east end of D Division that was long thought to be the burial place of all others executed at Pentridge. Then in 2006, Heritage Victoria used archaeologists to seek other remains there – but they could only locate Ryan's. However, the National Trust supplied a plan that seemed to be the layout of a different burial ground that was rectangular in shape, covering an area about twenty-five metres long by seven metres wide, contained by an iron fence and accessed through a gate. Such an area was located, and subsequent investigations revealed that it had indeed been used as a mass burial ground for prisoner remains from Melbourne Gaol. Two mass graves were discovered there – one containing the remains of the other nine prisoners executed at Pentridge, and the other holding the remains of the four reburied in 1937. Eventually two more mass graves were located in this site; they contained seventeen bodies of prisoners executed in the late 1800s and early 1900s at Melbourne Gaol. A third mass grave containing fifteen bodies was later located a short distance away, and was found to contain the first lot of bodies relocated to Pentridge. This grave was thought to have been made by workmen who had inadvertently uncovered the bodies and reburied them in this new site. All Melbourne Gaol prisoner remains were in coffins or burial boxes, and were passed on to the coroner to determine identification.

Naturally, there was much interest as to whether Ned Kelly's remains had been found. During the investigations, a man informed Heritage Victoria that he knew the whereabouts of a skull – stolen from the Old Melbourne Gaol – which was considered likely to be Kelly's. After he handed the skull in to the coroner, DNA testing determined that it was not Kelly's, but was likely to be that of the nineteenth-century murderer Frederick Deeming. Forensic investigations also revealed that DNA could be obtained from more than thirty sets of the remains – including those of Ned Kelly, which were found in a box originally used to store axe handles.

In September 2010, the coroner announced that the remains of posthumously pardoned Colin Campbell Ross, believed to have been wrongfully convicted of the murder of a schoolgirl, had been identified, and a month later his ashes were passed on to his family. The remains of Ned Kelly and Ronald Ryan have also been exhumed and handed on to relatives. Kelly has since been buried in his final resting place at Greta cemetery, close to his mother's grave. All other remains have been reburied in the triangular area at the end of D Division, thus ensuring they will remain at Pentridge.

CHAPTER 7
WILLIAM JOHN O'MEALLY

Of the 1200 inmates in Pentridge, there was no bigger name than William John O'Meally's. By the early 1970s, O'Meally had served eighteen years imprisonment for the murder of Constable George Howell, a crime he always claimed he hadn't committed. Originally sentenced to death, O'Meally had been reprieved after a change of government, but his papers were stamped 'Never to be released'.

O'Meally was born Joseph William O'Meally at Young, New South Wales, on 25 November 1918, the third of four children to Joseph and Eileen O'Meally. His father, a farm labourer, spent most of his earnings at the local hotel, and the marriage was an unhappy one. When O'Meally was eleven, the family moved to Sydney, where all four children were made wards of the state and fostered in friends' homes. When the children turned fourteen, the government endowment ceased, and they were turned out to fend for themselves. Young O'Meally was cast adrift in 1932, when Australia was in the throes of the Depression. In 1933, his parents divorced.

O'Meally soon took to 'jumping the rattler' – illegally riding the trains around country New South Wales, joining an army of unemployed drifters. He recorded his first conviction in January 1936 at Murrumburrah Police Court under the name Joseph Thompson, the first of his many aliases, when he was found guilty of 'trespassing on railway property'. Sentenced to two days hard labour, he chopped wood at the local police station. A week later, he was sentenced to five days hard labour at Wagga over a similar charge – riding on trains without a ticket.

In June that year, O'Meally fronted the Children's Court at North Sydney on the first of several charges he'd face for assaulting police. Sentenced to three months imprisonment, he was sent to the notorious Gosford Reformatory, where conditions were very harsh. He escaped and made his way home, but his mother turned him in to the police, and he was then sent to Yanco Reformatory. On release, he headed for Queensland where, under the alias of Gene Thompson, he was sentenced to six months with hard labour in June 1937 for stealing an overcoat. During this stint in prison, he began practising a new persona, speaking with what he thought was a Canadian accent and telling all comers that he was Canadian born.

Over the next few years, O'Meally gained further convictions in Sydney for assaulting police and for a range of property offences. In July 1938, he was sentenced to twelve months in prison for receiving stolen property. Convinced by his claim of Canadian birth, the judge recommended that he be deported after serving his sentence, but O'Meally's father later disabused the authorities of this idea, telling them he was born in Young, no matter how strenuously he denied it.

By now, O'Meally was familiar with several lock-ups, including Sydney's tough Long Bay Prison. Among all his criminal activities, he somehow managed to marry, but his new wife soon found that marriage alone wouldn't keep him out of jail.

Not long after his release on the receiving charge, he was again arrested for house-breaking but failed to appear in court. With a warrant out for his arrest, he fled to Brisbane, where he fell foul of the law again. In February 1941, he was sentenced to a month's jail on each of two stealing charges, and he'd barely been released when he was again sentenced to eighteen months for house-breaking and stealing.

On his release, he returned to Sydney, where he was soon back in court, this time under the alias Lawrence Rivette. Convicted yet again of house-breaking, he was given eighteen months jail in June 1942. He received the same sentence for the same offence in September 1945. While he was in jail, his wife sued for divorce in April 1946, pointing out to the court that he'd spent three-and-a-half years in jail during their five-and-a-half years of marriage. Then, in 1947, police in New South Wales again issued a warrant for his arrest on charges of stealing and illegally using a motor vehicle. At this point, O'Meally decided to try his luck in Melbourne.

He didn't get far. In November 1947, he was sentenced to three years in Pentridge on seven counts of stealing. On gaining early release, he tried to steal a car the same day. Appearing in court under his old alias of Gene Thompson in June 1950, he received a month for the attempted vehicle theft and was fined for assaulting two policemen and using indecent language. On a short trip back to Sydney after that incident, he informed his mother, 'Long Bay is a palace compared to Pentridge.'

He now took up lodgings in bayside St Kilda, and around this time he claimed he became connected with a gang of thieves who raided homes and cars. O'Meally would pay cash for these stolen goods, then sell them on to a 'fence'. This would be the crux of his defence against a later murder charge.

Two months after his release from Pentridge, he was back there again. He'd been given three months imprisonment for assault on a police constable at St Kilda. It reportedly took six policemen to transfer him to Russell Street Police Headquarters.

After he was next released, O'Meally briefly gained

employment at Heatherton Sanatorium, where he began a relationship with a fellow worker, Lois Evers. Soon they were living together at her parents' Oakleigh home, and they married in May 1951. According to O'Meally, there was friction with Lois's family after his brother-in-law discovered that he had a criminal record.

When the newlyweds moved to a small three-roomed house in Bonbeach, Lois's sister noticed several items around the home that she suspected were stolen. A party for Lois's father's birthday ended in an altercation between O'Meally and his in-laws. O'Meally claimed that his in-laws wrote to police about this incident and also informed them that stolen property had been seen at his home. This letter would contribute to O'Meally's downfall over a far more serious charge than theft.

THE CRYSTAL PALACE

Constable George Howell arrived for night shift at the East Malvern police station late in the afternoon of 30 January 1952. Life was looking good for George. He was living in the popular bayside suburb of Bonbeach, and was looking forward to marrying in a little over a month's time. He'd joined the police force in May 1948, serving at Russell Street and Malvern police stations before being posted to East Malvern the previous year. He'd recently been assigned to investigate a spate of thefts from cars in the vicinity of the Crystal Palace Theatre in Dandenong Road, Caulfield.

At about 10.15 pm, Howell left the station and rode his bicycle to the theatre, arriving a little before 10.30. Numerous cars were parked in the area immediately outside the theatre. He entered the foyer and spoke briefly to the theatre manager before going back outside. Surveying the row of cars, he noticed a man crouching and acting furtively around a Morris Minor. When Howell approached the car and challenged the man, he swung around, struck Howell full in the face with his bag, then spun around and dashed away from the parked cars, with Howell in hot pursuit.

Witnesses would give varying accounts of what happened next. At about 10.35 pm, two friends, Edna Wilkinson and Lorna Bailey, were leaving the theatre when they heard sounds of scuffling behind a car parked quite close to the front of the theatre. A few seconds later, two figures ran out from the line of cars about a metre apart and made a wild dash directly toward a nearby railway viaduct. The man in front appeared much shorter than the man behind, who was swinging a torch. The man in front also appeared to be wearing a Donegal or tweed coat, which was flapping about; the women couldn't tell whether he had a hat on, but the man at the back was bare-headed.

The two men reached the left opening of the viaduct, then disappeared from view. Curious, the women set out after them. About halfway to the viaduct, they heard groaning, 'as though somebody was struggling, and then something dropped to the roadway'. A few seconds later, they heard a shot.

A little further from the scene, engineer Norman Byrne was standing with his daughter on the footpath outside a shop in Dandenong Road when his attention was drawn to the area in front of the Crystal Palace Theatre. There, he saw a man running west, at a right angle to the viaduct, with a policeman about three metres behind him. According to Byrne, the two ran right across two plantations and a tram line, then veered back towards the viaduct, though they were zigzagging rather than running in a straight line. When they reached the left side of the viaduct, the policeman caught the other man on the footpath at the entrance, up against a brick wall. There was a scuffle, and the policeman stepped back, or was pushed, and fell to the ground. The man in front seemed to be hitting the constable with a torch, which was going on and off. Neither man had headgear, he believed.

The two then ran out of his view under the viaduct. Byrne got into his car with his daughter and drove under the viaduct into Normanby Road, which runs parallel to the railway line. A police constable was lying on the roadway, just around the corner. Byrne pulled up, had a quick conversation with the constable, who'd been shot and was writhing in agony, then drove to a nearby telephone box and called the police.

Misses Bailey and Wilkinson had now reached that side of the viaduct and found the badly wounded policeman lying on the road. Miss Bailey immediately recognised him as local constable George Howell. Almost directly under him was a tan satchel, and close by were a black hat and a long torch. While Miss Wilkinson did her best to make Howell comfortable, Miss Bailey went for assistance.

Though the witnesses' accounts varied in detail, they agreed that Howell had chased a man to the Normanby Road side of the viaduct, where he was shot at point-blank range. The mortally wounded policeman had staggered a short distance and collapsed as the gunman fled.

Bystanders did what they could to assist the stricken policeman, and eventually an ambulance arrived to rush him to the Alfred Hospital, where he underwent emergency surgery. Though near death, he was able to give detectives a description of the wanted man: he was about 173 cm (5 feet 8 inches) tall, with a ruddy, round face, about 26 years of age and solidly built.

Accompanied by Misses Wilkinson and Bailey, the police returned to the cars outside the theatre. By now, they had the hat and satchel found with the wounded policeman. At the edge of the plantation, they picked up a two-cell torch, some loose keys scattered on the ground, and a policeman's cap. Other police found a brandy flask, a pair of tinsnips and a screwdriver, all thought to have been the gunman's. Closer inspection of the black hat revealed that it was quite an unusual one – large (size 7¼), London-made and distinctively styled. These articles would become vital evidence in the subsequent trial.

Over the next couple of days, George Howell battled for his life, but in the early hours of Friday 2 February the gallant 26-year-old passed away. The investigation now became a homicide, and Melbourne's underworld was turned over in the hunt for the person responsible. The police investigation was governed by the mantra, 'find the person in possession of these articles on the night of the murder, and you've found the killer'. The newspapers published photographs of the black hat and satchel, which were soon identified as having been stolen in two house burglaries – the hat from a Toorak home, and the satchel from a house in Malvern. Police also found a new witness – a taxi driver named Walter Feltham, who had picked up an 'agitated' man not far from the crime scene a short time after the shooting.

A little over a week after the shooting, William O'Meally was arrested for the murder. Acting on a tip-off, detectives raided O'Meally's home in the early hours of 5 February, looking for stolen property that would connect him with the hat and the satchel. At the time, O'Meally was in bed with his pregnant wife, Lois. During the raid, the detectives impounded several articles of stolen property and took them away. O'Meally was taken to Russell Street Police Headquarters, where he was interrogated and placed in a line-up along with ten others, in the hope that he'd be identified by Feltham. The taxi driver failed to identify any of the men in the line-up as being his mysterious fare, but later identified O'Meally as he crossed Russell Street in the company of detectives.

In early March, O'Meally faced the Coroner's Court, and at the conclusion of the hearing, the coroner committed him for trial on a charge of having murdered Constable George Howell. The coroner said: 'The circumstantial evidence and verbal evidence given, in my view, point directly to O'Meally as the man who fired the shot and murdered Constable Howell.'

THE TRIAL

Before O'Meally's Supreme Court trial, his counsel inexplicably moved to have Howell's description of his killer as ruddy and round-faced ruled inadmissible, though it would appear to have been evidence in O'Meally's favour, not against him. The judge at the trial, Acting Justice Coppell, was only too pleased to concede to the defence's request.

The trial that followed went for ten days, and the courtroom was packed with spectators, who waited in queues for hours. The Crown's case was entirely circumstantial, and police may have been hoping that the sheer volume of evidence would counter the fact that much of it was of low quality. There were four main points of disagreement between prosecution and defence: the differences between the eyewitness accounts, the claim that O'Meally had been seen near by, the significance of the items found at the scene and in O'Meally's house, and the portrayal of O'Meally as a person of ill repute by the Crown and the judge.

Witnesses Wilkinson, Bailey and Byrne gave their accounts of what they saw outside the theatre on the night of the shooting. Eyewitnesses rarely give exactly the same testimony, even when they are looking at the same event, but the women's account didn't tally with Byrne's in any respect. The defence emphasised the differences and suggested that there had actually been three men tampering with the cars.

There were numerous indications that Misses Wilkinson and Bailey had seen two different men from Mr Byrne. The women had seen the two men take a direct route to the viaduct, whereas Byrne saw two men follow a more oblique path. Byrne was also the only witness to see a wrestling match between the two, and neither Wilkinson nor Bailey recognised a policeman as one of the pair they saw.

Oddly, both parties said they had reached Howell first, and neither saw the other. Yet, given the short distance each had to travel to reach Howell, if they had seen the same 'chase', they should have arrived at virtually the same time.

Another witness, Robert Lee, told the court that he was driving east along Normanby Road on the night of the shooting, and as he approached the railway viaduct, he saw two people running from under it. He didn't take much notice, but when he reached the viaduct, Howell was lying on the road. Lee got out of his car and rendered assistance to the constable, who was also being attended to by two women, one of whom he thought was Miss Wilkinson. From Lee's evidence, it is clear that after Howell was shot, there were at least two other men at the scene who were capable of running.

One of the police also changed his evidence between the inquest and the trial in one significant respect. At the inquest, two policemen gave conflicting accounts of where two items of property – a brandy flask and a pair of tinsnips – were found. One of these locations wasn't in a direct line between the plantations and the viaduct, supporting Byrne's view of a more indirect chase, but by the time of the trial, both police were in agreement that they were found on the tram tracks that ran under the viaduct, which supported the women's account.

The claim that O'Meally had been sighted near the scene of the crime rested entirely on the evidence of taxi driver Walter Feltham, who had picked up a fare while he was driving by Caulfield Park, about a kilometre from the viaduct. Feltham described how 'a gasping and very excited man' jumped into his cab and asked to be taken to St Kilda. He told the court the man was 'jumping around the cab like a madman and was looking everywhere'. When Feltham asked whether he'd lost anything, he replied, 'Yes, my b—— mate.' (Feltham said he didn't want to swear in court.) 'I lost the b—— about half an hour ago', but he said he didn't want to wait for him.

Feltham offered his passenger a cigarette, but he was so upset he lit the wrong end. As they were travelling towards St Kilda, a police car passed them and his fare said, 'There go the f—— wallopers.' In later evidence, the term 'wallopers' was described as an unusual one by Detective John O'Connor, who also testified that O'Meally used that expression to describe police.

In court, Feltham emphatically identified O'Meally as the man he'd driven to St Kilda, pointing to him and declaring, 'That is the man. O'Meally's the man – I'd know him anywhere.' But several of Feltham's statements belie his confident claim. In an informal note included in the prosecutor's case file, a junior counsel described him as an 'unreliable witness', and the remark seems justified.

For example, Feltham claimed that he drove under the viaduct at about 10.50 that night and 'noticed nothing out of the usual'. This claim is hard to believe. At that time, Howell would have been lying on the road two or three metres to Feltham's left, and people were rushing to the policeman's aid – including some who were flashing torches to alert motorists to pull over.

Feltham also had difficulty explaining why he'd failed to identify O'Meally at the line-up and had only identified him when he was clearly marked out as a suspect walking in company with police. Feltham excused this by saying he'd 'given O'Meally the benefit of the doubt' because he'd had a haircut and grown a small moustache since he last saw him, but it's difficult to see how this could have changed his appearance sufficiently to avoid recognition. His passenger,

Feltham said, had long, shaggy hair and had kept running his hands through it – a habit police said was one of O'Meally's mannerisms.

Feltham also said that his fare spoke with 'an accent like an Irish, Lancashire or Yankee brogue'. Detective O'Connor implied that this indicated O'Meally was their man, as he spoke like 'a Newcastle or Sydney Yank'. The descriptions were vague and contradictory, but the defence allowed them to ride.

Detective Tremewan said that O'Meally had changed his appearance after the murder by cutting and dyeing his hair, and that he'd developed a short moustache – mainly painted on – to alter his appearance, the inference being that he was doing it to fool Feltham, the only person who had placed O'Meally in Caulfield that night. But relatives and others swore that O'Meally's hair was always jet black, and that he more often than not had a moustache.

Tremewan reported that when police raided O'Meally's Bonbeach home, they found stolen property from the Toorak home of a Mr Phillip Carney, who had identified the black hat found at the scene of the shooting as his. They'd also found other stolen property from the home of a Miss Noel Tadgell, who had identified the satchel found at the scene as hers. These links, he told the court, indicated that O'Meally was the killer.

On cross-examination, however, the defence was able to establish that cigarettes had been found stubbed on the floor at the scene of the burglaries, establishing that whoever broke in was a smoker, whereas O'Meally had never smoked.

The prosecution called an expert witness, Mr Harold Wignall – a chemist at the state laboratories – who told the court that he'd examined paint spots taken from articles found at the scene of the shooting and had found them microscopically similar to freshly painted surfaces in the

O'Meally home. This evidence was largely refuted by defence experts, who claimed that Wignall's tests could not be used to draw conclusions about similarities in the paint. The paint spots on the articles found at the scene were far too old to compare with paint used very recently at the O'Meally home. An analytical chemist and a paint technician with Glazebrooks Paints who appeared for the defence both agreed that Wignall's faulty testing made his results unreliable.

In O'Meally's defence, his wife, Lois, testified that her husband hadn't left their Bonbeach home on the night of the shooting. Under oath, she told the court that at the time of the shooting, she was in an advanced stage of pregnancy. She'd been very ill, and her husband had stayed up all night looking after her. This alibi evidence formed the major part of O'Meally's defence, as did the evidence that O'Meally was a non-smoker.

In an unsworn statement from the dock, O'Meally said he was looking after his pregnant wife on the night of the shooting. He couldn't have been the man chased by the constable as he could hardly walk, let alone run, having recently burnt his feet stamping out a backyard fire. He denied being the fare in Feltham's taxi, and pointed out that Feltham hadn't identified him in the line-up. He further stated that he was a non-smoker and Feltham's fare was a smoker, as was the house-breaker who stole the property found in his home.

O'Meally explained that he was the 'receiver' of the stolen items, not the thief. He denied ever having any of the articles found at the scene of the crime in his possession, and told the jury that the black hat, which had been tried on him, was far too big. He also told the jury he cut his own hair, which he often dyed black, and wore a moustache from time to time as the mood took him.

The prosecution had made much of two items: a set of car

keys found among the keys at the scene of the crime, and a street directory containing a loose map of Apollo Bay, which had been found at O'Meally's home. Both had disappeared from a car parked opposite a church on a day when O'Meally and his wife were attending his sister-in-law's wedding there. But O'Meally denied ever having the stolen car keys and claimed that he'd found the street directory on the road near the church on the day of the wedding.

In his closing remarks, Mr Maloney, the defence counsel, told the jury, 'Unless you find that O'Meally is the only man who could have killed Howell, you should find him not guilty.' He pointed to the discrepancies in the eyewitnesses' accounts of the chase, maintaining that they had seen two different 'chases', and that only Byrne had seen the policeman chasing his killer. There were at least two men tampering with the cars, he said, and O'Meally wasn't one of them. He was at home with his wife, as she'd testified.

In his summing up to the jury, Acting Justice Coppell was cavalier in dismissing these discrepancies between the eyewitnesses' accounts of the chase. 'A suggestion was put to you that there may have been a second, or possibly a third man, taking part in this enterprise of tampering with people's motorcars. There is not a shred of evidence to support that suggestion.' He also suggested that the taxi driver's description of his fare's mannerisms, speech and language confirmed Detective O'Connor's evidence, and called it a 'gratuitous slur' when O'Meally suggested that O'Connor hadn't told the truth. In hindsight, however, it can be seen that without Feltham's evidence, O'Connor's claims about O'Meally's verbal habits were worthless.

The judge pointed out that Wignall had found similarities between flecks of paint found on various items and the paint newly used at the O'Meally house, but made no reference to the defence rebuttal of these findings. In regard to O'Meally's statement that he had blisters on his feet from stamping out a fire, Coppell suggested the jury should examine his sandals and decide 'how badly burned you think the feet of a man would be if the sandals were no more burned than those appear to be'.

As to the items found at the scene – the hat, the satchel and the car keys – the judge asked: 'Who but the man who committed all three thefts could have part of the proceeds of the same three thefts in the same area on the same night? Who could have dropped the keys, the satchel, and the hat except the man who broke into all three?'

This remark goes to the heart of the most contentious aspect of the Crown case. Much of the evidence presented in court depicted O'Meally as a man of bad character, the suggestion being that he was responsible for the burglaries, even though he'd never been charged over them. Justice Coppell placed so much emphasis on O'Meally's past record during his summing up that Crown Prosecutor Winneke raised the issue of prejudice with the judge almost immediately after the jury retired to consider its verdict.

The court didn't wait long to hear the outcome of the judge's tirade. After only a four-hour deliberation, the jury returned a guilty verdict. When it was delivered, a distraught O'Meally leaned forward in the dock and said, 'Yes, I was charged, yes, I was charged, but I am innocent, I could not do it.' Mr Justice Coppell then pronounced sentence of death. The judge asked O'Meally if he had anything to say as to why he should not be sentenced to death, and he replied, 'Yes, I am innocent.' With all the contradictory and conflicting evidence, it's hard to see how a court today would have found him guilty beyond *reasonable* doubt.

UNDER SENTENCE

Having been sentenced to hang, O'Meally was transported to Pentridge and placed in a condemned cell to await his fate. He appealed his conviction to the Full Court, mainly on two grounds: that prejudicial evidence given against him had made it obvious to the jury that he had a criminal record; and that witnesses had seen two and possibly three other men running towards the viaduct other than the constable and the gunman. This appeal was unanimously rejected. The court found that 'there was ample evidence to support the verdict'. A further request to appeal to the Privy Council was also rejected. Several months later, however, O'Meally received news that the Executive Council had commuted his death sentence to life imprisonment without remission.

Under these circumstances, escape was never far from O'Meally's mind. In the first year of his incarceration, he was sent to the labour yards for possessing escape equipment. He became extremely unpopular in prison, because his rebellious behaviour resulted in other prisoners losing privileges. His keepers considered him disruptive and incorrigible, while other prisoners thought him arrogant and vain.

In his autobiography, *The Man They Couldn't Break*, O'Meally claimed that he'd decided to highlight his plight to people he thought might be able to help him, but these efforts only landed him back in the punishment block. He wrote to Constable Howell's family, pointing out that if indeed he'd shot Howell, the constable would have recognised him, as they knew one another, being near neighbours in Bonbeach. The family simply took the letter to the police. He also claimed to have written to Princess Margaret, stating that he'd been convicted of a crime he hadn't committed. He'd written to her because he'd read that while she was on a visit to South Africa, a man whose brother had been wrongfully convicted and imprisoned threw a petition into her car as she drove by. The brother was later released. When he sent this letter, O'Meally said, he didn't realise that royalty don't receive their mail until it has been thoroughly checked. The princess's secretary returned his letter to Pentridge, and O'Meally was given three months in the labour yards on bread and water.

In May 1954, O'Meally was unintentionally involved in one of the most sensational incidents in Pentridge history. Fellow B Division inmate Robert Walker, who at the time held the title of 'King of Pentridge', began brooding over the life sentence he'd received for shooting his wife's lover the previous year. He'd written his life story in his cell at night, and had these memoirs smuggled out to his wife, Rita, who had sworn to wait for him. After he'd completed this task, he conceived an incredible plan to avenge some wrongs he believed had been done to him by killing eight men – four prisoners and four officials – having had a gun smuggled into the prison over the farm wall.

Walker had originally harboured ideas of escape, but changed his mind and instead decided he'd die in the 'Big House'. From his cell – No. 142 on the fourth tier – he wrote:

> Here is my final plan, and only death will prevent me from carrying it out as I want it. I am going to rub out eight men. It grieves me not to be able to give you a detailed description of each one's reaction as they stare death in the face. These are the eight, or should I include myself and say nine, who will get theirs.

Walker then named four prison officers and four prisoners, including O'Meally. He continued, 'These are the eight lowest specimens of humanity one could find.' He reflected on the irony that while his wife was 'planning a little house for the future, I am planning a little massacre for the present. By the time you read this, I'll be dead, but I know for sure a few will die with me.'

On 26 May 1954, Walker put his plan into action. He reported in sick instead of going to work in the tailor's shop. He saw the prison doctor, then returned to B Division and asked Chief Prison Officer Maguire for a confidential talk. At 2.20 pm, Walker was ushered into Maguire's office, where he produced a revolver, levelled it at Maguire's head and demanded that Deputy Governor Fox be summoned. As soon as Fox entered the office, Walker held the gun to his head and demanded that O'Meally and three other prisoners be brought up from their work gangs and be sent to their cells.

While this was being arranged, Walker threatened the division writer and ordered him to tie Maguire and Fox up. Shortly after, the four prisoners from the gangs were heard walking through the division, heading to their cells. Walker then demanded that Senior Prison Officer Asche be called to the office. When he arrived, Walker escorted him at gunpoint through the division and into the 'circle', where he handcuffed him to a desk by one hand.

But Walker made a mistake: he placed his revolver on the table and went to lock the entrance gate. Asche managed to get his free hand onto the gun, and as Walker turned back, Asche fired at him, but missed. In the struggle that followed, Asche was punched and kicked in the face. After regaining the gun, Walker raced to 'murderers' row'. He knew which cells to go to, and fired into the first of them. His target saved himself by falling unharmed to the floor, fooling Walker that he'd been hit.

The crazed Walker then ran to O'Meally's cell, but before he could fire, some armed warders appeared and challenged him to drop his weapon. Walker was beyond reasoning. He turned his gun on the warders, who immediately fired, hitting him in the foot. Enraged, Walker hobbled into his cell. For several seconds, an eerie silence fell over the division.

Then the sound of a shot echoed through the corridors. The armed warders crept carefully along the tier until they neared Walker's cell. Using a mirror, they peered through the trap of his cell door and saw him slumped in a corner, bleeding from a wound to the right temple. He was rushed to the Royal Melbourne Hospital and died shortly afterwards. A few days later, he was given an armed police escort on his last ride to Cheltenham Cemetery. Among the people waiting there was a relative of Constable Howell, Mr P. Howell of Sandringham, who said, 'I have come here to pay tribute to a man who might have killed O'Meally.'

ESCAPE AND RETRIBUTION

On Saturday 27 August 1955, O'Meally was granted permission to attend a weekend football match on the prison oval. During the match, he heard that four other prisoners were going to attempt an escape. Their plan involved waiting until the finish of the match, and then making a dash from the oval at the final bell. They'd be armed with a smuggled shotgun and rifle, which had probably been brought in and hidden near the football ground.

At the conclusion of the match, the four prisoners, two of whom were now armed, bailed up the warders and marched to a tower overlooking the oval, suddenly joined by O'Meally. Using the warders as shields, they marched them to the southern wall. There, they took a rope and began to climb. Now they had no hostages to protect them, bullets from other warders' rifles began to rain around them.

The first two prisoners over the wall raced to a nearby Singer car, ordered its occupants out and drove off. Two others managed to commandeer a panel van from a nearby street and quickly disappeared, but O'Meally wasn't so lucky.

Having been left behind by the others, he crawled into the rear of an unoccupied house in nearby Richards Street. He lay there in high grass for some time until police, acting on a tip-off, surrounded the house and closed in on him with guns drawn. As he was taken away, a newspaperman asked police if O'Meally had said anything about the whereabouts of the missing escapees. 'I told them nothing, fella,' O'Meally yelled through the bars of the police wagon. It wasn't a wise thing to be seen as a 'dog' around Pentridge.

O'Meally wasn't the first to be recaptured, however, as two of the other escapees had crashed their stolen getaway car not far from the prison. The other two made good their escape, remaining free for a week before robbing a Collingwood jewellery store and being recaptured when attempting their getaway.

O'Meally later told a court hearing that he was wrongfully incarcerated and that he'd been 'forced to escape' to highlight his plight and to try to establish his innocence. Although Justice Gavan Duffy allowed O'Meally to make public his claim that he'd been wrongly convicted, he sentenced him to four years for the escape, to be served concurrently with his life term. Sent to the punishment section, O'Meally was kept in the labour yards for thirteen months.

He was now getting considerable publicity, particularly through the Melbourne *Truth*. He'd become an embarrassment, especially to security at Pentridge, which was also taking a hammering from the press.

O'Meally's next – and last – escape attempt was in early 1957. It was to bring fearful retribution to him and his mate, John Henry Taylor, who had also been involved in the previous escape. They aimed to take advantage of a visit to Pentridge by the magistrate who came periodically to hear charges laid against prisoners for misdemeanours committed within the prison. These hearings took place in the prison governor's office, only a few metres from the main entrance to the jail. The pair planned to have themselves charged with breaking some regulation, and then take the magistrate and the governor hostage during the hearing. Taylor had contacted a friend outside to send him a handgun.

O'Meally and Taylor staged a fight in the B Division exercise yard and were duly charged. At 11 am on the day of the magistrate's visit, they and fourteen other prisoners were marched from their work gangs to the front section of the prison, where they were lined up outside the governor's office. After some time, the two would-be escapees became aware that the large iron grille gate through which traffic entered the prison was occasionally opened and shut to allow trucks through.

At around midday, the gate opened again. With a nod of their heads, the pair dashed for the opening and reached it just as the gate was about to shut. O'Meally grabbed a guard while Taylor tackled the gate operator. A shot rang out, and the guard on the gate fell to the ground. Undeterred, the escapees pushed their way out through the gate and into the reception area, where they locked some other guards up, then quickly made their way through the still-open gate.

Much to their surprise, the two tower guards on either side of the prison entrance were unaware of what was going on below. This allowed Taylor and O'Meally to stroll over to a garage opposite, where they commandeered a Holden utility that was being repaired. By now, the locked guards had freed themselves and rushed into the street in pursuit.

With Taylor at the wheel, the utility raced down O'Hea Street at high speed, hotly pursued by three vehicles full of armed guards. Twice the bonnet of the utility flew up, and when O'Meally jumped from the vehicle to shut it, their pursuers closed in. Screaming around the corner of Sussex Street, Taylor lost control and crashed the utility into a fire hydrant. The escapees were quickly surrounded by guards, thrown to the ground and hogtied. Sent back to the punishment section, the escapees learnt that the gatekeeper had survived, and that they'd be charged with escape and attempted murder.

At their trial in the Supreme Court, O'Meally again told the court he'd participated in the escape in an endeavour to establish his innocence of the crime for which he'd been imprisoned. He thrust a bundle of papers towards the judge, claiming they contained new evidence that would clear him of the constable's murder. O'Meally said, 'The only wrong thing I have done in jail is to try and escape because I am an innocent man.' When his turn came to enter the witness box, Taylor admitted having a gun, but claimed it accidentally discharged when the warder struggled with him at the main gate.

The judge, Justice Hudson, found O'Meally and Taylor guilty of the armed escape and also of 'occasioning actual bodily harm'. Ten more years were added to O'Meally's life sentence and seven to Taylor's sentence. The judge then dropped a bombshell when he sentenced the prisoners to be privately flogged with the cat-o-nine-tails. He fixed the number of strokes at twelve, telling the escapees he believed they were beyond reform. After the sentence was delivered, the judge told O'Meally he'd refused to read his papers, as 'there was no relevance to this case'. In response, O'Meally told Justice Hudson, 'The only thing flogging does to a man is scar his mind.'

There was much public outcry about the prospect of the floggings, and thousands signed petitions, which were sent to authorities in an attempt to have them stopped. Particularly outspoken against them was Dr Norval Morris, a long-term commentator on the O'Meally case who would later become an internationally recognised expert on the

197

criminal justice system and prison reform. Morris bitterly opposed such corporal punishment, saying, 'O'Meally is being punished for being O'Meally.' However, an appeal to the Full Court against the punishment was dismissed by a majority decision.

On the morning of Tuesday 1 April 1958, O'Meally and Taylor were taken to a section of A Division where a large triangular frame awaited them. In his autobiography, O'Meally gave a vivid account of the flogging. They were told to remove their shirts, and Taylor would be the first man flogged. Present in the room were the prison governor, seven guards and a doctor. When Taylor had received his punishment and was taken away, O'Meally was placed on the triangle with his arms raised upwards and sideways, and his hands manacled to the front legs of the triangle. A leather belt was put around his neck and another around his body to cover the kidney area. A masked man – the flagellator, who was also the hangman – stood by with the cat-o-nine-tails.

The governor read the sentence aloud and gave orders for the punishment to proceed. Stepping quickly forward, the masked flogger raised the cat, which crashed against O'Meally's back. At the Governor's count, the prisoner then received his full punishment. O'Meally described the flogging thus:

> The tails of the cat whined through the air and exploded on my right side. I gasped loudly as the savage blow knocked the wind from my lungs. The pain was excruciating. I bit my tongue and my mouth filled with blood. I vomited. With each stroke the flogger drew on all his strength to exact maximum suffering, and thus took out the absolute hatred authority had for me.

Taken back to the newly created H Division, the two escapees were thrown back into their separate cells. They would be the last men flogged in Australia.

O'Meally was to endure the following twelve horrific years in H Division – 'where there was no night or day, only an endless twilight', as he described it. He was to be constantly bashed, starved, humiliated and debased. For whatever debts he owed to society, he'd pay a price like no other. For twelve long and bitter years he survived all the brutality and ill-treatment H Division guards could muster.

He spent the first six years of his incarceration in the division in solitary confinement, breaking rocks by day and isolated in his cell at night. The latter half of his time was a little better, as he was working in the company of a few other prisoners in one of the two industry yards.

O'Meally had resigned himself to spending his remaining days in H Division, but in early May 1970 he was told he'd be transferred to B Division. He said that on release, the first thing he did was to get down and kiss the grass – something he'd not seen in all those years.

His quick-marching made him a conspicuous sight for a considerable time around B Division, but normality gradually began to return. After some months, the quick march became a very brisk walk. In his book, O'Meally told of his difficulties adjusting to life after H Division. He attributed his return to normality to the deep breathing he practised in his cell of a night. It was a long time before he became less conspicuous among his fellow inmates, though. O'Meally was to spend several more years in B Division before a brief stint in Castlemaine Prison. At his own request, he was returned to Pentridge, where he was then housed in the more relaxed A Division.

Agitation for his release grew during the latter 1970s, with television star Don Lane taking up the cause. Lane took a film crew to Pentridge and interviewed O'Meally in his cell. During the interview, which was aired on *The Don Lane Show*, Lane promised O'Meally he'd do all he could to help him, as he thought his sentence and subsequent treatment had been inhumane.

Shortly after this, on 4 July 1979, O'Meally was taken from Pentridge to the Social Welfare Department in Melbourne, where he was told he was to be given immediate parole. Ironically, his parole papers were signed by the man who'd prosecuted him at trial – Sir Henry Winneke, then Governor of Victoria. O'Meally had served a total of twenty-seven years – fourteen of them in Pentridge's maximum-security sections and six in solitary confinement – and had been the last man to be flogged in Australia. He headed to Queensland, still maintaining his innocence of the crime for which he'd paid so severely.

It was reported that as recently as the mid-1990s, O'Meally attempted to have his case reopened. It was also reported that a man who claimed he was at the scene that night, pilfering from cars, told a lawyer that O'Meally's version of events was true. However, it is of little consequence to O'Meally now. According to relatives, he died in 2011 in Brisbane at the remarkable age of 92. To have reached such an age after all the punishment he'd received suggests that perhaps he *was* the toughest man in Pentridge after all.

B Division skylight looking up from the circle

B Division cell block

(above left) View from interior of underground, or 'blind' cell, B Division

(above right) Interior of underground cell showing pit into which a prisoner could be lowered

View from chapel, showing fire damage caused by rioting prisoners in 1978

Entrance to chapel, B Division

Recently excavated foundations of 'airing yards' in B Division

B Division exercise yard entrance

(left) B Division cell
(right) Painted cross on tunnel floor, H Division

Entrance to H Division tunnel

H Division cell. Prisoners originally had to do without cupboards
like the one on the end wall

Main entrance internal gate through which O'Meally and
Taylor escaped in 1957

Exterior main entrance

Lonely rose against a wall

D Division, where executions took place

E Division entrance

B Division Chief Prison Officer's office where Robert Walker held hostages in 1954

H Division reception area and Chief Prison Officer's office

H Division entrance

Internal guard's tower

Walkway in guard's tower

(overleaf) Aerial view of Pentridge circa 1920. The letters superimposed on the photograph identify the divisions as they were known in the 1960s. Note the 'airing yards' at the lower left of A Division and the H Division labour yards.

Main entrance from square

William John O'Meally
twice escaped from
Pentridge and was the
original inhabitant of
H Division
Examiner (*Launceston,
Tasmania*) 24 May 1952,
courtesy Trove

(*right*) Andrew Gordon
Kilpatrick, the 'Barwon
Murderer' and one-time
'King of Pentridge'
Examiner (*Launceston,
Tasmania*) 11 September 1953,
courtesy Trove

(*below*) Robert Peter Tait,
callous murderer of a
defenseless old lady

O'MEALLY GUILTY OF MURDER

MELBOURNE. — William John O'Meally (28) was found guilty by a Criminal Court jury last night of the murder of Constable George Howell. He was sentenced to death by Mr. Justice Coppel.

AFTER pleading his innocence, O'Meally, in tears, cried out to his wife, "Cooky, Cooky, Cooky, darling."

Weeping hysterically, she ran from the crowded but hushed court with her mother

The judge then began the death sentence and, as it concluded, O'Meally slumped to the floor of the dock, despite the efforts of two warders to keep him upright.

confusion," he replied: "Yes, I was charged. I am, I say, innocent. I couldn't do a think life this. I have been found guilty of—I couldn't—

I was fond of my wife and child. I couldn't honest."

At this stage O'Meally's wife and her mothr burst into tears and O'Meally cried, "Cooky, Cooky, Cooky, darling."

The two women ran from the court and the judge began the sentence.

After leaving the court to

ALLEGED CONFESSION TELLS OF BRUTAL COLAC MURDER

MELBOURNE.—The story of how a hacksaw was allegedly used to cut the head and hands from the body of a man on a river bank at night was unfolded in the Geelong Coroner's Court yesterday.

TWO Colac men were committed by Mr. Steedman, S.M., for trial on a charge of having murdered Donald Brooke Maxfield (22), labourer, Murray St., Colac, whose mutilated body was found in the Barwon River on August 1.

They are Andrew Gordon Kilpatrick (33), boilermaker, Murray St., Colac, and Russell William Hill (22), labourer, Gellibrand St., Colac.

Det.-Sgt. F. J. Adam said he interviewed Hill at Hamilton on July 31.

In an alleged statement, Hill said that Kilpatrick had urged him to get rid of "Chitters" Maxfield because Maxfield had been with him (Hill) when he broke into Sears in Colac and had made a statement against him to the police.

Referring to a meeting between Hill and Kilpatrick at Goodall's garage, Colac, on May 13, the statement went on: "Kilpatrick said to me, 'Chitters Maxfield has got to

come around here tonight with a .22 rifle. Now is our opportunity to get rid of im.'

"A Bit Dubious"

"I was a bit dubious of doing it. We had a few drinks of beer and then Maxfield arrived. Maxfield had a drink with us.

"We had a general conversation and then Andy picked up an iron bar about 18 inches long by about 1¼ inches thick off a bench and hit Maxfield on the side of the head with it.

"He then hit him on the head four or five times and he went down on his back and blood was spurting all over his face and all over the floor. He was unconscious and groaning and we both lifted him into the back of the car."

Still Alive

The alleged statement went on to say that at Queen's Park, Maxfield was still alive and he said, "You

"Andy pulled him out of the car and hit him with the butt of a .45 pistol a couple of times. I think that was where he died," the alleged statement said.

Hill was also alleged to have said that at the Barwon bridge over the Barwon they stopped the car and carried Maxfield to the river

(left) Daryl Francis Suckling almost committed the perfect murder when Jodie Larcombe disappeared

(right) Leith Ratten (left) with Ernie Sigley. Was the shooting of his wife deliberate or accidental?
Newspix

(left) James Edward 'Jockey' Smith was labelled 'Public Enemy No. 1' by the media

(right) Leigh Robinson took the lives of two girlfriends who rejected him

(left) Derek Ernest Percy, a sadistic paedophile murderer who took his secrets to the grave

(right) Christopher Dale Flannery, branded as 'Mr Rent-a-Kill' over alleged contract killings

(below) Laurence Joseph Prendergast (centre), acquitted of murder and disappeared in mysterious circumstances
Newspix

CHAPTER 8
ANDREW GORDON KILPATRICK

Very few murderers actually look the murderous type, but even when Andrew Kilpatrick was in his fifties, it wasn't hard to imagine that he'd been fearsome in his younger days. Kilpatrick, a tall, heavily built man, had at one time been recognised as the 'King of Pentridge'.

Andrew Gordon Kilpatrick, born in 1919, had a long history of violence. Educated at the prestigious Geelong Grammar School, he joined the Victorian police at a young age. After eighteen months of service, however, he was dismissed for assaulting a superior officer.

In April 1943, he volunteered for service in the Royal Australian Navy, but again his penchant for violence brought his career to an abrupt end. In July 1944, Ordinary Seaman Kilpatrick, 25, was court martialled on twelve charges, including acts of sabotage on a warship in New Guinea's Milne Bay. Kilpatrick was described as an extremely powerful man who had terrorised other members of the crew. He was accused of holding another seaman over the ship's side and threatening to drop him overboard.

It was alleged that Kilpatrick had thrown hand grenades into his ship's motorboat and discussed a plan to use grenades to blow up the ship's galley in protest at the quality of the food. In the course of the hearing, however, it became obvious that Kilpatrick was not the only sailor disaffected by the regime on his ship, and that other naval ratings felt they were being treated like children.

The day after the motorboat was blown up, authorities found an anonymous letter saying: 'It could have been a bomb. Anyone of you pigs or you rats could have been on the end of it. Wake up to yourselves. Give the men a fair go. Peace be with us. Amen. (Signed) The Gohst.' The next day, a message was posted on the ship's notice board saying: 'Warning. Rats undermine foundations of peaceful homes and breeding vermin are easily stamped out. (Signed) The Gohst.' Police alleged they had asked Kilpatrick how the word 'ghost' was spelt, and he'd given the same spelling as that used in the letters.

At the conclusion of the court martial, Kilpatrick was found guilty on ten of the twelve charges, including theft, desertion, and having written and sent anonymous threatening letters. He was expelled from the navy and sentenced to twelve years in prison, but he only served two.

Kilpatrick's next known court appearance was just three years later, in 1947. Now a labourer living in the western Victorian town of Colac, he broke into a factory at Sylvania, south of Sydney, with two other men, and stole equipment to the value of £600. Police surprised them as they were attempting to conceal the stolen gear. All three bolted, but Kilpatrick was brought down by a policeman's bullet. Newspapers reported that he appeared in court on a stretcher with his body encased in plaster, and it was feared he might be crippled for life. In fact, he'd spend the next two years in a wheelchair. He pleaded guilty to factory breaking and was released on a three-year good behaviour bond. The judge said he was satisfied that Kilpatrick had already been punished enough.

But in 1953, Kilpatrick was at the centre of a gruesome murder that received much publicity, after a man's dismembered body was discovered dumped in the Barwon River at Geelong. Kilpatrick and his younger accomplice,

Russell Hill, might well have got away with the crime had it not been for a separate police investigation, led by Detective Sergeant Fred Adam, into a series of break-ins around Colac. The wily Adam soon centred his attention on three locals who he suspected were behind the robberies – Andrew Kilpatrick, now 33, Russell Hill, 22, and their friend Donald Brooke Maxfield, a 22-year-old Colac labourer. Subsequently, Hill and Maxfield were charged with shop-breaking and released on bail.

On 10 May 1953, Police Constable Ross Chester was riding his motorbike around Colac streets when he noticed two men loitering near a store. When he challenged them, one of the men threatened him with a pistol while the other circled behind him and dragged him from his motorbike. Chester was then bashed and hit several times over the head with the pistol. Badly hurt, he was taken to Colac Hospital for treatment. He was later awarded the Police Valour Badge for 'outstanding tact and courage' in the execution of his duty.

Police lost no time charging Andrew Kilpatrick and Russell Hill for maliciously wounding Constable Chester with intent to do bodily harm. A jury acquitted them on this initial charge, but they were later convicted on the lesser charge of 'wounding with a weapon' and sentenced to twelve months imprisonment. They appealed against their sentence, but before the appeal could be heard, the two men were arrested on a far more serious charge – the murder of their partner in crime, Donald Maxfield.

Detective Adam launched a new investigation after Maxfield failed to appear in court over the shop-breaking charge, having disappeared from his home on 13 May. Adam decided the quickest way to discover what had become of Maxfield was to put pressure on Russell Hill. The older, more experienced Kilpatrick had already claimed he knew nothing about Maxfield's mysterious disappearance.

On 31 July, Adam questioned Hill at Hamilton police station and put him under pressure to confess. Hill quickly cracked and admitted that he and Kilpatrick had killed Maxfield in the belief that he was going to implicate them in other burglaries in the Colac area. After he'd made a written statement to Adam, Hill was charged with murder.

In Geelong next day, Hill showed detectives where Maxfield's body had been thrown into the river. Some hours later, police interviewed Kilpatrick at a house in Geelong West and showed him a copy of Hill's statement. Police later alleged that on reading the statement, Kilpatrick had snarled, 'The squealer. If I get my hands on him, I shall fix him for keeps. If I knew he was going to squeal, I would have done him also.'

The next day, a Harbour Trust diver found a headless body in the Barwon River. Covered with sacking, the body had fencing wire wrapped around it and had been weighed down with a 40-kilogram rock. A short time later, the diver found a kerosene tin – punctured with holes and weighed down with stones – embedded in the muddy river bottom. When opened, this tin contained Maxfield's head and hands.

THE BODY IN THE BARWON TRIAL

What became known as the 'Body in the Barwon' murder trial began sensationally on 20 October 1953, when counsel for Hill attempted to have his statement declared inadmissible into evidence, because Hill now claimed it was made under duress. Hill told Justice Martin that when he was interviewed in the CIB room at Hamilton police station, he told detectives he didn't know where Maxfield was. The detectives' response had been to give him a bashing. Hill said:

> My shoes and socks were taken and I was belted several times with a piece of rubber. I was dragged by the hair

onto the floor and pushed in the stomach. I was put in a chair and punched. My nose started to bleed. My arms were twisted.

Hill said that his statement was only partly true. He now declared that Kilpatrick had committed the murder, and that he'd only helped him to weigh the body down with a stone when they found it floating in the river some time later.

After submissions from counsel, Justice Martin declared the statement to be fairly obtained and therefore admissible as evidence. There may have been truth in Hill's claim, however. Detective Adam wasn't known as 'Thumper' without good reason.

Crown Prosecutor Winneke said in his opening statement that Maxfield had disappeared from his home in Murray Street, Colac, on the evening of 13 May after having dinner with his parents. 'Nothing was heard or seen of Maxfield until his body was taken from the Barwon River,' Mr Winneke said.

A hushed courtroom then heard that in the course of the murder, Maxfield's skull had been shockingly damaged by severe blows. Detectives, who had been trying to track Maxfield down, didn't know he'd been murdered until Hill confessed to them and told them where the body was. When questioned by detectives, Hill had broken down and said, 'I'm glad it's come to this – poor Chitters [Maxfield] is dead, and Kilpatrick killed him. I want to tell the truth and get it off my mind. It's been driving me crazy.'

Winneke told the court that Hill and Kilpatrick had met at a Colac garage on 13 May and decided to kill Maxfield. He read out Hill's statement, which said:

Andy Kilpatrick mentioned to me several times that we should get rid of Maxfield. I knew Andy meant I should kill him, as he probably would give evidence against me at my trial for shop-breaking. Kilpatrick said to me, 'Maxfield has got to come around here tonight with a .22 rifle. Now is our chance to get rid of him.'

I was a bit dubious of doing it, but we had a few drinks of beer and then Maxfield arrived. We had a general conversation and then Andy picked up an iron bar about eighteen inches long and hit Maxfield on the side of the head with it. He hit him on the head four or five times and he went down on his back. He was unconscious and groaning, and we both lifted him into the back of the car. Andy also put two kerosene tins in the back of the car. We mopped up the blood on the floor with water, and Andy put a hacksaw in the car.

We then went out to Queen's Park and Andy said, 'There's a waterfall up there – it would be a good place to put him.' After I stopped the car and we got out, Andy opened the door and dragged him onto the grass. Maxfield was still alive and he said, 'You bastard.' Then Andy pulled him out of the car and hit him with the butt of a .45 pistol. I think that was where he died. We carried him along a track and got some of the way up, but the going was too rough and we decided to turn back.

By this time all his clothes were dragged off him. We bundled him back into the car and drove to Prince's Bridge. I stopped the car and Andy pulled him out again. We both carried him down to the river bank, where Andy said, 'Now we will cut off his head and his hands and they won't be able to identify him.' He got out a hacksaw and cut off his hands and then his head. Andy said, 'You put the head and hands into a tin'. We put his clothes into the other tin and threw both tins and the body into the river just near the Prince's Bridge.

Investigating Detective Sergeant Frederick Adam told the Court that Hill had attended the Hamilton police station on 31 July, where he made a full and frank statement to him concerning the death of Donald Maxfield. After concluding his statement, Adam continued, Hill had also said, 'About a fortnight after the murder we were going to Melbourne on a motorcycle and saw the sack floating near the river bank. We came back and tied a big rock to it and sank it.'

Adam further told the court that when interviewed about the murder, Kilpatrick was asked if he'd hit Maxfield with a revolver. Kilpatrick had replied, 'Yes, a couple of times.' Adam said Kilpatrick then added, 'Listen, he was dead before we cut him up.' Adam also told the court that unidentifiable bloodstains had been found on a Webley & Scott .45 revolver found in a house where Kilpatrick had been living.

Adam declared that Hill's statement had been made voluntarily, and that he'd not physically assaulted Hill in any way, nor had he even spoken to him harshly. He also expressed his belief that Hill feared Kilpatrick. As a result, they'd been kept apart from each other since they were arrested. He further denied the allegation that he'd told Kilpatrick police would make up their own evidence unless he told the truth.

The government pathologist, Dr Keith Bowden, confirmed that Maxfield's head and hands had been sawn off, probably with a hacksaw, and that the severe injuries to his skull were consistent with blows struck with an iron bar or a pistol butt. Maxfield probably would have died within half an hour of these wounds being inflicted, he observed, but he believed that he had been drowned after the head injuries were inflicted, after which his head and hands had been amputated.

A Colac taxi driver, Max Benson, and a passenger, Colin Thomas, testified that on 3 June, Hill and Kilpatrick were travelling to Melbourne in Benson's taxi when they stopped near a bridge over the Barwon River. Hill and Kilpatrick had left the taxi and gone under the bridge for about ten minutes. Thomas also identified a .45 revolver among the exhibits in court as similar to one belonging to Kilpatrick.

At the conclusion of the Crown's case, the defence called Hill's mother, Mrs Ruby Hill, who told the court that on the night of 13 May, she'd gone to a picture show in Colac, and when she returned home at about 11.15 pm, her son was in bed reading. She also told the court she always did her son's washing and hadn't noticed any traces of blood on his clothing after that night.

Both accused men gave evidence in their own defence, each claiming he was at his mother's home on the night of the murder. When it came to Hill's turn in the witness box, his story diverged markedly from the one in his statement. He agreed that Kilpatrick had raised the idea of getting rid of Maxfield on 13 May, and said he told Hill to be at the garage at about 7 pm. Hill said he'd agreed 'just to pacify him', but he didn't go. He went for a walk and sat in a park in case Kilpatrick called for him at his home.

He didn't see Kilpatrick until the next day, when they met in a hotel and Hill was 'roasted' for not turning up. Kilpatrick said he'd had to go through with it by himself. He'd hit Maxfield on the head with an iron bar while they were having a few drinks together in the garage, then taken him to Geelong, where he'd cut off his head and hands, dumping everything into the Barwon.

Hill claimed that a couple of weeks after the murder, the two of them had gone to Melbourne, and on the way, Kilpatrick had shown him the spot in the river where the body was. He claimed he could see a bag floating in the water, so on their way back that night, he helped Kilpatrick to wire a large rock to the body in order to sink it.

Hill repeated the claim that his written statement had been made after detectives 'pushed him about'. He knew

Kilpatrick didn't like squealers and continued to associate with him after the murder because he feared Kilpatrick might do him harm.

When it came to his turn in the witness box, Kilpatrick said that certain evidence given against him had been made up. He claimed detectives had threatened to frame him if he didn't own up to Maxfield's murder. He categorically denied planning or carrying out the murder with Hill, claiming that Detective Sergeant Adam had said to him: 'If you say you killed Maxfield, we'll see you get off lightly.'

Cross-examined by Hill's barrister, Mr Cohen, Kilpatrick denied the claim that the previous week, while they were both in custody, he'd suggested that Hill should take the blame for the murder. He also denied that he'd ever discussed Maxfield with Hill at all, though he did say he'd 'heard rumours' that Maxfield had made a statement against Hill to police. He further claimed that Hill had told lies in court as well as in his statement to police.

Kilpatrick denied ever owning a .45 revolver or any other gun, and couldn't account for Hill swearing that he did. When asked why he hadn't made an official complaint to Inspector Donnelly about detectives saying they'd make up evidence, Kilpatrick said he thought if he did so, Donnelly would just laugh at him. He was adamant that he'd been home at his mother's house on the night of the murder, and that he was nowhere near Prince's Bridge that night. He also denied that he'd spoken to Hill about Maxfield's death at a hotel the day after the murder, and stated, 'At no time did I get Hill to help me to tie a rock to a bag in the river.'

In his summing up to the jury, Crown Prosecutor Winneke pointed out that though both accused had denied any part in the murder, police couldn't have recovered Maxfield's body when they did if Hill hadn't made admissions the day before. He further pointed out that although Hill claimed that police used force to obtain his statement, he hadn't complained previously – not even to the magistrate at the inquest into Maxfield's murder. He also described Kilpatrick's story as hard to believe, asking why three detectives would conspire to fabricate evidence to convict a man of murder.

Against this, Hill's counsel told the jury that it was highly unbelievable that a young man like Hill could have planned and committed such a callous, cold-blooded murder. In turn, Kilpatrick's counsel put it to the jury that Hill was 'clutching at the last straw' by blaming his client, and that his lying was in strict contrast to Kilpatrick's straightforward evidence. He also questioned why Hill hadn't protested if – as he claimed – Kilpatrick had suggested that they murder Maxfield, Hill's closest friend. He also pointed out that Hill had a motive to kill Maxfield, but Kilpatrick didn't.

In his directions to the jury, Justice Martin told them that if they believed Hill's statement was made entirely freely, they must regard it seriously. He pointed out that the firmness of Hill's notes and signature on his statement suggested he hadn't been coerced.

The jury obviously agreed, as later on the evening of 22 October 1953, it returned with guilty verdicts against both Hill and Kilpatrick. When the judge's associate asked if they had anything to say before sentence, an ashen Hill shook his head, then almost in a whisper replied, 'No, sir.' Kilpatrick calmly and clearly responded, 'I am not guilty.'

Justice Martin then told the prisoners, 'You have been found guilty on what I regard as clear and convincing evidence of a horrible and cruel murder, planned in cold blood and completed in circumstances of the utmost barbarity.' He sentenced them to death. The State Executive Council commuted the death sentences on 14 December, sentencing Kilpatrick to life imprisonment without remissions and Hill to twenty years without remissions.

KILPATRICK IN PENTRIDGE

From the time of his admission until the early 1960s, Kilpatrick was a man to be feared in Pentridge. In May 1954, after the sensational death of the reigning 'king', Robert Walker, Kilpatrick became the dominant personality in B Division. In an article in Melbourne's *Argus* newspaper, Maxwell Skinner, another B Division prisoner of long standing, was glowing in his praise of Kilpatrick. He wrote:

> Kilpatrick is now emerging as the B Division 'king', taking the place of Robert Walker. He is one of the strongest willed men I have met, and men's personalities seem to melt in his hands. He is more than 6 feet high and this with his 17 stone makes him a frightening figure. Under the showers, he rubs his body vigorously for minutes with a tough bristled brush. He is mad on physical fitness and could probably break the back of any man in the jail.

But things went wrong for Kilpatrick early in the 1960s, after he was given the prized job of disc jockey for B Division. Some young toughs in the division took exception to his on-air remarks and gave vent to their opposition physically. According to Governor Ian Grindlay in his memoirs, *Behind Bars*, Kilpatrick was bashed and given a kicking in his cell after he described the younger prisoners as 'mugs' for carrying on around the prison and having privileges taken away from the older prisoners.

The prison grapevine agreed that this was the reason for the attack on Kilpatrick, but had a different version of the punishment. It was said that Kilpatrick had been given a 'helping hand' down the stairs leading from the top tier in B Division, and a razor had been used to slash his face when he reached the bottom. Whatever had happened to him, by the

1970s Kilpatrick was far from the fearsome man he'd once been. He was in poor health, extremely quiet and docile around the prison. Russell Hill, his accomplice in Maxfield's murder, had been released from Pentridge in 1969.

CHAPTER 9
ROBERT PETER TAIT

A tall, ginger-haired prisoner often seen around the jail, Robert Peter Tait was forever whistling. His favourite tune was 'The Green, Green Grass of Home', which never seemed to end. As you passed, he'd pause to say 'Good morning' in a broad Scottish accent. To anyone who was willing to pass the time of day with him, he'd cheerily introduce himself as 'Jock'. It was noticeable that the prisoners shunned him, as they did other inmates convicted of violence against children or the elderly and defenceless. Having murdered an elderly woman, Tait was one of the 'rock spiders', as they were generally known.

Tait had gained notoriety in 1961, when he brutally and sadistically murdered the mother of Anglican minister George Hall at the Hawthorn vicarage of the All Saints Church. A loner and an alcoholic, Tait was also a sexual deviant. Little wonder he was always whistling. He was probably the luckiest man alive to have escaped execution for this terrible crime. His reprieve came so late that his grave had already been dug within the prison grounds, he'd been weighed and measured to ascertain the drop required for a successful hanging, and the hangman had tested the mechanics of the trapdoor.

* * *

Tait was born in Glasgow, Scotland, in 1924. At the age of eight, he fell from the roof of a building and was hospitalised for some months with severe head, back and leg injuries, and after that he was placed in a school for children with learning difficulties. He served a stint in the Royal Navy as a stoker, and during that time he became a heavy drinker. He also engaged in homosexual activities during this time.

After the war, he married a Lithuanian woman, and together they migrated to Australia in 1952, but his alcoholism and violence placed the marriage under strain. His wife soon left him after enduring much sexual humiliation and several beatings.

Tait soon fell foul of the law. His drinking habits worsened, and his sexual fantasies became increasingly violent. By 1954, he'd begun to wear women's underwear. Then, during 1959, he violently assaulted a 70-year-old librarian at the Christian Science Reading Room in St Kilda, punching her several times, attempting to throttle her, then stealing money from her.

Tait was soon captured and sentenced to three years imprisonment, which he served at the prison on French Island, east of Melbourne in Westernport Bay. After almost two years, he was granted parole on the condition that he abstain from drinking, but he made little or no attempt to abide by this condition. He soon began to go from one hotel to another around Melbourne, using whatever money he could scrounge.

When his resources dried up, Tait decided to go to the All Saints vicarage, where he later claimed he intended to borrow some money. He'd previously made contact with the vicar, George Hall, a couple of years earlier, after Tait allegedly found a set of keys in the door of a factory in nearby Glenferrie Road. Tait gave Hall the keys and asked him to hand them in to police, as he said he was afraid they might accuse him of stealing them. Later, Tait went back to the factory and was given a £1 reward for his honesty.

Tait arrived at the vicarage in the late afternoon on 8 August 1961. After knocking at the front door and failing to get an answer, he made his way to the rear entrance and knocked there. Again there was no answer. Mr Hall was away attending a meeting, while his mother, who lived with him, was asleep in the back room. Tait decided to let himself in, entering through the unlocked door. He began to ransack the house in search of money, but Mrs Hall heard noises and went to investigate.

Ada Ethel Hall was 82 years old and quite frail. She was active in the church and was always willing to help anyone in need. Startled by the noise, she called out to the intruder, demanding to know what he was doing in the house. Tait punched the defenceless old lady to the floor and rained blows on her with a torch until she apparently lost consciousness. Tait sexually assaulted the frail old woman, ripping the clothes from her. He dragged her into a bedroom, threw her onto a bed and inserted the torch violently into her vagina. Tait washed Mrs Hall's blood from himself and stole a leather case, some money and some panties from the old lady's bedroom before furtively leaving the scene of the crime.

Later that evening, George Hall found his mother and raised the alarm. A massive hunt for her killer followed. Investigating detectives later found Tait's fingerprints on a wooden box in the study.

That night, Tait checked into the Orrong Hotel in Armadale, where he drank at the bar, and stayed the night under the alias of Tom Jones. A couple of days later, he hitchhiked to South Australia, where he stayed for some days. He visited two more vicarages in Adelaide, seeking money, and went to a Presbyterian manse, where he was given a job. A short while later, he broke into the manse when nobody was there, stealing jewellery, a clock and some women's panties.

On the run again, Tait hitched a ride with a truck driver

to Port Augusta, where he gave the driver a brooch for his kindness. The truck driver felt this was so odd that he reported the incident to police. As a result, Tait was arrested and charged with breaking, entering and theft from the manse.

Police soon noticed a good deal of similarity between this crime and the now well-publicised robbery and murder at the vicarage in Melbourne. Interviewed by Melbourne detectives, Tait quickly admitted committing the crime at the Hawthorn vicarage. He said, 'I was there. I did it. I did not know she was dead until I read about it in the papers next day.' He was immediately extradited back to Melbourne, where he again made a full confession to police.

In a Supreme Court trial before Mr Justice Dean, Tait readily admitted his crime, but pleaded insanity. He was supported in this plea by Dr Guy Springthorpe, a psychiatrist, who contended that during the attack on Mrs Hall, Tait was overcome by an 'irresistible impulse' and that the use of the torch was 'a horrible form of sadistic behaviour'. However, two psychiatrists from Pentridge Prison gave evidence for the prosecution that Tait wasn't legally insane. They argued that Tait knew what he was doing and that it was wrong. The jury accepted their view and found Tait guilty of murder. Mr Justice Dean then pronounced the death penalty.

Two appeals followed, one to the Court of Criminal Appeal and one to the High Court, but both failed. The Executive Council didn't commute the death penalty, as had been done for every death sentence imposed since Jean Lee and her accomplices faced their fate in 1951. The time and date for execution were announced: it would be at 8 am on Monday 22 August 1962 – almost twelve months after the crime.

The Premier of Victoria, Henry Bolte, was determined that Tait would hang. His Liberal government was backed by the Country Party, which strongly supported the death penalty. They believed that a large majority of Victorians were in favour of capital punishment, and that such a vile crime demanded an execution as a deterrent to others.

Surprisingly, however, an avalanche of protest followed the announcement of the execution date. The Labor Opposition moved to abolish capital punishment, but the proposal was defeated. Religious groups took up the protest and even the victim's son, George Hall, pleaded to the authorities for Tait's life to be spared. Hall declared that he'd do anything to save Tait from being executed, as he didn't believe in the death penalty no matter how heinous the crime.

Tait was granted finance to appeal to the Privy Council in London, and his execution was deferred pending this appeal. In Melbourne, the protests continued while his case for leave to appeal was waiting to be heard in London. But in October, the Privy Council refused Tait leave to appeal and a new execution date was announced – 22 October 1962 at 8 am.

Tait's counsel decided that the only way he could be saved from the hangman's noose was to have him found medically insane; they moved to do so, but the government refused legal aid to Tait for further psychiatric assessment. To counter this move, a group of barristers and solicitors offered to provide their services free to assist Tait in having his sanity further tested. A petition was filed in the Supreme Court appealing against the government's decision, together with statements from two psychiatrists, who asserted that they'd examined Tait at Pentridge and found him to be insane. They maintained that Tait was suffering from sadism, transvestism and compulsive alcoholism, and that his mental condition was deteriorating. Again, the government produced a report from another psychiatrist that Tait was 'sane, normal and rational'. The Supreme Court then dismissed the appeal.

A further appeal was made to the Full Supreme Court, which began its hearing on 17 October, five days before the scheduled execution. As time was short, Sir Henry Winneke, the Solicitor-General, announced that the execution would again be deferred to allow the court to make its judgement without the pressure of an impending execution. Meanwhile, the storm of protest against the execution continued unabated, and there were large demonstrations against Bolte for his stance on it.

On 30 October, the Full Court rejected Tait's appeal and Premier Bolte announced the execution would take place two days later. The drama continued later that afternoon when the trial judge, Mr Justice Dean, began hearing an appeal for a reprieve from the death sentence. This appeal too was rejected after the judge voiced his opinion that at the time of the trial, Tait didn't show signs of insanity. Tait's legal representatives then moved for special leave to appeal to the High Court, which began its deliberations next morning and quickly ordered that Tait be given a reprieve pending the result of their hearing. This was Tait's fourth reprieve, and by now a grave had been dug for him within the prison grounds.

The High Court was still deliberating when Henry Bolte made the shock announcement that Tait would have his sentence commuted to life imprisonment, as he'd now been certified insane. He'd be sent to the Ararat Mental Home with papers marked 'Never to be released'. Bolte explained that the number of reprieves granted to Tait had made his mental condition deteriorate, and he was now legally insane.

After a time at Ararat, Tait's mental condition improved, and in early 1963 he was returned to Pentridge to serve his sentence. He had much time to contemplate his luck over his brush with the hangman – having already ordered his last meal, and knowing his grave had been dug in the surrounds of D Division. His relief was probably heightened when Ronald Ryan was executed some five years later. Many believed that

Bolte's determination to hang Ryan was compounded by Tait's narrow escape from the noose.

Tait was never released from prison, and died there in 1983, having served 21 years imprisonment. He'd beaten the hangman, but couldn't escape the grim reaper.

CHAPTER 10
DARYL FRANCIS SUCKLING

An inmate of A Division in the early 1970s, Daryl Suckling had been in and out of prison and mental institutions since the age of eleven. He was serving a sentence for burglary and stealing, but it was his future offences against young women that would gain him notoriety as a sexual deviant of the worst possible kind.

Suckling was a short, round-shouldered, hollow-chested individual who was difficult to keep at arm's length. He was ever ready to assist around the education office, and more often than not, his approach was overwhelming. There was something about him that rang alarm bells, and it was obvious that he had the same effect on his fellow inmates.

Suckling's favourite topic was drugs. The best drugs of all, he insisted, were 'rohies' – the popular term for rohypnol, a powerful prescription drug that produces disinhibition and amnesia when used in combination with alcohol. Suckling would use this drug with lethal effect later in his criminal career.

A cell in A Division wasn't a true fit for Suckling, as he had a record a mile long, but he was there for protection because he'd run into trouble with other prisoners. Prison psychiatrist Dr Allen Bartholomew had described Suckling as a 'psychopath' and 'a gross example of personality disorder' for whom psychiatry had 'little to offer' – an assessment that would prove chillingly accurate. A detective closely involved in a subsequent murder investigation of Suckling described him as 'a cunning, ruthless and vicious deviant'.

AN INSTITUTIONAL LIFE

Daryl Francis Suckling was born in April 1936 at Portarlington, a coastal town on the Bellarine Peninsula, 28 kilometres east of Geelong. His father walked out when Daryl was young, and his mother struggled to support her six children. Young Suckling became rebellious at school and soon fell foul of the law, receiving convictions for house-breaking and stealing.

At the age of twelve, he was sent to Morning Star Boy's Home in Mt Eliza, which was run by the Franciscans as a training centre to give delinquent boys exposure to rural life. Suckling would later claim that he lived under constant threat of sexual abuse by the older boys. He complained to the priests directly and also through his mother, who worked at the home for a time, but nothing was done to stop the perpetrators. Suckling claimed that he began deliberately committing offences that would land him in jail, where, he said, 'at least I was safe ... from assaults'.

For decades after that, Suckling was in and out of prisons and mental asylums, running up a huge number of convictions, mainly for burglary and stealing. While he was detained at Pentridge in 1964, Dr Bartholomew reported that he had 'poor memory, and some defect in intellectual capacity', a 'psychopathic personality' and suicidal tendencies. Later that year, Suckling was placed in J Ward at Ararat Mental Hospital, where he spent several months. By the late 1960s, Suckling, now in his early thirties, was back in Pentridge over burglary charges.

In 1973, he swallowed some pins and was sent to the Royal Melbourne Hospital; he escaped, but only for a very short time. When he was eventually released from Pentridge,

Suckling changed his modus operandi in crime, but not for the better: he began molesting women and young girls.

In 1978, Suckling attacked a young girl and sexually abused her. He was initially charged with abduction and rape, but these charges were reduced to a single charge of carnal knowledge, to which he pleaded guilty. This saved the girl the added ordeal of cross-examination in court, but it was to have dire consequences for others.

Suckling was imprisoned for twelve months on the carnal knowledge charge. While in Pentridge, he became friends with a man by the name of Mark Carni. The friendship would have major consequences for both of them.

WYARAMA STATION

When Suckling was released from Pentridge, he sought Mark Carni out. Carni had recently married a woman called Sophie, and she was expecting a child. The baby, a girl, was born soon after Suckling's release, but there were few celebrations, because her father was already back in jail. Under Suckling's influence, Mark had continued his life of crime, and the two men committed several burglaries together. Then tragedy struck the Carni family. Sophie was returning home from visiting Mark in Ararat Prison when she was involved in a car accident and the baby was killed.

For several years, Suckling was in and out of prison, accumulating an extraordinary number of convictions, including rape, indecent assault and burglary. In October 1987, he was asked if he'd like the job of caretaker at Wyarama Station, a property of some 14,500 hectares (36,000 acres) near Pooncarie in south-western New South Wales. Suckling accepted the offer, moving his few worldly possessions there in his old Landcruiser.

The property was in a remote location, about halfway between Mildura and Broken Hill. Suckling's tasks were mainly routine maintenance, but the locals quickly realised he was totally out of his environment, and some grew suspicious of the new caretaker. The Healys, who part-owned Wyarama and another nearby sheep station, didn't much like the shifty, slouching, seemingly nervous newcomer.

In about March 1988, Suckling told locals, including the Healys, that he had a niece in Melbourne who'd developed a drug habit, and that he was going to bring her to Wyarama to help cure her of the addiction. Shortly after, Suckling headed off to Melbourne in his Landcruiser.

When he arrived in Melbourne, he tracked down Sophie Carni and discovered that her husband was still in prison. He arranged to take her to a restaurant in Dandenong, and picked her up in St Kilda. On the outskirts of Dandenong, Suckling said he had a surprise for her: a necklace and a silver Citizen watch. As he was putting the necklace around Sophie's neck, he pulled a knife on her and held it to her throat, then handcuffed, blindfolded and gagged her. He forced her to drink Southern Comfort and take drugs. When the effects wore off, Sophie found she had a chain around her neck, and Suckling was holding the end of it. He drove all the way back to Wyarama, where he forced Sophie into the house, still wearing the chain.

For the next couple of days, Suckling repeatedly raped Sophie and forced her to pose naked while he photographed her. She was convinced that he intended to kill her, as he'd already threatened to cut her up and bury her separate parts in different places so that if anybody found her, they wouldn't know who she was. He also told her that he 'had a body buried down the road already'.

On the third day of Sophie's captivity, Eddie Healy – a near neighbour and part-owner of the station – called in and told Suckling and Sophie to go to his place to pick up some gas cylinders. Before they left, Suckling warned Sophie there would be terrible consequences if she didn't go along with his story about her being his drug-addicted niece. But before the night was out, Sophie managed to speak to the Healys' governess out of Suckling's earshot and tell her that Suckling wasn't her uncle, but had actually kidnapped and raped her. The governess passed the message on, and police were called. When local constable Nick Skomarow arrived, Sophie told him how she'd come to know Suckling and what he'd done to her.

Investigations soon showed that Sophie herself had a criminal record and had used a number of aliases. She'd previously been charged with burglary, fraud and taking contraband into a prison. Her story about Suckling, however, had the ring of truth. Police inspected Suckling's bedroom and verified Sophie's story from items found there. They then arrested him. When they called up his criminal record, they found 137 convictions listed on six typed pages, with offences committed in Victoria, New South Wales and Queensland.

Police also confiscated a camera, where they found nude photographs of Sophie and two other girls, one lot of which looked as though they'd been taken in Suckling's Landcruiser. The girls looked as if they'd been drugged, and detectives began to suspect that at least one other girl had been taken to Wyarama for similar purposes.

A new search of the property turned up various articles, including a purple T-shirt dress similar to that shown in the photos of one of the unidentified girls. The same girl was also photographed wearing the jewellery Suckling had given Sophie as presents.

Police later found a piece of paper on which was written: 'Jodie – 27/12'. Detectives began to suspect that Suckling's claims of having a 'body buried down the road' was probably no idle boast. Just who was the woman in the photo?

Police found the purple dress stuffed into Suckling's bedroom cupboard, and also found a dental plate that wasn't

Sophie's in a paper basket. Detectives now set out to discover who the mystery woman was. They soon discovered that a prostitute working in St Kilda named Jodie Maree Larcombe hadn't been seen around her usual haunts since about Christmas 1987. Although police could find no evidence that she was dead, they now had a strong suspicion that Suckling had murdered her.

Jodie had been involved in the drug scene since the age of sixteen, when she became involved with a dealer. Six months after her twenty-first birthday she disappeared, and hadn't contacted family or friends since. Her criminal record revealed she'd spent time in Pentridge – in fact, she'd only been released a few days before she disappeared. Her convictions were mainly for drug use and prostitution.

Further investigations revealed that police had already interviewed Suckling over the abduction of a girl from St Kilda, who'd narrowly escaped his clutches by jumping naked from his car after he'd handcuffed and stripped her. Picked up by a passing motorist and taken to police, this girl had probably saved herself from a terrible ordeal.

Police soon established that Daryl Suckling had been near the area where Jodie operated when she went missing. Further enquiries revealed that she'd disappeared on Boxing Day 1987, wearing the dress found at Wyarama. Relatives also confirmed that she owned some jewellery found there, and a dental technician had identified the dental plate as one he'd made for Jodie Larcombe.

Pooncarie postman James Wembridge also had a story to tell. In early December 1987, Suckling told him he was going to Melbourne to visit his niece. Then on 27 December, Suckling called in at his house and announced that his Landcruiser had got a flat tyre on an unmade road when he was on his way back from Melbourne, and he needed help. When they reached the vehicle, it was facing in the wrong direction for anyone returning from Melbourne, and Wembridge noticed drop sheets, clothing and a travel bag piled on the passenger side. When Wembridge went to get a jack from the Landcruiser, Suckling wouldn't let him open the passenger side door, so Wembridge used his own jack to change the tyre.

A couple of days later, when the postman called at Wyarama, he saw Suckling washing his vehicle. The inside had been hosed out, and Suckling had used so much water that the vehicle had become bogged. When Wembridge asked Suckling why he'd been out on the unmade road, Suckling claimed that it was a shortcut, but Wembridge knew better. Police now believed Jodie was in the Landcruiser, either dead or heavily drugged. They again searched Wyarama for signs of digging, but to no avail.

In early April 1989, Suckling was charged with Jodie's murder while awaiting trial for the abduction and sexual assault of Sophie Carni. However, in November that year, when Suckling faced Wollongong Court charged with Sophie's abduction, it was too late. Sophie had died some four months earlier from a heroin overdose. As the victim couldn't now be cross-examined in court, the judge directed the jury to find Suckling not guilty. Suckling was still facing a charge over the abduction of the St Kilda woman who'd escaped naked from his car, but his run of luck continued. The charge was dropped after the victim fell from a train and suffered head injuries that left her with a defective memory.

In preparing the case against Suckling for the murder of Jodie Larcombe, detectives were given the go-ahead to use Sophie Carni's case as part of the prosecution under the use of 'similar fact' evidence – evidence that is identical, or almost identical, to the current case. Without a body, this was going to be of significant assistance to the prosecution when the case was heard. In October 1990, however, the New South Wales

Director of Public Prosecutions 'no-billed' the case due to lack of evidence. The prosecution couldn't go ahead, mainly because of the lack of a body.

Early in 1991, Suckling was jailed for four years on charges of fraud, having made several applications for Department of Social Security payments using varies aliases. He was sent to Goulburn to serve this sentence, and while there, he confided to an inmate that he'd murdered a prostitute and got away with it. The prisoner passed this on to police, who decided to put a wire on him, but the plan came unstuck when another inmate brushed up against him and discovered the wire.

While this was occurring, a married couple went to police and informed them that Suckling had shown them nude photographs of women they were later able to identify as Sophie Carni and Jodie Larcombe. The women had been handcuffed and in chains when the photographs had been taken. He'd also virtually told the couple that he'd killed Jodie, and that searchers had 'run over her hundreds of times' in their search.

In late 1993, another prisoner from Goulburn approached police, telling them that Suckling, his cell mate, had boasted about murdering a girl and getting away with it. As this prisoner had just been released and Suckling was about to be, it was arranged that the two of them should take up accommodation together, while police monitored the place with listening devices. Police gave this prisoner the alias of 'Collins'. In one recorded conversation, Suckling explained how he'd buried Jodie's body, then returned later to dismember it with an axe. He'd been discussing ways in which they could drug Collins's girlfriend and dispose of her body if things went awry. Eventually, talk got around to putting her corpse in the same place as Jodie's. Suckling explained how he'd drugged Jodie and driven her from Melbourne to Wyarama, where he'd killed her and cut up the body.

Armed with this new evidence, the DPP agreed to prose-cute Daryl Suckling for the murder of Jodie Larcombe. When the case was tried in the New South Wales Supreme Court in May 1996, Suckling entered a plea of not guilty. The prosecutor argued that Suckling had a desire to dominate women in order to satisfy his perverted sense of power, and then to have the ultimate power by taking the woman's life. The court was told that various items identified as Jodie's had been found in Suckling's bedroom at Wyarama, and also that he'd taken obscene photographs of her in his vehicle. A crucial witness was one of Suckling's sisters, who testified that he'd contacted her, wanting her to say that she was the owner of the purple dress found at Wyarama. She'd quickly refused his request. Other items of evidence included Jodie's dental plate – also found in Suckling's bedroom – the piece of paper with 'Jodie – 27/12' written on it, and the recorded conversations in which he'd spoken about Jodie's murder and body disposal.

Suckling made an unsworn statement from the dock in which he described his movements around Christmas 1987 as an 'innocent journey' that would become a nightmare. He claimed that the last time he saw Jodie Larcombe was on Christmas Day, and that she'd been alive when he left her to return to Wyarama Station. He explained away his recorded accounts of Jodie's murder as 'boasting, fantasising, and making it all up – never believing that anyone would take it seriously'. He further claimed that Collins had a reputation as a 'dog' in jail and said he was aware that Collins was wired. Suckling had deliberately said what he did 'because he wanted gory bits in'.

The jury deliberated long and hard over a couple of days before returning with a verdict of guilty. The judge was scathing in his remarks, declaring that the offence was in 'the worst class of cases of murder', and that he'd impose the maximum sentence, jailing him for life without remission.

Suckling appealed his conviction, but before the appeal was heard, Jodie's mother committed suicide. The horrific details of what Suckling had done to her daughter were too much for her to live with, and she shot herself, thus becoming another victim of Daryl Suckling. His appeal was eventually dismissed, and a further appeal to the High Court of Australia also failed.

Two things seem certain – that Jodie's body will never be recovered, and that Daryl Suckling will never be released into the community again. He has joined an exclusive list of murderers who have been sentenced to life, never to be released. At the time of writing in April 2015, he is incarcerated in a high-security jail, where he is likely to spend the rest of his days.

CHAPTER 11
LEITH McDONALD RATTEN

One inmate of A Division who didn't have the manner or appearance of a murderer was the quiet, reserved and seemingly shy Leith Ratten, who was serving a life sentence for murdering his wife with a shotgun when she was eight-and-a-half months pregnant. It was difficult to associate him with the acts attributed to him.

What was in no doubt was that Ratten was there, holding the shotgun when it went off, killing his wife almost instantaneously. What *was* in doubt was whether he discharged the shotgun deliberately or accidentally. Ratten consistently maintained to the day he died that it was an accidental shooting. His claim received the backing of many influential people, including politicians, lawyers and even his own children.

Those who observed him at Pentridge were all of the opinion that he seemed a genuine, decent person, quite out of place in the prison environment. He was popular with inmates and prison officers alike. Pentridge Governor Ian Grindlay was moved to say of Ratten: 'He is a thorough gentleman. Well educated, intelligent. Everybody wishes there were 200 or 300 like him out there.' Grindlay added, 'On face value you would say he was innocent.'

Certainly, he didn't exhibit any traits of the cold, calculating killer implied by the scenario the Crown presented at his trial, a man who'd shown no mercy whatsoever to his heavily pregnant wife, blasting her with a shotgun and then setting up a scene in their kitchen to support a claim of an accidental shooting. In the 1970s, Ratten mounted a series of unsuccessful appeals aimed at proving he was the victim of circumstantial evidence that had brought about a grave miscarriage of justice.

Was the prosecution case proved beyond reasonable doubt? Was guilt the only reasonable conclusion to draw from the facts? In this case, the onus seems to have been on Ratten to prove his innocence rather than on the prosecution to prove his guilt.

THE AFFAIR

Born in 1939, Leith McDonald Ratten married Beverley Joan Smith in Melbourne in 1960. Christina, their first daughter, was born two years later, and in 1963 they had a second daughter, Sally.

The following year the Rattens moved to Echuca, a town on the Murray River. They soon became involved in the Anglican Church, where Leith played the organ. At the weekends, he enjoyed fishing and shooting. By day, he worked as a surveyor while Beverley attended to home duties and cared for their two girls. The Rattens quickly became friendly with their neighbours, Peter and Jenny Kemp, who also had two young children. Peter and Leith began to go fishing and shooting together at the weekends.

In 1966, Bev Ratten gave birth to a third daughter, Wendy, and not long after, the Rattens moved to 52 Mitchell Street, Echuca. Around this time, Peter Kemp took up a position as a salesman of fishing and camping equipment at Barmah, some thirty kilometres from Echuca, and the Kemps moved there in 1968. The Rattens and the Kemps maintained their friendship, though, and Peter and Leith still often went shooting together.

Peter's new job kept him away from home for most of

the week. In early 1969 – with Peter's permission – Leith began taking Jenny Kemp for driving lessons. Their friendship became closer, and soon they were having an affair. A few months later, Bev discovered she was pregnant with their fourth child. This was welcome news to Bev, as for some time Leith had been talking about applying for a surveyor's position in Antarctica, and she hoped this news would change his mind.

In early 1970, local gossip about an affair between Leith Ratten and Jenny Kemp reached the ears of Peter Kemp, who told his wife to discourage Leith from visiting when he wasn't at home. Jenny's response was the reverse of what her husband wanted: she asked Leith to leave Bev and move in with her. Leith tried to stall, saying he'd wait until Bev had the baby, but on 5 May 1970, he and Jenny attended a solicitor's office to discuss divorce and custody.

Jenny and Peter now agreed to separate and sell their home. Bev appeared outwardly happy, although a close friend would later say that when she visited, Bev seemed to have been crying. Leith later explained this by saying that Bev was upset because he'd put in for the job in Antarctica, which would take him away from home for twelve months if he was successful.

THE FATEFUL DAY

On 7 May 1970, Leith went to Jenny's house and tried to dissuade her from packing up and leaving that day. When she asked whether he'd told Bev that he wanted to leave, Ratten said that he'd told her the night before that he'd leave after she had the baby. He'd then slept in the lounge while she slept in the bedroom.

Over the day, Leith repaired the washing machine, making two trips to the hardware store to buy hoses. Shortly after 11 am, he switched his office telephone through to the house.

He went home and took out his guns to clean, including an old side-by-side shotgun that he hadn't used in recent times. In fact, Peter Kemp was the last person to use that gun; he'd taken it to a local gun dealer, and afterwards told Leith it was in need of repair.

At 1.09 pm, Leith's father, Stanley, rang him to ask if Bev needed more nappies for the baby. As they spoke, Stanley heard Bev's voice in the background. When the conversation finished at 1.12, Leith returned to the kitchen to continue cleaning the guns, and Bev came in from the den, where she'd been vacuuming.

Shortly after, Janet Flowers, a telephonist at the Echuca exchange, answered a call from the number Echuca 1494. She plugged in the line, opened the 'speak' key and said 'Number please.' She was shocked to hear a high-pitched, hysterical voice say, 'Get me the police please – 59 Mitchell Street,' then hang up. Janet immediately contacted the police and spoke to Constable Holley, telling him that police were needed at the address she'd been given.

Constable Holley and Senior Constable Shaw rushed to the address, while Constable Lawrence Bickerton telephoned Miss Flowers to get more details about the call. The telephonist couldn't throw much more light on it, but put Bickerton through to the Ratten number. The call was answered straight away, and Bickerton heard a high-pitched voice scream, 'Help me, help me, for God's sake come quick.' Bickerton checked the address and headed to the Ratten home in the company of Detective Moxham.

Holley and Shaw were the first to arrive at 59 Mitchell Street, where four-year-old Wendy was standing at the front fence, crying. They quickly knocked and went in, encountering a distraught Leith Ratten just inside the door. 'In the kitchen, quick,' he cried. There, the two policemen found Bev Ratten lying face up on the floor. Ratten babbled, 'The baby, too, the baby, too, oh my God.' A doctor was quickly summoned. Shaw felt for a pulse, but couldn't find one.

In the kitchen, police found a rifle, a rifle case, a gun case, ammunition and various cloths, oils and cleaning gear on the table. On a chair was a shotgun, broken at the breech. Next to the table sat a Gladstone bag holding ammunition and a variety of cleaning materials. On the floor at the entrance to the den – where the telephone was – lay the gun that had killed Mrs Ratten, a side-by-side shotgun that was between forty and sixty years old.

Ratten was beside himself and kept crying, 'I killed her, I killed her.' He explained to the two policemen that he'd been cleaning the rust off a shotgun in the kitchen when it suddenly went off, hitting his wife, who was standing near by. He told them he hadn't used the gun for some months and that it had been out in the garage unloaded. He rambled on about Bev making coffee while he was cleaning the gun, and said that he never kept shells in his guns. As he was giving these details, Shaw picked up the old shotgun and broke it apart. As he did so, the barrels came off in his hand and a spent cartridge fell from one of them. A cartridge was stuck in the other barrel, but he couldn't get it out.

By this time, Bickerton and Moxham had arrived at the house, and Moxham also began to investigate the shotgun. He noticed that the forepiece had been removed, which was why the gun had come apart. He found the forepiece lying on the kitchen sink, re-assembled the gun, and was then able to eject the stuck cartridge from the barrel. Both this cartridge and the spent one had the impression of a firing pin on the cap. The police also found a green scouring pad with rust on it lying at the entrance to the den.

Mrs Ratten's body was taken to Bendigo Base Hospital for autopsy, and Ratten was taken to the local police station to make a statement.

Shaw asked him, 'Who rang here?'

Ratten replied, 'I did. I rang the exchange and asked them to send an ambulance.'

He was examined by a doctor, who found that he was unfit to give a statement until later that night.

To the police officers' surprise, Jenny Kemp turned up at the station. She'd gone looking for Ratten that afternoon and found out he was there. She told police that Ratten wouldn't have been capable of shooting Bev. She said it was more likely to be suicide, as Bev had just recently learnt of their affair.

This visit threw new light on the shooting as far as police were concerned. They asked Jenny to make a statement. If they hadn't suspected murder before her arrival, they were certainly suspicious now. The homicide squad was called in from Melbourne, and detectives were soon on their way to Echuca to interview Ratten.

They began questioning him later that evening. He told them he'd taken a day off work and had been repairing the washing machine before deciding to clean his guns, which he had in the house. He'd gone to the garage to get his cleaning gear and noticed the old rusted shotgun there. He'd decided to clean it as well as his other two guns, which he kept in the house and normally cleaned in the kitchen or the lounge.

Just after 1 pm, he'd received a phone call from his father in Melbourne. Shortly afterwards, he resumed cleaning the rust off the shotgun in the kitchen by the sink while his wife was making a cup of coffee at the bench. The gun had suddenly gone off, and Bev had collapsed to the floor.

He was asked to explain the position he and the gun were in, and also where Bev was standing when it went off. He told the detectives he couldn't remember what angle he was holding the gun at, but he was sure it was at waist height. He explained that he used ICI Blue Star plastic cartridges, some of which he kept in a canoe in the garage, and others in the den. He had a strict rule of always unloading the guns before they came back to the house so that he knew they weren't loaded. He had no idea how the gun came to be loaded, or how it came to discharge.

The detectives now had the result of the autopsy performed by Dr Robert Charlton, who found that the fatal shot had hit Bev several centimetres below her left armpit, and would have entered on a downward angle of 45 degrees. It was now put to Ratten that his wife was on the floor or kneeling when she was shot, and that his explanation of the shooting was at odds with Dr Charlton's estimate of the angle. Ratten rejected this suggestion; the shooting had been exactly as he had described it, he said.

Ratten was also questioned about how the gun could have fired. The safety catch should have come on automatically when the gun was broken. He couldn't provide any explanation for this. Asked why each cartridge bore the mark of a firing pin, he said he remembered hearing a click when cleaning the gun. He couldn't recall when he'd last cleaned the gun, but told the detectives that Peter Kemp had taken it to a gun dealer some months ago, and said he or Peter might have cleaned it then. He couldn't account in any way for the gun being loaded.

When questioned about the call from his house to the telephone exchange, Ratten insisted that *he* had made the call, and it was to try to get an ambulance to the house, not to call the police. The detectives then put it to him that the call had been made by Bev in fear of her life, but Ratten continued to insist that he'd made the call.

The detectives asked Ratten whether he and Bev had been unhappy, and whether they'd been arguing. They suggested to Ratten that all wasn't well with their marriage. Ratten denied this. He agreed that he'd been having an affair with another woman, but he said it was only casual. He agreed when detectives suggested he'd told Jenny Kemp that Bev would never agree to a divorce. He was taken back to the house for a re-enactment of the shooting and told he'd be charged with murdering his wife.

THE TRIAL

At the inquest into Bev's death and in the lead-up to the trial, there was a lot of publicity in the media about Ratten's affair with Jenny Kemp. His legal team moved to have the trial shifted to Melbourne, believing he'd be unable to have a fair trial locally, but they didn't succeed. The trial eventually took place in Shepparton, about seventy kilometres from Echuca.

During the trial, the prosecution told the jury that Ratten had deliberately shot his wife because he wanted to eliminate her in order to continue his relationship with Jenny Kemp. To support this contention, prosecutors cited the angle of the shot, and the medical opinion that it came from above. There was much discussion of the fact that both cartridges in the gun bore the mark of a firing pin. The prosecution contended that Ratten had tried to fire the gun, but the first cartridge had stuck, so he had to pull the second trigger in order to make the fatal shot. An expert police witness supported this argument, maintaining that the gun couldn't go off unless the trigger was pulled. There was also the evidence of the telephonist Miss Flowers, who maintained that the call from the Ratten home had been made by a woman.

The prosecution also contended that Ratten couldn't have been holding the gun as he said he was, because he'd have been injured or bruised. Rather, the prosecution said, he'd been holding it up to his shoulder in the normal firing position.

Ratten was portrayed as deliberately setting the scene up to suggest an accidental shooting. A Birko water heater had been found lying on its side on the bench with a small amount of water around it, supporting his contention that Bev was making coffee, but the prosecution pointed out that Rattan was left-handed and the handle of the Birko was on the left, while Bev, who was right-handed, lay on the floor with her right fist clenched. Ratten had said he had no idea how the Birko had been knocked over while some eggs close by were undisturbed.

The prosecution claimed that when police arrived, there was no blood about for some time. They suggested that this proved Mrs Ratten had only just been shot, and had made the phone call for help. The defence, however, pointed out that the autopsy report had said that the spleen and abdominal tissue had blocked the wound, making it impossible to accurately estimate the time of death.

Ratten said he ran to the phone in the den immediately after his wife was shot, but the prosecution suggested that this showed a lack of care for his wife. Then, when the police arrived, he didn't make any effort to go to the kitchen to help her. The defence rebutted this suggestion, pointing out that there was little Ratten would have been able to do for her, and that if he'd done what the prosecution suggested, he'd have been attacked for not going to the phone.

The prosecution also used the telephone call from his father as evidence against him, arguing that it enabled Ratten to claim – with the corroboration of his father – that all was normal in the house, setting the scene for an accident to occur. Then the call to Miss Flowers, which Ratten claimed was from him, asking for an ambulance, was actually from his wife, calling for police. Finally, when Constable Bickerton was put through to the house, the prosecution said the caller should not have known it was police, as Bickerton said he didn't identify himself.

In deciding how to organise the defence, Ratten's counsel faced a difficult decision: if they called their own expert witnesses to refute the prosecution's, they'd have lost the right to give the final address to the jury. Instead, they called character witnesses in Ratten's defence, and all testified that he was a highly respected member of the Echuca community. Ratten himself also took to the witness box, maintaining that the shooting was accidental.

In their address to the jury, the defence contended that an extramarital affair was hardly sufficient reason for a man to want to murder his wife, but was more likely to cause him to leave home. It was pointed out that Ratten had maintained from the very outset that he didn't intend to leave his wife and become permanently involved with Mrs Kemp. Counsel stated that it was unheard of for a married man to murder his wife because of an affair, and pointed out that applying for a job in Antarctica was hardly the action of a man who wanted to get involved with another woman.

Not having called expert witnesses, the defence couldn't attack Dr Charlton's evidence that the angle of the bullet didn't square with Ratten's explanation that the gun went off accidentally as he cleaned it. Instead, the defence argued that it would have been foolish in the extreme for Ratten to have fired the gun with the forepiece off – particularly with the type of ammunition used – as he was likely to have seriously injured himself by doing so. The defence also claimed that the police had dismissed Ratten's claim of an accidental shooting without first testing its validity, and that no tests had been conducted on the gun to see whether it could have misfired. The defence further pointed out that testing should have been undertaken to see if the gun contained reloaded shot, which Ratten didn't use, but Peter Kemp did. If in fact reloads had been used, it would suggest that Kemp, not Ratten, had loaded the gun.

In his summing up, the judge, the Chief Justice, Sir Henry Winneke, warned the jury against judging the case on the morality of the accused man. He was fair to Ratten, posing several questions favourable towards him, particularly about the telephone calls. He pointed out that it was improbable that Rattten would speak in a relaxed way to his father, then 'immediately put the phone down, and almost immediately go back into the kitchen and deliberately shoot [his wife] in her pregnant condition'. Winneke also reminded the jury that they shouldn't base their verdict on Ratten's infidelity. He said: 'We are in a criminal court, we are not in a court of morals here; we are dealing with human beings'.

The Chief Justice also pointed out that if accidental shooting remained a reasonable hypothesis, 'then the Crown has not established the elements of the charge beyond reasonable doubt, and the accused must be acquitted'. The jury, however, obviously didn't consider accident a reasonable hypothesis. After ten hours deliberation, it returned a verdict of guilty of murder. Ratten was then sentenced to death, but his sentence was later commuted to a sentence of 25 years imprisonment with a minimum of 20 years before parole.

After the jury's decision, it was revealed that at least one juror had misunderstood the judge. The foreman of the jury was reported to have said that he thought the judge believed the prosecution had won and was just trying to be fair by making remarks favourable to the defendant. Ratten's counsel, Jack Lazarus, commented, 'In my more than twenty years at the bar, I had never seen an innocent man convicted of murder until I heard the death sentence passed on Ratten.'

APPEALS

Ratten was sent to Pentridge and classified to A Division to serve his sentence. Over the next few years, his lawyers undertook four separate appeals, one of which involved the exhumation of Beverley Ratten's body in 1973. Ratten's first two appeals, to the Full Court of the Supreme Court of Victoria and then to the Privy Council in England, were related and mainly based on the reliability of the telephonist's claim that she had heard a female voice. Since the trial, Constable Bickerton had revealed that when he rang the Ratten home, his call was answered by someone with a high-pitched, hysterical voice, which he couldn't conclude was male or female. Ratten's lawyers argued that it was dangerous for Miss Flowers to decide she could differentiate when Bickerton couldn't. The defence contended that this constituted fresh evidence, but both appeals failed.

The State Full Court conceded that there were several circumstances that could indicate an accidental shooting, but also said that the jury could have found several circumstances indicative of a deliberate shooting, particularly the fact that the gun was loaded and required a pull on the triggers to discharge it, which would have necessitated a conscious and deliberate act by the defendant – all reasonably compelling a conclusion that the shooting wasn't an accident.

The appeal to the Privy Council was based on the argument that the telephonist's evidence was hearsay and should not have been admitted. This appeal too was dismissed.

Yet there was widespread doubt about Ratten's conviction. His supporters included senior Federal and State Members of Parliament, as well as several prominent barristers, who believed that a great miscarriage of justice had occurred. They believed that Ratten's consistent explanation – including his inability to explain how the gun came to be loaded and fired – pointed to innocence rather than guilt. They further believed that the jury might have been swayed by his sexual affair, and that he'd been found guilty because of his marital infidelity.

Liberal MP Don Chipp was one of Ratten's strongest supporters. Chipp was to claim that over dinner one evening, the trial judge had said of Ratten, 'That man is absolutely innocent.' A decade later, however, Chief Justice Winneke had altered that to, 'I have never formed a view as to either the guilt or innocence of Ratten.'

Chipp asked Peter Brett, Professor of Jurisprudence at the University of Melbourne, to examine the case. Brett reported that, in his opinion, the Crown case against Ratten couldn't be supported. He found that doubt surrounded Ratten's motives and the phone call made to Miss Flowers. Furthermore, he found that Dr Charlton's conclusions about the angle of the fatal shot were highly doubtful. Other experts had told him that Bev's injuries were more consistent with a horizontal shot, thus supporting Ratten's claims rather than Dr Charlton's findings. Brett further stated that it was almost anatomically impossible to devise positions in which Ratten was 1.5 metres away from Bev when the gun discharged and fired a shot that entered her body at a 45-degree angle, as the prosecution had claimed.

Brett also concluded that the affair with Mrs Kemp was no reason for Ratten to have brought about the death of his wife. Also, if the jury had been aware of the new information from Constable Bickerton, Brett concluded they probably wouldn't have placed the same importance on the evidence of Miss Flowers.

He also raised questions for which no answers had been provided. If Ratten knew that Bev had called for help, why would he go ahead and kill her? Why had he switched his work phone through to the house, enabling her to later call for help? How could he have got Bev from the den – where the phone was – to the kitchen, shot her, answered Bickerton's call and set the scene for an accidental shooting, all in the space of a few minutes? If Mrs Ratten was in fear of her life, why didn't she seek help from neighbours?

Brett also cast serious doubt on the Crown's case that the gun couldn't be discharged accidentally. He found it could easily be discharged by pressure from a tightened overhead grip. He was also concerned about police interference with the gun. When Senior Constable Shaw picked it up, he broke it open. Had the safety catch been locked, it too would have broken open. As Brett put it, 'If the safety catch was on, a factor of great assistance to Mr Ratten's case was destroyed by Mr Shaw's act.'

Brett handed his report to Chipp, who then passed it to the Victorian Attorney General. As a result, Mrs Ratten's body was exhumed and examined by Dr John Laing to investigate the questions raised as to the angle of the shot. But Laing reported that he agreed with Charlton's findings.

In 1973, Ratten submitted a petition for mercy to the Governor of Victoria, claiming fresh evidence that the angle and distance of the shot didn't support the Crown case. It was also submitted that Janet Flowers's voice identification was unreliable and that fresh evidence threw a different light on the markings on the cartridges. This appeal was forwarded to the Full Court.

At this hearing, expert evidence was given as to the accuracy of Dr Charlton's findings. Although Dr Laing supported these findings, many eminent defence experts refuted them. Other evidence raised the possibility that a mark could be left on the right-hand barrel of the gun if a shot was fired from the left-hand barrel, thus eliminating the theory that there had been two attempts to fire the gun. However, this appeal too was dismissed, the judges concluding that there had been no miscarriage of justice, and even suggesting that Ratten may have killed his wife in the heat of an argument.

Ratten appealed these findings to the High Court in 1974, but again without success. In rejecting this appeal, Chief Justice Sir Garfield Barwick said the case against Ratten was very strong and there was evidence he meant to shoot his wife. 'There was ample motive for the pressure on that trigger to have been deliberate. The applicant was infatuated with another woman to the point he'd agreed on her pressing suggestion to leave his wife and children and set up house with her.'

Ratten's supporters continued to campaign. In the late 1970s, the ABC produced a documentary on the case in their series *Beyond Reasonable Doubt*. It was researched and scripted by lawyer and writer Tom Molomby, who also produced a book on the case entitled *Ratten: The Web Of Circumstance*. Molomby had formed the belief that Ratten was innocent from reading the transcript of his trial, and he provided logical explanations of the circumstances that led to his conviction. Molomby explained his aim was to show 'that what Ratten is alleged to have done is full of contradictions and inconsistencies, and quite outside the limits of normal human conduct'.

Molomby pointed out that Dr Charlton was inexperienced in forensics or gunshot wounds. He'd actually failed practical examinations for membership in the College of Pathologists of Australia, and this was only his third experience of a gunshot wound. Molomby also believed that Miss Flowers was mistaken in believing that the high-pitched voice she heard was that of a female. He maintained that Ratten had called for assistance by ambulance, and had been saying this in panic before Miss Flowers said, 'Number please', and that the word she mistook for police was 'please', which he'd said a couple of times in a sobbing, hysterical voice. In evidence, Miss Flowers had acknowledged that the caller could have been speaking before she answered the call, and that she could have missed hearing an ambulance being asked for.

Molomby made a number of cogent points. He argued that the motive provided by the prosecution was nonsensical, as Ratten had applied for a job in Antarctica – hardly the act of someone wishing to continue an affair and resorting to murder to do so. The only way the shot could have occurred as it did was very much as Ratten demonstrated. Ratten had answered all questions put to him by the prosecution without wavering in any of his evidence throughout. The fact that Ratten had always said he couldn't explain how the gun came to be loaded, or how it came to fire, was a greater indicator of innocence than guilt, as a guilty person would most likely have concocted a story about it.

Molomby also emphasised the perils in arguing that the situation was planned. This would have meant that in five minutes, at the most, between the shooting and the arrival of police, Ratten had to set the scene for an accidental shooting, including the cleaning of the guns. This was to say nothing of the fact that in three minutes or less, between the father's call and the one to Miss Flowers, Mrs Ratten had suddenly become afraid of her husband and was ringing hysterically for police.

Molomby was also critical of the police conduct, pointing out that they'd handled items that could well have been fingerprinted, and if the gun had been recently loaded, the cartridges should also have been fingerprinted, as should the Birko and the telephone. Most importantly, testing should have been done on the stuck cartridge to see if it was rusted in. If so, this would have pointed strongly towards Ratten's innocence, because if the gun was already loaded when he picked it up, it's easy to believe that he wasn't aware of it.

Misgivings about Ratten's guilt persisted. Colin Howard, the Hearn Professor of Law and Dean of the Faculty of Law at Melbourne University, wrote after reading Molomby's book: 'I share the author's belief that there can be no doubt left that Ratten did not murder his wife'. He also commented that it remained a mystery how the jury managed to find Ratten guilty of murder.

Molomby then decided that the type of ammunition found

in the gun was pivotal to the case. As Ratten used factory loaded ammunition, and not reloads as Peter Kemp did, if another type of ammunition was in the gun, that would support Ratten's claim that he didn't know it was loaded and that someone else had loaded it. This possibility hadn't been investigated in the twelve years since the shooting. However, a request for an examination of the cartridges was refused.

After a change of government, legal aid was granted to Ratten to have the cartridges examined on his behalf by a forensic expert. The expert's findings were that the fired cartridge was too distorted to form a conclusion, but the live round was almost certainly a reload. He stated: 'I am very strongly persuaded that the live round in evidence was a reload of a cartridge case fired earlier.' This decision was arrived at from visual inspection only, as he wasn't allowed to interfere with the cartridges. The expert further revealed that if he could have opened up the unfired cartridge, he could have been certain, but just from its external features, he was 'strongly persuaded'.

Shortly after this, Ratten was unexpectedly released from prison in July 1983. A model prisoner, he'd served 13 years of a 25-year sentence. With maximum remissions, he'd have been eligible for release in a further fifteen months.

He was reunited with his now adult daughters, Christine, Sally and Wendy, who had been raised by his brother and his wife during his incarceration. Shortly after, he applied for employment as a surveyor in Queensland and was accepted. But tragedy struck again in 1988 when Ratten's youngest daughter, Wendy, aged just 22, collapsed and died at her office desk as a result of blood clots on her lungs.

Leith Ratten died – still maintaining his innocence – on 20 January 2012 in Brisbane. Family members, including his daughters, remained convinced he was wrongfully convicted and earnestly believed the shooting was an accident. In his obituary they wrote that he was 'the loved husband of Bev', and that he was 'now reunited with Mum'.

Postscript: Recently, Ray Mooney told me about an incident at Pentridge in which Leith Ratten had cried out under much stress. Ray told me that Ratten's voice was so shrill he'd have sworn it was a woman's. Could this account for the most damning piece of evidence used against Ratten – Miss Flowers believing the hysterical voice she heard on the telephone was a female's?

CHAPTER 12
JAMES EDWARD 'JOCKEY' SMITH

'Jockey' Smith had a lifelong passion for horses. A short, stocky prisoner often seen around B Division in the early 1970s, 'Jockey' not only went by that name and was the size of a jockey, but had actually been a professional jockey in his earlier life. A safecracker or 'tankman', Smith was the SP bookmaker in B Division, and was a general livewire around the place. He was doing five years for possession of explosives and had recently been in 'the slot' – H Division – which gave him the status of a 'real crim'.

James Edward Smith was born in Colac in October 1942, the second of eight children. At an early age, he developed a love of horses and quickly became a skilled rider. When the Smith family moved to Geelong, Jimmy was able to pursue his passion, and at the age of fifteen he brought home his first horse. On turning sixteen, he became an apprentice jockey. He won several races around the western district of Victoria, but opportunities were scarce and soon dried up. He next took a position with an owner-breeder, but his boss soon reneged on their deal, and Smith found himself working for virtually no wages. By way of revenge, he stole some goods from the owner's shed, believing they were owed to him. The owner thought otherwise and called the police.

Smith then embarked on a series of petty thefts around Geelong, leading to his first jail sentence in 1961. By now, he'd 'graduated' to safe-blowing. His first conviction came when he and three others were charged with shop-breaking and stealing after guns and stolen items were found hidden under a hedge behind the grandstand at the Geelong Racecourse. As a result, eighteen-year-old Smith would spend eighteen months in the bleak bluestone jail at Geelong.

Smith had barely served this sentence in 1962 when he was back in prison again on similar charges, this time for six months. His racing career was put on hold. Not only did he now carry the baggage of a criminal record, but he'd also gained weight – a change that has brought many a promising jockey's career to an end.

THE RYAN CONNECTION

Around this time, Smith met Ronald Ryan at the races, and the two teamed up. One night, they stole a quantity of goods from Foy and Bilson's store in Murray Street, Colac. As he drove the truck containing the stolen goods toward Geelong along the Princes Highway, Smith was pulled over and arrested. Riding in his car behind, Ryan managed to avoid detection and made good his getaway. Smith was loyal to a fault and took the rap alone, receiving two-and-a-half years.

Ryan must have thought his luck was in, but it was definitely out. A few months later, he was sentenced to fourteen years for theft and possession of explosives. It was while serving this sentence that he escaped from Pentridge, allegedly shooting a warder in the process. This was the crime that would send him to the gallows in February 1967.

Meanwhile, Smith, having been released in 1966, was soon in trouble with the law again, sentenced to two years for receiving stolen goods. Smith appealed and while out on bail, he planned a raid on Pentridge to free his old mate Ronnie Ryan, who was awaiting execution there. His plan was to lead a gang of ex-prisoners in an assault on the grim fortress. They were to use explosives to gain admission through the front gates at night, then, fully armed, they would make their way to Ryan's cell and free the condemned prisoner. This would have been no mean feat, as Ryan wasn't being held in the D Division condemned cells but in the maximum-security H Division.

When Ryan heard of the scheme, not wanting further bloodshed, he sent a message through Father John Brosnan to alert Ian Grindlay, the prison governor. Together, Grindlay and Ryan devised a plan by which Ryan would send Smith and his mates a message through a former prisoner known as Jogger, calling off the 'bust-out' attempt. When Jogger first heard of the scheme, he described it as 'bulldust', but he'd changed his mind by the time he returned from delivering Ryan's message. He declared Ryan's mates 'desperate and determined'. They had cars, guns, gelignite, ropes and grappling hooks at the ready, and had planned to take hostages. But they reluctantly called off their planned assault, respecting Ryan's wishes.

Four months later, Smith was sentenced to five years jail for possession of explosives – sticks of gelignite, which he claimed police had planted in his Holden utility. He was eventually paroled on 3 May 1972. Having spent so much time in Pentridge and received the 'treatment' in H Division, Smith had now completed his education in criminal practice.

ON THE RUN

In 1973, Smith was tried on several more charges: conspiracy to commit armed robbery; possession of unlicensed firearms; loitering with intent; and assault by kicking. Found guilty on the loitering charge, he received three months imprisonment, with a further seven days for the firearms offence. From then on, he appears to have decided to avoid facing court. Over the next four years, Smith was constantly on the run from the police.

In 1974, while being interviewed at a police station, Smith

managed his first successful escape from custody, though he was recaptured the following day. Released on bail, he again absconded and held up the ANZ Bank at the Prahran Market with four accomplices. The haul was $107,000, a fortune at that time. A month later, the same gang grabbed the payroll of an after-care hospital in Collingwood, adding $6733 to their loot.

By now, Smith had decided things were getting a little hot for him in Melbourne, and he set his sights further north. With one of his accomplices, he flew to Sydney, unaware that he was under police surveillance for the armed robberies. At Bondi Junction, Smith and three others were arrested by police wearing bulletproof vests, and Smith was charged with conspiring to rob the Eveleigh railway workshops at Redfern. Freed on bail of $10,000, Smith later failed to appear at court, preferring to head back to Melbourne.

He was soon arrested sunbaking on the beach at Sandringham. Two days later, he pulled off an audacious escape from D Division. During a visit from his girlfriend Valerie, Smith relieved an elderly visitor of his pass, then used it to escort Valerie through the south gate. Shortly after, the couple disappeared into nearby Sydney Road, where they separated.

Accompanied by Valerie, Smith again headed for New South Wales, where he managed to keep ahead of the law for the next twelve months, continually moving from place to place. Then, in January 1976, two policemen, Constables Ambrose and Love, were on highway patrol around the Sydney suburb of Kingsford when they pulled over an Austin sedan that was being driven without lights. The car suddenly took off with the police vehicle in pursuit, and several shots were fired towards the police car. The Austin collided with the kerb and came to a sudden halt. The driver bolted, chased by Constable Love, but managed to escape. Meanwhile, a passenger got out of the Austin, and when Constable Ambrose called on him to surrender, he fired several shots, one of which hit Gerry Ambrose in the stomach. Police in New South Wales and Victoria were soon alerted to the shooting, and Terry Keith Clark and Edward James Smith became wanted men.

Even after that, Smith was able to lie low under an assumed name. He moved to the Nowra district, south of Sydney, where he trained and raced horses under the alias of Doug Cumming, which he later changed to Tom Cummings – a thinly veiled reference to the two leading horse trainers of the time, Tommy Smith and Bart Cummings.

On 13 June 1977, leading Sydney bookmaker Lloyd Tidmarsh was surprised by three masked men and shot dead at his home in the southern suburb of Kogarah. It was a futile killing, as the bookmaker had already banked his day's takings, so there was no gain for the bandits at all. Tidmarsh's daughter, Michelle, overheard one of the intruder's voices, which she was to describe as 'rough and gruff'. The only other clue came from a neighbour who'd noticed part of the number plate of a vehicle leaving the scene with its lights off.

In early September 1977, an armed robbery at the South Hurstville branch of the Commercial Bank of Australia netted about $180,000 for the balaclava-clad robbers, who escaped under fire from a security guard. During the heist, one of the bandits removed his balaclava, and he was later identified as Smith.

The media were now calling 'Jockey' Smith 'Australia's most wanted man'. Later that month, the police organised a huge manhunt, which culminated in his arrest at a telephone box in Bomaderry. Smith was charged with 'maliciously attempting to discharge a loaded firearm with intent to do grievous bodily harm', as detectives claimed he attempted to fire on one of them with a revolver. Though no civilian witness came forward to support this charge, a jury believed the prosecution's version of what took place, and Smith was given fourteen years imprisonment.

Now that Smith was in custody, many of his old crimes came back to haunt him. He was taken to Sydney, where he was placed in Katingal Special Security Unit at Long Bay Prison. Tried over the shooting of Constable Ambrose, he was initially found guilty of attempted murder and sentenced to life imprisonment, but the verdict was quashed on appeal some twelve months later. The problem was that the only witness had been Ambrose, and he'd given varying descriptions of the man who had shot him in the darkness. The only other evidence the jury could rely on was a hotly contested 'confession' supposedly given to police by Smith, who was hardly the confessing type.

Smith also faced several committal hearings and further charges of armed robbery, though several of these charges were eventually dropped. When he was tried over the robbery at the Commercial Bank branch in South Hurstville, the judge had to dismiss the jury and abort the trial due to adverse media coverage. A retrial was never held.

During one of these trials, police took Lloyd Tidmarsh's seventeen-year-old daughter Michelle to hear Smith defending himself in court. After listening to him for some time, Michelle declared that his voice was the one she'd heard in her house the night her father was shot. Smith was duly charged with Tidmarsh's murder, a charge he hotly denied. Before his trial, 'Jockey' alleged he'd been bashed by police and 'framed on the charge'. While in Long Bay Prison, he married his long-time girlfriend, Valerie Hill, who was also now in prison over charges in connection with the South Hurstville bank robbery.

Before fronting court over the Tidmarsh murder, Smith was tried for having made a 'malicious attempt to discharge a firearm' at a detective outside the telephone box in Bomaderry. He defended himself against the charge, but without success. He was found guilty and once again sentenced to life imprisonment, with fifteen years to be served before being eligible for parole. Smith then faced a charge of conspiring to rob the Eveleigh Railway Workshops at Redfern in 1974. Once again he defended himself unsuccessfully, this time receiving a further fourteen years, with a non-parole period of ten years.

Finally, almost six years after bookmaker Lloyd Tidmarsh had been gunned down in his home, Smith faced trial over the murder. Michelle Tidmarsh told the jury she'd heard the voices of the men in the house before her father was shot, and repeated her claim that Smith's voice was the one she'd heard threatening her father. It was also explained to the court that police had to get this highly unusual form of identification as Smith had refused to take part in an identification parade.

Defending himself once again, Smith continued his poor record as a barrister when, after one of the longest murder trials in New South Wales history, he was found guilty and sentenced to life imprisonment. He was also found guilty of robbing Tidmarsh's home, for which he received sixteen years, and the theft of the car used in the commission of the crime, for which he received a further five years – though all these sentences were ordered to be served concurrently.

All wasn't lost for Smith. On appeal, he was granted a retrial on all three counts, mainly because of doubts concerning Michelle's voice identification and the scantiness of the evidence connecting him to the car used in the murder.

Smith's luck held further. The New South Wales Attorney-General, after weighing up his options, decided not to proceed with the second trial. The detective who had taken Smith's confession before the trial had since been dismissed in disgrace from the New South Wales police force, and another key detective in the case had died. This now left

Smith to serve his life sentence for shooting at the detective at Bomaderry, together with the fourteen years he received for the Redfern conspiracy charge.

For several years, Smith was imprisoned in New South Wales. He was then transferred back to Melbourne at his own request to face his outstanding Victorian charges, including escape from legal custody, and by Christmas 1989 he was in A Division at Pentridge. His luck continued to hold, as the new charges only added a month to his previous sentence.

Having completed his time in Victoria, 'Jockey' returned to Long Bay Prison in New South Wales to have his life sentence re-determined under the new 'truth in sentencing' regulations. His sentence was now set at fifteen years with an additional ten years parole, but on appeal, the sentence was further reduced to fourteen years.

With good behaviour, Smith was released in February 1992, having been in custody for almost fifteen years. His wife, Valerie, had been living in a flat in Bondi, and Smith went there to be reunited with her. He was unaware that a masked gunman lay in waiting for him in the stairwell above her flat. As Smith and Valerie went to enter the flat, Smith was shot several times at close range. Critically wounded, he was taken to St Vincent's Hospital at Darlinghurst, where he was placed on life support and operated on. Despite his massive wounds, he survived. It was rumoured that the shooter was a former husband of Valerie's, but no charges were ever laid over the shooting.

Smith couldn't help himself, though. He was soon back to his criminal habits, being caught shoplifting from a Grace Brothers store. He pulled a gun on security staff who had detained him, then fled, bailing up a motorist and taking off in his car.

Smith now headed for country Victoria and a date with destiny. He holed up in a farmhouse at Glenlyon, near

Daylesford, with the escapee Christopher 'Badness' Binse. At 8.20 pm on 5 December 1992, Smith left the farm in a white Ford panel van, unaware that the house was under surveillance by police looking for Binse. As fate would have it, the watching police didn't follow the van, as they were focused on apprehending Binse and didn't realise who was driving it.

Smith was heading for Creswick, but his driving caught the attention of Senior Constable Ian Harris, on routine patrol, who decided to follow the van. Harris radioed Ballarat D24 for a vehicle check and was told the panel van had recently been stolen from Northcote. By now, Smith had become aware that he was being followed, but he didn't realise the van was stolen.

Harris continued to tail the van until about 8.45 pm, when it reached Creswick and pulled into the Farmer's Arms Hotel. Harris parked close by, and began what he expected to be a routine stolen car interception. He got the shock of his life when the van's driver pulled a gun on him. Harris quickly put his arms in the air as Smith levelled his pistol at his chest. Smith then attempted to take Harris's revolver from its holster – screaming at him not to touch it, and that he was going to kill him.

While hotel patrons watched on, Smith fired a couple of shots into the ground and one into the air as he grappled with Harris. Darren Neil, a hotel patron who had seen what was going on, suddenly drove his car straight at Smith, momentarily distracting him and giving Harris the chance to draw his own gun. The policeman fired three shots, two of which hit Smith, killing him instantly.

'Jockey' Smith's race was over. Patrons emerged from the hotel, and a couple of them tried to revive him. Others simply stood around in shock. News of Smith's death soon spread, and it wasn't long before television crews were on the scene, which had quickly been sealed off with crime-scene tape.

For Ian Harris, the event marked the beginning of a period of personal pressure. Smith's death was yet another in a long list of Victorian police shootings, which had given rise to much media criticism of the force. To make matters worse, it was rumoured that Smith had been on a police 'hit list'. Harris and Neil were traumatised over the shooting – as were Neil's young boys, who had been in his car with him.

Both Harris and Neil were later recognised for their bravery. Ian Harris was awarded the Police Valour Award, and Darren Neil was presented with the Star of Courage in a ceremony at Government House. Harris was also cleared by a coroner of any doubts as to his actions at the Creswick Hotel. In July 1994, after a week-long inquest, the coroner found that Harris had shot Smith 'in lawful self-defence'.

After a turbulent criminal career, James Edward 'Jockey' Smith was finally laid to rest at the Geelong East Cemetery.

CHAPTER 13
LEIGH ROBINSON

A young A Division prisoner who always made his presence felt around the jail was 22-year-old Leigh Robinson. He'd recently been reprieved from execution for the murder of his seventeen-year-old ex-girlfriend, whom he'd stabbed with a kitchen knife in a raging frenzy at her Chadstone home. His new sentence was thirty years hard labour, with a minimum of twenty years.

An enthusiastic participant in the prison's performing arts, Robinson was an outgoing, confident young man, and it was obvious he liked to be in control. This desire had already led him to a long sentence at Pentridge, but he'd commit a similar crime some thirty years later on a girl who wasn't yet born.

THE ROAD TO MURDER

Born in 1948, Robinson had an unsettled upbringing, his parents having divorced when he was four years old. He lived with his grandmother and later with an aunt, before returning to his mother's care. Young Robinson developed a rebellious attitude towards others, particularly women. He left school at thirteen, having been expelled from Oakleigh High School, and apparently was in the army for a time. In his late teens, he came to the attention of police, mainly for theft and tampering with cars. By the age of nineteen, he was working as a labourer and boarding in the home of an old army mate in the Melbourne suburb of Chadstone.

A man named Harold Dunn, who lived four doors away,

then offered Robinson a part-time job as a carpet layer. Robinson soon became attracted to Dunn's sixteen-year-old daughter Valerie, and the two went steady for about twelve months. Then Valerie decided to break it off. Robinson had become increasingly domineering and often resorted to physical violence. He was also still pilfering from cars and milking them of petrol, and he'd been convicted of breaking into a garage in Oakleigh and stealing some tools. Harold Dunn was remarkably tolerant of this behaviour, and even put up bail for Robinson after he broke into the garage.

Robinson was greatly upset when Valerie called off their relationship, and he threatened her with a gun. One day, she'd been out with a girlfriend when Robinson bailed them up outside her home, abusing her and threatening 'to kill anyone who gets in the way'. He forced her into his car and drove off with her, before finally calming down and driving her home.

Police were called to a later incident after Robinson produced a gun in a car. Harold Dunn was approached to speak to the agitated young man and persuade him to hand over the firearm he was brandishing. Oddly, Robinson wasn't charged over this incident.

By now, Valerie's family were becoming deeply concerned about her relationship with Robinson. Her sisters did everything they could to dissuade her from having anything to do with him. Valerie too was living in dread of him. In an apparent attempt to put the relationship behind her, she reunited with a former boyfriend, sixteen-year-old Des Grewar, a local motor mechanic.

Robinson later told police that around this time he began having fantasies about killing Valerie. In one recurring fantasy, the two of them would be killed in an accident in his car. Robinson continued to work for Harold Dunn, but he became morose over his breakup with Valerie and resentful of her new boyfriend.

On the day of the murder, 8 June 1968, Robinson was out working with Valerie's father, who asked him to take some gear to his house in Margot Street. When he arrived there in the late afternoon, Robinson found Valerie with Des Grewar. Robinson asked her to go out with him, but she was reluctant to do so. At this, Robinson flew into a violent rage, grabbing a kitchen knife and stabbing Valerie twice in the stomach. She collapsed to the floor, screaming out for help to Des, who was in another room. Des rushed to the kitchen, where he found Robinson stabbing Valerie. Grewer vainly attempted to help her, but was himself stabbed in the stomach. Robinson was in a frenzy, though he never said anything during the savage attack. Des and Valerie tried to run to the front door, but Robinson began stabbing Valerie frantically in the back to stop her leaving. Des managed to reach a neighbour's house and raise the alarm, but Robinson continued stabbing Valerie until she lay dead on the floor. She'd been stabbed sixteen times, twice in the front and fourteen times in the back.

Robinson then returned to Harold Dunn's car and drove away. He tried to ring Valerie's house from a public telephone box, 'to see if she was still alive', he later said, and he then rang a detective he knew. Next, he drove to a friend's home and confessed to the murder. His friend accompanied him to police at Cranbourne, where he again confessed and handed over a kitchen knife. Police quickly came to the conclusion that Robinson couldn't handle the fact that Valerie had refused to obey his demands.

At his Supreme Court trial in November 1968, Robinson made an unsworn statement from the dock in which he told the court that he could remember bending down and kissing Valerie as she lay on the floor, but he couldn't remember stabbing her. 'Everything went funny', he said. He explained that he'd been feeling depressed and frustrated for months before the murder, and he simply didn't know what he was doing. 'I really loved her, I didn't want to hurt her. I remember Valerie on the floor and she looked as though she was hurt', he said.

The jury deliberated for less than an hour before finding Robinson guilty of the murder of Valerie Dunn, and Justice George Lush sentenced him to death. After the sentence was delivered, Robinson sat down, put his head in his hands and wept. Asked if he had anything to say, he replied, 'No, sir.' State Cabinet later commuted his sentence to 30 years hard labour, which he served at Pentridge. Strangely, he was never charged with the attack on Des Grewar.

IN AND OUT OF JAIL

While serving his time in A Division, the outgoing Robinson made several friends from the entertainment world through his involvement in the performing arts at the prison. Among them was Gil Tucker, a popular television actor who later gave Robinson character references when he was in trouble with the law. Transferred to the minimum-security prison at Morwell River, Robinson escaped, but was soon recaptured and returned to Pentridge.

In 1983, fifteen years into his sentence, Robinson met the Parole Board. He managed to convince its members that he was rehabilitated and deserved a second chance. The Parole Board agreed to release him, but Des Grewar wasn't happy; he even went to Russell Street Police Headquarters in a vain attempt to have Robinson charged with attempted murder.

After his release, Robinson began living with a woman named Gena, a mother of five he'd met in Pentridge, where she'd taught soft-toy making. Robinson took on the role of stepfather to her children. Around 1987, he appeared on a television discussion program in which he insisted that he had the right to a normal life and that his past was just that – past. His reformed ways didn't last, though. In 1991, he was back in prison, serving two years on fourteen counts of receiving stolen goods, one count of burglary and two of unlawful possession.

Released again in 1993, Robinson married Gena, but before the wedding, one of his stepdaughters went to police and told them he'd been sexually abusing her since she was thirteen. He was charged and sentenced to five years imprisonment. In his sentencing statement, Justice Smith told Robinson that he was guilty of a gross betrayal of the trust given to him as a father figure, and emphasised the psychological trauma he'd caused, including insomnia, fear, suicidal thoughts and drug and alcohol abuse.

By the time his sentence ended, his marriage to Gena was understandably over. Robinson now took a job as a casual truck driver and moved into an old caravan on his employer's property in Pearcedale. He also worked at repairing trucks.

A FATAL RERUN

In Pentridge, Robinson had made friends with a man called Jeffrey Greenbury, who was serving ten years in prison for murdering a 70-year-old man in a caravan park at Seaford. When Jeffrey got out, he introduced Robinson to his 33-year-old sister, Tracey, who was a single mother. Tracey formed a relationship with Robinson, who was now 60, but it very quickly soured. Like Valerie Dunn some forty years earlier, Tracey became fearful of his overbearing and aggressive nature. Tracey's father, Max, did everything he could to discourage his daughter from associating with the man. When discussing his past with Tracey's parents, Robinson had admitted that he'd been imprisoned over a girl's death, but claimed he'd killed her in a car accident.

In events that were eerily familiar, Robinson threatened Tracey with a gun and told her not to push his buttons. He even phoned Max and described the terrified look in his daughter's eyes as he pointed the gun at her head. Again, Tracey's parents begged her to stop seeing Robinson, telling her to go to the police and report his behaviour. Tracey by now was determined to end the relationship, and she told Robinson she no longer wanted to see him. Rejected again, he responded as he had before.

On 28 April 2008, ten days after his threat to kill Tracey, Robinson descended on her home at Frankston. Although it was a cold, wet April morning, Tracey followed Robinson out to his car, where she saw a 12-gauge shotgun half-hidden by a tea towel. After an argument, and in fear of her life, Tracey made her way to the house of a neighbour, Leoni Coates, with Robinson in close pursuit.

Leoni, who was home from work, heard scratching noises and someone sobbing at her front door. There was also 'a very soft knocking very low down', Leonie later recalled, and her immediate thought was that there was a child outside. Opening the door, she found Tracey cowering on the step, pleading with her for help. At the same time, Leoni noticed the barrel of a gun poking at Tracey, and looked up to see Robinson holding the weapon.

Tracey crawled into the passageway of the house and lay there face down, frozen with fear. Robinson, without saying a word, leant across Leoni and cold-bloodedly shot Tracey in the back of the head. Leoni stood transfixed, waiting her turn to be shot, but the assassin just grinned at her, calmly turned, walked off to his car and drove away.

Just as he'd done forty years before, Robinson made some telephone calls before giving himself up to police through an intermediary. He called his ex-wife, phoned the father of Tracey's two children, and informed his boss he wouldn't be working for him any more. His boss had heard of the murder over the radio, so he wasn't surprised.

At his trial for Tracey's murder, Robinson pleaded not

guilty. He admitted he'd chased Tracey down the street, but maintained that he'd discharged the weapon accidentally. From the dock, he joked with his guards and appeared totally unconcerned about the gravity of his charge. He waved to supporters in the public gallery and shook his head when evidence was given against him. The jury was given an insight into Robinson's callous nature when Tracey's ex-husband told them about his telephone conversation with Robinson, who'd said, 'Yeah, come and get your kids – they've got no mother.' Though the jury was unaware that Robinson was already a convicted murderer, it took just one hour's deliberation to find him guilty.

On sentencing day some four months later, in late January 2010, the cold-hearted killer faced Justice Simon Whelan. A defence forensic psychologist, Elizabeth Warren, told the judge that she'd interviewed Robinson three times since his trial and had diagnosed him with 'intermittent explosive disorder', which meant that he 'acts rapidly on impulse and aggression resulting in violent actions'. She told the judge she believed he could be rehabilitated.

Before the hearing, Robinson had been in a jovial mood, laughing and joking with his guards. His attitude changed, however, when Justice Whelan addressed him for sentencing. The judge told him that he'd terrified Tracey, even though she'd posed no threat to him. Justice Whelan said:

> Motivated by annoyance at some parts of your relationship with her, you chased her down a suburban street in broad daylight, carrying a loaded and cocked shortened shotgun. When you caught her, you callously shot her in the back of the head as she was attempting to crawl away from you before the eyes of her petrified neighbour. You now have taken the lives of two women who were in a relationship with you and have deeply damaged the lives

of all those who were close to them. There is a pressing
need to permanently protect the community from you.

To an outburst of applause from Tracey's family and friends,
Justice Whelan sentenced Robinson to life imprisonment
without parole.

OPEN
OUTWARDS

CHAPTER 14
DEREK ERNEST PERCY

G Division, originally built in the 1870s as a reformatory, was converted into a psychiatric unit in 1958. The unit, which accommodated up to 46 inmates, aimed to assess and provide treatment for prisoners who were found to be mentally unwell. Average treatment time was relatively short, but the unit also housed longer-term prisoners who'd been charged with serious offences and found not guilty on the grounds of insanity, as a result of which they were serving an unspecified amount of time at the Governor's pleasure. These inmates were generally considered to be a danger to the community. They were treated until they were cleared for release from detention when they were no longer considered a threat to community safety.

Such a prisoner was Derek Ernest Percy, who in July 1969 had committed an atrocious murder on a young Warneet schoolgirl. There was no doubt that Percy had committed the crime. An eyewitness had identified him and his car when he abducted the girl, and he'd later been found washing blood off his clothing. He'd also led police to the girl's body in an isolated paddock. The horrendous acts involved in the murder almost certainly influenced the jury at his trial to find him not guilty on the grounds of insanity. It was difficult to accept that any sane person could commit such an atrocity on a fellow human being.

Though there was no doubt that Percy was responsible for this crime, the investigating detectives doubted that it was a 'one-off' murder. As they spread their net wider, they began to suspect Percy of involvement in a spate of unsolved murders of young children around Australia during the 1960s, though he never confessed to any of these crimes.

YVONNE TUOHY

Twelve-year-old Yvonne Elizabeth Tuohy was a bright, happy girl whose parents ran the Warneet General Store and a boat-hiring service on Victoria's Westernport Bay. Yvonne had a good friend, eleven-year-old Melbourne boy Shane Spiller, who regularly came to Warneet, where his parents had a weekender.

On 20 July 1969, the two friends set off for a picnic on the beach. Yvonne took some sandwiches that her mother had prepared for them and Shane carried a small tomahawk, which he planned to use to cut some wood.

They made their way along a track through some tea-tree scrub to nearby Ski Beach. As they walked by a car park, the two friends noticed a man – who Shane would later say 'looked like bad news' – sitting in the driver's seat of a station wagon. Being a bit of a car enthusiast, Shane noted that the vehicle was a light-coloured Datsun with a luggage rack on top. He also observed that it had a couple of rugs in the back and a parking sticker in the rear window with 'Navy' inscribed on it. The two youngsters continued along the track, eventually arriving at Ski Beach.

Sitting in the Datsun was Derek Ernest Percy, a young naval rating on leave from the nearby Cerberus base. Percy watched intently as the youngsters walked by along the track leading to the beach. He quickly took a dagger from under the seat of his car and set off on foot in pursuit of the children. Yvonne had become temporarily separated from Shane, who had headed off to the right of the beach, and Percy soon caught up with her. Shane turned back and saw with horror that the man from the car was with Yvonne, holding a knife to her throat.

For a short time there was a standoff, as Shane would later describe it, with Percy holding his knife at the terrified girl's throat while at the same time trying to coax Shane to come to him. The young boy waved his tomahawk at Percy to keep him away. Percy snarled, 'Put that down or I'll hurt the girl.' Then he said to Yvonne, 'Tell your friend to come back here.'

In desperation, Shane decided to go for assistance. He ran through the tea-tree, yelling for help as he went. Behind him, he heard Yvonne scream, 'Shane, Shane, help! He's going to cut my throat!' A nearby group of picnickers heard Shane's cries for help, but didn't go to assist; they later said they thought it was just children playing. After he'd run some distance, Shane saw Percy drive off in his Datsun with a terrified Yvonne. He ran on in a similar direction until he reached a road, where a passing motorist picked him up.

Police were notified, and Shane gave them a detailed description of the man and his car, including the naval insignia on the back. Armed with this information, homicide detectives raced to the nearby Cerberus naval base, where they found a cream-coloured Datsun station wagon in the car park. Shortly after, they located its owner, Derek Percy, busily washing his clothing in a laundry. Before leaving, police looked in Percy's locker and seized a diary containing graphic descriptions of the torture and murder of children.

Though Shane Spiller was in a state of shock, he went with police to the naval base and identified the Datsun. He later chose Percy as the attacker from a line-up.

Percy was taken to Frankston police station for a lengthy interrogation. Later, he was put in a police vehicle and directed detectives to a spot in Devon Meadows, some distance to the east. After a couple of turns and a bumpy ride along a dirt road, Percy indicated a paddock and told the driver to stop. 'She's in there,' he said.

Entering the paddock, detectives shone their torches on the ground where Percy was pointing, and there they saw a sight that would live with them forever. Lying on the ground was the body of a young girl – or what was left of her. Her wrists had been tied firmly behind her back, and a filthy piece of rag had been jammed tightly into her mouth, which had been covered by a cloth gag. Her throat had been cut from ear to ear – a cut so deep she'd almost been decapitated – and an enormous wound ran the full length of her torso, exposing her intestines. Distraught at the sight, the detectives led Percy from this horrific scene. Little was said on the return journey to the police station.

When Percy's case came to trial in the Supreme Court, psychiatrists gave evidence that he had an 'acute psycho-sexual disorder'. On the sixth day, he was found not guilty on the grounds of insanity. This verdict may well have saved Percy from the noose. The judge ordered that he be held in custody at the Governor's pleasure.

Had Percy been sentenced to a long term in a mainstream prison, he undoubtedly would have been a target for attack as a despised 'rock spider', and a particularly sadistic one. Furthermore, he'd probably have been released around the mid-1980s, when he'd still have been a menace to children. The situation would have been similar if he'd pleaded guilty.

Though Percy was now under lock and key, there was still another victim. Shane Spiller was never able to cope with what had happened. It haunted him that he hadn't stayed with his terrified friend.

In his early teens, Shane began drinking heavily, using alcohol as a crutch to help him with his fears. He later moved to Wyndham, a village in southern New South Wales, where he continued to battle his demons. He told people he could still see the murderous look Percy gave him when he identified him as the killer, and he often imagined that Percy was coming after him.

Living off a disability pension, Shane continued to drink heavily and used drugs. In 1998, police contacted him to inform him that Percy's case was to be reviewed, and that there was a possibility he might be released. Fortunately, at the review, Justice Eames found that Percy wasn't fit to be released and would probably be a greater risk than before. For Shane Spiller, however, this was small consolation.

In 2000, Shane applied for crimes compensation and was granted $5000, which was later raised to the maximum of $50,000 on appeal to the Victorian Civil and Administrative Tribunal.

In August 2002, Shane Spiller disappeared. It has been speculated that he may have been murdered for his crimes compensation payout; he may also have died from a drug overdose or committed suicide. But many of those who knew him believed he'd simply taken off. What happened remains unknown, but there is little doubt that without his ingenuity, Derek Percy would have murdered again.

WARNING SIGNS

Derek Ernest Percy was born in Strathfield, a suburb of Sydney, in September 1948. When he was eight years old, he and his family moved to Victoria after his father, Ernest, took up a position with the State Electricity Commission. They lived in the Melbourne bayside suburb of Chelsea for two years before relocating to Warrnambool on the west coast of Victoria. These seaside locations suited Ernest well, as he was a keen yachtsman.

Three years later, Ernest moved his family again, having obtained a promotion at work. This time, they settled at Mount

Beauty, a country town in north-eastern Victoria. Although now living inland, the Percys continued to participate in yachting. Ernest often competed in interstate competitions, and the family accompanied him in a caravan.

Derek attended Mount Beauty Higher Elementary School, where classmates remembered him as intelligent and physically fit, though with very few friends. By doing odd jobs around the town, he saved up enough money to buy a second-hand red bicycle with racing rams-horn handlebars, and he was often seen riding it around the town.

During 1964, a number of women in Mount Beauty had their underwear taken from clotheslines – 'snowdropping' as the practice is known – and young Derek Percy was a red-hot suspect. Students at the school reported that they'd seen him in the bush wearing a pink negligee, and cutting and stabbing at a pair of female underpants with a knife. When they reported this, however, they weren't believed.

In January 1965, two young girls were murdered at Sydney's Wanda Beach. An identikit portrait of a suspect was widely circulated, and some residents of Mount Beauty believed it looked like Derek Percy. Later the same year, Percy inexplicably failed his Leaving Certificate at Year 11.

The Percys made yet another move in 1966, this time to Khancoban in southern New South Wales. Afterwards, the 'snowdropping' ceased in Mount Beauty, but it began around Khancoban. At Khancoban, Derek sexually assaulted a 6-year-old girl, but his father managed to have the matter dealt with 'in-house', assuring the girl's father that the incident would never be repeated.

Percy was now also writing about violent sexual fantasies, which he'd continue to do for years to come. His parents and grandmother came across some of these writings and were appalled by them, but nothing seems to have been done to seek treatment for him. Apparently, the family decided that it was all part of Derek's sexual adjustment as he grew up.

Ernest Percy made yet another move in 1967. He quit his job with the Electricity Commission and purchased a Shell service station in Newcastle. Derek attempted Year 12, but didn't complete the year. He dropped out of school and worked at his father's service station for a short time, then joined the navy.

In March 1968, Percy was posted to the aircraft carrier HMAS *Melbourne*, but the ship was in dry dock in Sydney Harbour for a year, so Percy stayed on the naval base HMAS Kuttabul. He took eighteen days leave in August 1968 and headed for Melbourne. He was later sent to Victoria's Cerberus naval base and was stationed there when he committed the atrocious murder of Yvonne Tuohy in mid-1969.

A psychiatrist who assessed Percy after his arrest for the Tuohy murder concluded that he had 'many psycho-sexual abnormalities' and was 'highly likely to have killed other children'. Detectives investigating Yvonne's murder came to a similar conclusion. To add to their suspicions, another twelve-year-old girl came forward to identify Percy as the man who had attempted to abduct her earlier in the year when she was riding her bicycle near the Cerberus base. Fortunately for this girl, she was able to escape. Certainly if it hadn't been for the powers of observation – and the fortunate escape – of Shane Spiller, Percy may well have succeeded in many more such attacks.

Suspicious homicide detectives began to re-investigate several unsolved child murders and abductions that had occurred in recent years around Australia. In order of occurrence, these were:

- the Wanda Beach murders of Christine Sharrock and Marianne Schmidt, both aged fifteen (Sydney 1965);
- the abduction and presumed murders of the Beaumont

children – Jane, aged nine, Arnna, aged seven and Grant, aged four (Adelaide 1966);

- the abduction and murder of Allen Redston, aged six (Canberra 1966);
- the abduction and murder of Simon Brook, aged three (Sydney 1968); and
- the abduction and presumed murder of Linda Stilwell, aged seven (Melbourne 1968).

There were links between these cases. Almost all involved the disappearance of children from a beach area, and they'd vanished without anyone seeing them taken. In some cases the bodies had been discovered, and there were quite similar mutilations of the victims. There was little evidence pointing to the person, or persons, responsible, but there were indications that Percy may well have been involved in some if not all of these crimes. By his own admissions, he was in the vicinity when each crime occurred, and others had observed him there. With the exceptions of the Beaumont children and Linda Stilwell, who all disappeared without a trace, the rest were the victims of a brazen, sadistic paedophile.

Could Derek Percy have been that paedophile? Certainly he demonstrated he was brazen and sadistic during the execution of the one crime for which he was caught. Fortunately, such individuals are rare, so the fact that he was in the vicinity when these crimes were committed casts much suspicion on him.

THE WANDA BEACH MURDERS

The first of these crimes occurred at Sydney's Wanda Beach on 11 January 1965. On that day, good friends and next-door neighbours Christine Sharrock and Marianne Schmidt, both fifteen, set off from West Ryde for a picnic at Cronulla Beach. They took Marianne's four younger siblings – Peter, aged ten, Trixie, aged nine, Wolfgang, aged seven and Norbert, aged five.

They caught a train from West Ryde to the beach, arriving a little before midday. After having lunch at Cronulla, the two older girls took the Schmidt children for a walk across the sandhills to Wanda Beach. There had been a strong wind all day, and it was too much for the smaller children. The two older girls left them to shelter behind a sandhill while they continued on their way. They didn't return. Both Peter and Wolfgang later said that they saw the girls talking to a blond-haired boy.

The children waited until late afternoon before walking back to Cronulla, where they caught the last train out at about 6 pm. They reached their West Ryde home a couple of hours later and reported the two girls missing. Christine's grandmother, with whom she lived, contacted Ryde police about 8.30 pm.

The following day, a teenage boy came across a body, mostly covered in sand, in the sandhills north of Wanda Beach. Detectives who arrived at the scene soon discovered that there were actually two bodies, those of the missing girls. Both had suffered a dreadful death at the hands of their killer. He'd buried them in the sand, but the strong wind had partly uncovered them. Police deduced that Marianne had been attacked first and that Christine had run away. The killer had chased her, hitting her over the head with an object and fracturing her skull, before dragging her back to Marianne. Each girl was stabbed several times with a knife, and the lower part of Marianne's swimsuit had been slashed. Like Yvonne Tuohy some years later, Marianne had her throat cut to the degree of near decapitation.

People who were around Wanda Beach that day saw a youth aged about nineteen, with light-coloured hair and a pale complexion, in the vicinity of where the two murdered girls were found. Others spoke of a 'surfie-type' youth with blond hair. This youth never came forward, nor was he located. The Wanda Beach murders remain unsolved.

Could Derek Percy have been the Wanda Beach murderer? There are key elements that fit Percy neatly into the frame. At the time, Percy was a fair-haired youth heading for seventeen, and people who knew him said he looked older. Percy always seemed to have a knife with him, and he'd been seen slashing at women's underwear in a similar way to the slashing of Marianne's swimsuit. People also told police that the Percy's had gone to Sydney that year for the summer holidays, and there was a national regatta at Botany Bay Yachting Club, near Wanda Beach, at the time of the murders. Also, Percy's grandparents lived in Ryde, less than two kilometres from the West Ryde station where the girls had caught their train to the beach.

During an autopsy on the bodies of the two girls, it was found that Christine had a blood alcohol level of 0.015, equivalent to her having consumed a ten-ounce glass of beer. Later readings of Percy's diaries revealed that he'd written about making a victim drink alcohol before a killing.

The similarities between the murder of Yvonne Tuohy at Warneet and the Wanda Beach murders are obvious. In each case, two children were set upon at a beach in broad daylight, though at Warneet one managed to escape. The victims were tortured and savagely knifed to death, including the ferocious cutting of the throats in a frantic overkill. And without the actions of Shane Spiller, the Warneet case could also have been an unsolved murder.

THE BEAUMONT CHILDREN

The disappearance of the Beaumont children from Adelaide's Glenelg Beach in 1966 is one of Australia's most tragic unsolved mysteries. It sparked a massive search for the three missing children, which included bringing a psychic from the other side of the world in a futile effort to discover what had happened to them. Their disappearance changed the thinking of Australian parents, making them far more aware of the dangers of allowing children to go out unsupervised.

On 26 January 1966, Jim and Nancy Beaumont's three children – nine-year-old Jane, seven-year-old Arnna and four-year-old Grant – asked their mother to let them go for a swim at nearby Glenelg Beach. Nancy had made arrangements to visit friends that day. She allowed the children to go, on the proviso that they return to their Somerton Park home on the midday bus. Before they left, she gave them eight shillings to buy some pasties for their lunch.

The three children boarded a bus to the beach at about 10.15 am. The driver later remembered the children leaving the bus near the beach and noticed that Jane had a copy of *Little Women* under her arm.

The children were also observed at the beach during the morning. A woman saw them playing under a sprinkler at Colley Reserve at about 11 am. A short time later, they were joined by a 'surfie-type man' wearing a blue swimming outfit, and the children began flicking their towels at him. Observers estimated that the man was about thirty years old.

The next sighting of the children was at 11.45, when they entered a Jetty Street milk bar to buy pasties and, significantly, a pie – the children had never bought a pie before. Jane paid for the purchase with a £1 note, whereas her mother had only given her coins.

Another woman saw the man and the three children return to the reserve area about midday. The children seemed happy with the man, and the woman later told police he dressed the children, seemingly to go home. Another woman noticed him walking with the children to the change rooms at Colley Reserve at about 12.15. The children waited on a seat outside, she was later to tell police. Shortly after, they walked away and disappeared from view.

There was one last sighting of the children that is considered by police to be accurate, though there were to be many more unconfirmed 'sightings', many of them hoaxes. The local postman, who knew the children, told police he saw them walking along Jetty Road towards the bus stop, but couldn't recall whether he saw them at 1.45, at the start of his round, or at 2.55, when he finished it. He was sure they were by themselves.

The children then vanished.

Nancy Beaumont met the midday bus, but when she realised her children weren't on it, she didn't feel there was too much cause to worry. They'd probably bought lunch, missed the bus, and would catch the two o'clock bus, she reasoned. When that bus arrived and left without any sign of her children, Nancy became quite concerned, but there was little else she could do but wait for the three o'clock bus.

When that bus came and went with still no sign of her children, Nancy Beaumont became alarmed. Her husband, Jim, came home from work at 3.30 pm, and both parents immediately set off for Glenelg Beach.

After a frantic and fruitless search of every possible place where they could imagine their children going, the Beaumonts reported the children missing to police at 7.30 pm, sparking an extensive search of Glenelg Beach and its surrounds. It was initially feared that the children may have drowned or even run away. It seemed incomprehensible that three children had been abducted from a busy beach, but when there was no sign of the children or their belongings, this almost unheard-of possibility became a reality.

Everything possible was done to find the children. Boat havens were searched at low tide; the Adelaide Hills were searched, as were rubbish tips; people in seaside suburbs of Adelaide searched stormwater drains and wells, and a suburban taxi fleet even joined in when it was discovered that Jim Beaumont had been an owner-driver with them. Police and the frantic parents responded to tips, sightings and hoax calls. These were to continue for years, but no trace of the children was ever found.

Later that year, Gerard Croiset, a psychic from the Netherlands who'd been given details of the case, contacted the Beaumonts to tell them their children were buried within half a mile of Glenelg Beach. He then flew to Adelaide and declared that they were buried under the concrete floor of a recently built warehouse. It was later ripped up, but no trace of the children was found.

The loss of their children and the subsequent publicity eventually took their toll on the Beaumonts, who separated.

Because the Beaumont children disappeared and left no physical evidence of who abducted them or what happened to them, it is difficult to do anything more than point a finger of suspicion for the crime. It has been reported that investigators have four main suspects, all of whom resembled the fair-haired man seen with the children on the day they disappeared. Each of these men – Bevan von Einham, Arthur Brown, James O'Neill and Derek Percy – had committed crimes involving the molestation and murder of children.

Percy answers the description of the person last seen with the children, except there is an obvious age discrepancy. However, Percy did look older than his years, and witnesses can give unreliable descriptions after an event of which they have not taken particular notice. Percy was heading for eighteen, so there is a fair margin to the man described as in his thirties, but there is also no certainty that the person last seen with them actually abducted them. Further, the postman saw them walking alone, quite possibly after these sightings.

Nobody has ever come forward to say they saw the children leaving the vicinity of the beach.

Those who say that it couldn't have been Percy have also compared the disappearance of the Beaumont children with the abduction of two girls from an Adelaide football oval in the 1970s, when Percy was in jail. They point out that there are similarities in the identikit pictures of suspects in the two cases. However, it could equally be argued that no-one saw the abductor of the Beaumonts, so what reliance could be put on an identikit? There was much controversy over the identikit drawing of the Beaumont suspect, with even the artist stating there had been problems.

By his own admission, Percy was in Adelaide and 'near the beach' when the Beaumont children disappeared. This was made known at a recent inquest into Linda Stilwell's disappearance, when an ex-policeman – an old classmate of Percy's – took the stand and told the court that when he was starting out in the police, the homicide squad had placed him in Percy's cell shortly after the Yvonne Tuohy murder to see what he could find out about murders involving children. Presenting himself as being there as a friend for his old classmate, the policeman managed to get from Percy that he'd driven through St Kilda on the day when seven-year-old Linda Stillwell was abducted from St Kilda Beach in August 1968.

When the topic of conversation got around to the Beaumont children, Percy said, 'I was in Adelaide at the time.' He also said that he'd 'been near the beach – nothing else'. Unfortunately, at this point the watch-house keeper, unaware of what was going on, told the young constable to leave. The policeman then had to reveal the purpose of his presence in the cell, and Percy realised his old classmate wasn't there to help him as a friend at all, but rather to learn his secrets. No further information was forthcoming, and it never has been since.

Confirmation of Percy's presence in Adelaide at the time came from two other sources – people living in Mount Beauty recall Percy holidaying in Adelaide at the time, and his brother agreed the family had been there. So it's considered likely that Percy was in Adelaide and 'near a beach' on the day the Beaumont children disappeared; that he resembled a suspect seen with them; and that he'd abducted and killed at a beach in a brazen way since. Not enough to charge him – but there is no better 'qualified' suspect.

ALLEN REDSTON

On 27 September 1966, six-year-old Allen Geoffrey Redston left his home in the Canberra suburb of Curtin to go to a nearby milk bar and disappeared. His body was found the next day, hidden among some reeds beside a creek, hog-tied and with cloth and plastic wrapped around his throat. Before his murder, it was reported that a blond-haired youth had been attacking other boys in the area, tying them up and putting plastic wrap over their heads. The suspect was seen riding a bicycle not unlike the one Percy rode around Mount Beauty. An identikit drawing of the youth bore remarkable similarities to Percy.

Later, after the Tuohy murder, Percy told police he'd been on holidays in the ACT during 1966, but couldn't remember when. Both Allen Redston and Yvonne Tuohy had been tied and gagged. Allen was hog-tied, and again there is a connection to Percy. When Percy stayed with his grandmother as a child, she'd put him in an empty room and hog-tie him if he misbehaved. Allen had also been bound with a tattered green-and-gold-striped tie, similar to one Percy wore when he attended school at Mount Beauty. The murder of Allen Redston remains unsolved.

* * *

In March 1968, while HMAS *Melbourne* was in dry dock, Percy lived at HMAS Kuttabul, the naval base on Garden Island, commuting to and from the suburb of Glebe.

In May that year, little Simon Brook, aged three, was playing in the front yard of his Glebe home while his parents were entertaining visitors in the house. When his father went to bring Simon in, he discovered the little boy was gone. His lifeless body was later found behind a block of flats about three hundred metres from his home. The labourer who found him was physically ill at the sight, later saying that 'only a raving maniac' could have inflicted those injuries. They bore striking similarities to the injuries on Yvonne's body some fourteen months later, and in his writings Percy described inflicting similar injuries on a three-year-old boy.

A truck driver had seen a boy resembling Simon holding hands with a fair-haired youth in the area at the time of his disappearance. An identikit picture of the youth created from the truckie's description bore striking resemblances to Percy. Later, Percy told police he was in the area where the child was abducted that day. He said that he'd driven his brother to work, turned off at the railway cutting where the body was found, and returned along the same route. When asked if he'd killed Simon, Percy said, 'I could have. I just don't remember.'

Years later, in 2005, an inquest was held into the death of Simon Brook. Percy was taken from a Melbourne prison to the inquest, but he didn't give evidence on the grounds of self-incrimination. The inquest lasted only two days before the coroner closed the hearing and referred the case to the Director of Public Prosecutions, stating that he believed 'there was a reasonable prospect that a jury would convict a known person in relation to the offence'. The DPP later decided there was insufficient evidence to make a case, but Simon's father is convinced Percy was the killer.

LINDA STILWELL

On Saturday 10 August 1968, Jean Stilwell's three children, Karen, Gary and Linda, left their Middle Park home and walked to nearby St Kilda pier, where they spent some time with other children who were fishing there. Karen soon became concerned that they'd be late home and urged Gary and Linda to go back with her, but they refused. Karen went home while the other two headed off to the amusement area known as Little Luna Park. Not long after Karen reached home, Gary arrived. He said that he and Linda had become separated, and he didn't know where she was. Mrs Stilwell then sent Karen to find Linda, but she had no success. Frantic with worry, Mrs Stilwell contacted police, but it was some hours before they mounted a search for the missing seven-year-old. There was no sign of Linda, and never has been since.

A couple of days after the disappearance, a woman came forward to tell police she'd seen a young girl matching Linda's description rolling along a grassy hill near the Lower Esplanade at St Kilda. Near by was a man whom she described as about thirty years old with an olive complexion and thin features, wearing a deep navy-blue spray jacket of the type used in sailing. When interviewed by his old schoolmate, now a policeman, Percy said he was on leave and in Melbourne at the time of Linda's disappearance. He had a map with a line drawn through St Kilda Pier. He also remembered having driven along The Esplanade in St Kilda on the way to the White Ensign Club for some drinks. When asked if he had killed Linda, he volunteered, 'Possibly – I don't remember a thing about it.'

Later, the woman who had reported she'd seen Linda rolling on the grass saw a photograph of Percy in a newspaper after the Tuohy murder and recognised him as the man she'd seen near Linda that day. She went to police and declared she was 'absolutely certain' it was Percy she'd seen, and she repeated her claim at an inquest into Linda's death. She also told the court she'd said to herself at the time, 'Go home little girl – you are in grave danger'.

This inquest was held after a court found in 2007 that Linda had been murdered, and her family had been granted crimes compensation. Like Simon Brook's parents, Linda Stilwell's family is convinced Percy was her killer. At the inquest in 2009, the family visibly shivered when Percy was brought from the prison to face them in court. Percy again refused to give evidence on the grounds of self-incrimination.

THE MODEL PRISONER

Throughout the time that Percy was incarcerated, he was a model prisoner. Given the position of writer in G Division, he enjoyed such activities as guitar playing, making model boats, stamp collecting, reading sea stories, and playing tennis and carpet bowls. He managed to retain a high level of physical fitness. Amazingly, he also received a fortnightly pension from the navy and was able to invest it.

Percy became Victoria's longest-serving prisoner, He outlasted Pentridge itself, remaining under lock and key for 44 years. In 2004, he applied for a transfer to the Thomas Embling Hospital to get treatment for his psycho-sexual problems, but the transfer was refused.

For all his good behaviour, his prison record had the occasional blemish. In 1971, security raided his cell at Pentridge and uncovered graphic handwritten details of what he wanted to do with children. In these writings, he fantasised about abducting multiple children and subjecting them to torture, mutilation and death. The horror of these writings belied his outward docility.

Some years later, his legal representative told a review hearing that he was a reformed character and hadn't fantasised about children since 1971. In 2007, however, police discovered that Percy had been lying. With inside help, he'd managed to have his writings smuggled out of prison and taken to storage depots – one in Pascoe Vale and one in South Melbourne. His subterfuge fuelled fears that, if released, he'd still be a monstrous menace to children.

Opinions vary as to whether Percy was mad or just plain bad, insane or just a cold, sadistic killer of the defenceless. For many years, he played the system to perfection. His inability to remember his crimes – for example, maintaining he couldn't remember murdering Yvonne Tuohy, even though he was virtually caught red-handed – baffled police and psychiatrists alike, particularly when he was able to recall details of other events that took place on the same day. One police source had little doubt about his mentality, stating: 'He's intelligent, cunning and pure evil. There is no way he is mad.'

Psychiatrists who assessed Percy mostly agreed that he had dangerous abnormalities but didn't suffer from mental illness. An earlier examiner of Percy, Professor Paul Mullen, wrote: 'I could find no evidence suggestive of psychiatric illness'. Dr Stephens, the co-ordinator of psychiatric services at Pentridge, wrote in 1984 that Percy was 'a highly dangerous, sadistic paedophile who should never be released from safe custody – he is not certifiable, neither is he psychiatrically treatable, and he is totally unsuited to a mental institution'. In 1992 another psychiatrist, Dr Neville Parker, disagreed with the jury's original verdict. 'There was nothing at the time to suggest that he was psychotic when he committed the crime, nor that he had a mental illness,' he said.

Many people who came into contact with Percy – including prison officers, psychiatrists, police and welfare officers – considered him the most dangerous man in Australia. One of his guards called him 'our Hannibal Lecter' – a reference to the sociopathic serial killer in Thomas Harris's novels.

After the Tuohy murder, notes were found in Percy's car. On a review of Percy conducted in 1998, Justice Eames said of these notes: 'The notes seized from Mr Percy's car after the killing of the young girl, disclosed that her abduction and death weren't spontaneous events but occurred very much as the notes anticipated that such events might occur.'

Percy didn't demonstrate any remorse for his actions. When talking to a psychiatrist in 1993 about Yvonne's murder, he said that she could have been 'hit by a bus a week later and died'. He was totally unconcerned about the murder.

Percy's response to questions about whether he'd murdered any other children was always, 'I could have, I just don't remember.' Pentridge psychiatrist Dr Alan Bartholomew once said: 'Percy has the capacity to repress memories of the crimes he committed ... It is not beyond the bounds of possibility that there is some other great harm been done in the past and there is no way of knowing it.'

* * *

A strong case exists that Percy was the Wanda Beach murderer, the Simon Brook abductor and murderer, and almost certainly the abductor and murderer of Linda Stilwell. Actually, it's not hard to accept that Percy murdered at least five children – though proving it beyond reasonable doubt is another matter – and there is a real possibility that, in total, he'd claimed nine.

In 2005, Percy was interviewed by Victorian and interstate police over the deaths of Christine Sharrock and Marianne Schmidt in 1965; the disappearance of the Beaumont children in 1966; the murder of Allen Redston in 1966; the killing of Simon Brook in 1968; and the abduction and presumed murder of Linda Stilwell in 1968. The cold case unit's review of these crimes – code named 'Operation Heats' – found several links between Percy and these cases. There was a remarkable similarity between Percy and identikit drawings done at the time. His writings, seized in 1969, contained references to unsolved murders. He was in the areas where several of the murders and disappearances occurred, and a new witness had come forward placing Percy at the scene of the Simon Brook murder. After facing hundreds of questions, Percy continued to be just as evasive as always, and simply 'couldn't remember'.

Percy continued his incarceration in a unique situation – he'd never been found guilty of homicide and had no prior criminal record. But there was one real public benefit to Percy's situation – he was never released. In 2013, however, Percy was found to have terminal lung cancer. He had little time left.

Before his death, Linda Stilwell's mother, Jean Priest, did everything in her power to have Percy give evidence at an inquest into Linda's disappearance and death, but her last chance of knowing her daughter's fate was taken away from her when Percy died. Shortly before his death, Percy gave evidence from his bed in St Vincent's Hospital to Coroner Iain West. During a 45-minute hearing, Percy varied his usual 'I can't remember' response by denying any involvement in her disappearance. But later, the coroner found that Percy had 'caused the death of Linda Jane Stilwell' as he was satisfied that the description of a man seen near Linda on the day of her disappearance was consistent with Percy, and that a description of a car near the scene was also consistent with Percy's. The little girl's family later expressed their satisfaction with the coroner's findings, which her mother described as 'a form of closure'.

There is still hope for a resolution to other murders Percy is suspected of committing. Just before his death, he voluntarily provided Victoria Police with a sample of his DNA, which will be tested against unsolved homicide cases in New South Wales, where he is 'a person of interest'. Though he was approached several times on his deathbed by police hoping to get a confession, he took his secrets with him when he died in the early hours of 24 July 2013.

CHAPTER 15
CHRISTOPHER DALE FLANNERY

A 'graduate' of Pentridge's infamous H Division, Chris Flannery was born and raised virtually in the prison's shadow, in the neighbouring suburb of Brunswick. During the early 1970s, he was housed in B Division at Pentridge along with his great mate and partner in crime, Laurie Prendergast, who also spent periods in H Division. At the time, the two were serving a seven-year sentence over a hotly contested rape charge. But it was what Flannery did after his release that made him one of the most notorious figures in the annals of Australian crime. His subsequent disappearance – presumed murder – in 1985 remains unsolved to this day.

Whether or not he possessed the qualities of a ruthless and remorseless killer before entering Pentridge, he certainly emerged with them. By the time he was released in 1972, Flannery was a hardened and embittered man, a loose cannon who was ready to take the dehumanisation he'd experienced in prison and inflict it on others. At the height of his powers, it is said that Flannery could command $10,000 for a bashing requiring the victim to be hospitalised, and $50,000 for a kill, with disposal of the body thrown in.

Flannery and Prendergast both forged their reputations in the criminal underworld after they were in Pentridge. Though they only occasionally worked together, their careers had much in common. Both were charged with murder, but never convicted. Rumour had them both as hired killers who'd accept a contract to kill. And eventually both would disappear in mysterious circumstances.

THE STREETS OF BRUNSWICK

Christopher Dale Flannery was born in 1949, the youngest of three children. When he was just a year old, his father left his mother to fend for her family, which also included a four-year-old boy and a three-year-old girl. When Chris was nine years old, he lost his grandfather, with whom he was very close. This death deeply affected him, and he soon became rebellious. He left school in 1963 at the minimum age of fourteen, and in the same year he received his first criminal conviction, being put on probation for house-breaking and stealing. Shortly after, he was sent to Morning Star Boys' Home for house burglary and stealing cars. The discipline there was extremely harsh, and the constant threat of violence created fear among its juvenile inmates. Here, Flannery met and befriended Alan Williams, who would later become a drug dealer.

On release, Flannery teamed up with his friend Laurie Prendergast, and they joined a gang of 'sharpies' on the streets of suburban Brunswick. The sharpies' hallmark was their natty dressing, and Flannery and Prendergast would both be sharp dressers for the rest of their lives. Together, the two embarked on a series of house break-ins and car thefts. At the age of seventeen, Flannery served a short time in Pentridge. He returned for a longer stint in 1968, after he and Prendergast were charged with rape and sentenced to seven years with a minimum of four years before parole. The charge was a contentious one, with the boys claiming the girl consented to sex in the rear of Flannery's car. She'd been out with them for drinks in the city, and the sex acts had taken place on the way back to her home in Reservoir.

The eighteen-year-old didn't say anything to her parents when she reached home, but later she told them she'd been raped, and police were called. She also informed police that Prendergast had stolen her handbag. At trial, both men pleaded not guilty on the grounds that the sex was consensual, but they were found guilty with 'mitigating circumstances'. They appealed, and a retrial was ordered on the grounds that the judge had misdirected the jury, but a further hearing in November 1968 reinstated the original verdict and penalty.

After they were sentenced, both Flannery and Prendergast were classified to B Division, but they also spent time in the punishment section. Flannery's first encounter with the dreaded H Division occurred while he was still on remand awaiting trial. He was sentenced to a term there for 'knocking out a fellow inmate and being insolent to a prison officer'.

Later, as I've discussed in chapter 3, Flannery played a key role in the rebellion that helped break down the reign of terror that was H Division. By now no stranger to the punishment section, he deliberately had himself sent there towards the end of his sentence in an attempt to break the system.

Flannery said his stints in H Division had 'broken' him. Like many other inmates, he'd been brutalised, humiliated and debased. Just how much effect it had on him is difficult to judge, but by the time of his release, he was a thoroughly hardened and embittered criminal.

FROM ROBBER TO STANDOVER MAN

During the latter stages of his incarceration, Flannery had corresponded with an old girlfriend, Kathleen, whose marriage had failed. The two were reunited when he was eventually released on parole. Kath had a son from her earlier marriage and was soon expecting another child to Flannery, but family responsibilities did nothing to dampen Chris's enthusiasm for crime.

In early 1973, Flannery and Prendergast were arrested

outside a Pascoe Vale bank where they'd planned an armed robbery. The police were acting on a tip-off from Prendergast's brother, Billy. Facing the prospect of another spell in Pentridge, Chris skipped bail and went to Western Australia, leaving Kath behind in Melbourne. He worked briefly in the mines, then took a job at David Jones under the alias of Ferguson. He was later joined by a pregnant 'Mrs Ferguson' and her son.

The dapper Ferguson was doing very well in his new job at the upmarket retailer until he decided to rob the store with the help of two Victorian armed robbers, Robin Holt and Archie Butterly. Shortly after the robbery, Holt was nabbed by detectives, who found a note with 'Rhodes Station' written on it – a clue that would lead to the robbers' undoing. Roger Rogerson, then a detective in the armed hold-up squad, found that the Sydney station of Rhodes was used for parcel delivery, and arranged to be notified when anything arrived from Western Australia. A short time later, a parcel came in from the west. When Flannery and Butterly arrived to pick it up, they walked straight into a police trap. After a fierce battle, they were arrested and extradited back to Western Australia. Flannery pleaded not guilty at trial and was acquitted, but Holt and Butterly were convicted and jailed for six years each.

Flannery was then extradited to Victoria, where he spent three years back in Pentridge, convicted on charges of breach of parole and conspiracy to commit armed robbery. On release, he married Kath and briefly turned his hand to legitimate security work, becoming a bouncer at Mickey's Disco in St Kilda. But he soon decided that he could make far more money as a standover man and contract killer.

In that role, he is believed to have been responsible for a large number of murders, gaining a reputation for his extreme violence. In May 1979, he met Sydney criminal Ray 'The Lizard' Locksley and drove him from Melbourne to Sydney.

On arrival at Liverpool, Flannery allegedly killed 'The Lizard' by shooting him four times.

In February 1980, barrister Roger Wilson disappeared on his way home from Melbourne to his property at Nar Nar Goon. It was later alleged that Chris Flannery and a man named Kevin Williams had flagged Wilson's Porsche down, masquerading as police. Wilson obligingly pulled over to the side of the road, where he was handcuffed, placed in the back of the 'police car', driven to a location near Pakenham, and shot in the head. Bleeding profusely, Wilson ran from the car into the bush. Flannery shot at him and missed, but eventually Wilson was trapped, at which point it's said that Flannery went berserk, emptying his gun into his victim. Wilson's car was driven to Melbourne Airport and left in the car park, but his body was never found.

Later, four people were charged over the murder: a work associate of Wilson's named Mark Alfred Clarkson; Flannery and Williams as the assassins; and Kath Flannery as an accessory after the fact, because she'd allegedly cleaned the car. Kath's charges were dropped after the committal hearing, but the others went to trial. During the hearing, it was alleged that Clarkson had paid Flannery $35,000 to kill Wilson. Asked if he had anything to say, Flannery said he only wanted to say he wasn't guilty of the charges. He added, 'I think the whole court has been a kangaroo court, and if you want to get me for contempt of court, away you go.'

A key Crown witness in the case was Williams's girlfriend, Deborah Boundy, who'd told police she'd overheard Williams and Flannery talk about 'killing somebody and disposing of his body'. It was said that Flannery told Williams that Boundy knew too much and should be killed. Around Christmas 1980, she disappeared, presumed murdered. Her body has never been found. After that, crucial elements of the Crown case against the accused men collapsed. Flannery, Clarkson and

Williams were acquitted in October 1981, after what was then Victoria's longest-running criminal trial.

Flannery's run of good luck continued. He was extradited to Sydney to face trial over Ray Locksley's murder, but the case against him was weak, and the jury failed to reach a verdict. A retrial was scheduled to be held in January 1984, but was adjourned until April after Flannery produced a medical certificate from Dr Geoffrey Edelsten certifying that he was unfit for trial. It was believed that Flannery arranged this to avoid being tried by a particular judge. Flannery was acquitted of Locksley's murder, mainly on a technicality over conflicting evidence given by a doctor who'd died between trials.

Flannery now decided to stay in Sydney rather than returning to Melbourne. Having obtained a position as standover man and bodyguard for the notorious Sydney identity George Freeman, he purchased a house in Arncliffe and moved his family from Melbourne to join him. He soon formed a friendship with Sydney crime figure Arthur 'Neddy' Smith, a physically large and powerful man with a reputation for violence who was eventually convicted of murder, rape, armed robbery and heroin trafficking. Smith's mate Graham 'Abo' Henry didn't share Smith's approval of the Flannerys. Henry later observed that Flannery wanted to become top dog in the Sydney underworld at the urging of Kath, whom he described as having 'delusions of grandeur'.

THE GANG WARS

Flannery is believed to have played an active and prominent part in what were dubbed the Sydney gang wars of 1984. He'd become a close associate of 'Neddy' Smith, but Smith was later quite scathing about Flannery. After the gang wars started, Smith said, Flannery 'got completely out of hand. He was continually fighting with his own team, especially the cops who were assisting him.'

The gang wars had numerous victims, and many of the murders were attributed to Flannery. These included the killing of drug dealer Daniel Chubb, who was shot on the road by two masked men outside his mother's home at Millers Point. An inquest heard that Chubb had been shot with either a Colt revolver or a .357 magnum, fired at a distance of no more than two metres. It was rumoured that Flannery was involved, but the crime was generally considered to have come about over a drug deal gone wrong.

Flannery was also said to be involved in the murder of the former painter and docker Les Cole. A contract was apparently taken out on Cole and given to Michael Sayers, an old friend of Flannery's from Pentridge. Cole was gunned down as he drove into his home. Though nobody was ever charged over Cole's murder, it is generally accepted that Sayers had done the job, possibly with Flannery's assistance.

It's said that in 1984, Flannery took on a contract that helped to bring about his downfall. The target of the contract was a Sydney detective, Michael Drury, who'd been working undercover to bust a drug operation being run by Flannery's old Melbourne mate, Alan Williams. After Drury had Williams charged with drug offences, Williams allegedly contacted Flannery and arranged for Drury to be offered a substantial bribe – reported to be $30,000 – to alter his evidence against Williams. Drury refused this offer, which he claimed came via Roger Rogerson, and he later refused even larger offers.

After it became obvious that Drury's co-operation couldn't be bought, it's said that Flannery met Williams and offered to kill Drury for $100,000. The terms of the contract required an up-front payment of $50,000 followed by the balance on the completion of a successful 'hit'. Williams agreed, and the first instalment was made.

On 6 June 1984, Michael Drury was washing the dishes in the kitchen of his home in suburban Chatswood when he was shot twice with a .357 magnum. The bullets were fired through the window by an assassin lurking outside under cover of darkness. Drury was rushed to hospital. Despite suffering massive wounds, he survived.

It was generally believed that Chris Flannery shot Drury, but he had an alibi – around the time the crime was committed, he and his wife were seen drinking at a club in the company of Roger Rogerson. Ironically, Williams was eventually acquitted over the drug offences, despite Drury's evidence against him. Rogerson was also acquitted on a charge of conspiring to murder Drury, and was found not guilty of having tried to bribe him. He has always maintained that he wasn't involved in the shooting of Drury. Williams, however, pleaded guilty to conspiring to murder Drury and was sentenced to fourteen years imprisonment.

In his autobiography, 'Neddy' Smith gave his version of what took place at the time of the Drury shooting and how Flannery came by his alibi. According to Smith, Flannery and Laurie Prendergast often swapped contract killing jobs with one another. If Flannery accepted a job, he'd arrange for Prendergast to do the actual shooting while Flannery was making himself obvious elsewhere. Then, when Prendergast took a job, Flannery would do the 'hit' while Prendergast arranged an alibi. So, on the night of the Drury shooting, while Flannery made himself obvious to patrons in a club, Prendergast was at Drury's home. Smith also saw the failure to complete a successful 'hit' on Drury as a poor advertisement for Chris Flannery as a gun-for-hire.

In January 1985, Flannery himself was the target of a 'hit'. As he and his wife walked towards the front door of their Arncliffe home, about thirty shots were fired at them from a green car parked in the street near their driveway. They took shelter in front of their car, and most of the shots missed, but Chris suffered superficial injuries to one hand.

Crouching behind the car, Kath Flannery caught a glimpse of the gunman, who was wearing a wig and false moustache, when he leant over to try and fix the rifle, which had jammed. He gave up and drove away.

When police arrived to investigate, Flannery told them not to 'bother asking questions – I'll sort it out myself.' He became certain that the shooter was Tom Domican, a well-known Sydney identity who had a reputation as an enforcer. This was the start of much conflict between Domican and Flannery.

According to 'Neddy' Smith, Flannery enlisted the aid of Laurie Prendergast, who drove him on a motorbike as pillion passenger to the police station at Kingsgrove, arriving just as Domican was leaving. Flannery fired on Domican but missed.

Flannery later made another attempt, firing at a person he thought was Domican leaving his Kingsgrove home in a car, but he had the wrong man; it was one of Domican's friends, who fortunately survived being shot in the neck. 'Neddy' Smith believed Flannery lost all respect in the criminal underworld over these incidents.

Later, police did charge Domican with the attempted murder of Chris Flannery, Kath Flannery having identified him as the shooter. He was found guilty and sentenced to fourteen years imprisonment, of which he served several years. In May 1992, however, the High Court found that the jury in his trial had not been sufficiently warned about the dangers of relying on Kath's identification, which had been made three months after the event. As a result, his appeal was successful, and he was released.

DISAPPEARANCE

In late 1984 and early 1985, Flannery's relations with the strongmen of Sydney's crime scene began to sour. Around that time, his mate Michael Sayers, who had moved from Melbourne to Sydney at the same time as Flannery, fell out with Flannery's boss, George Freeman. Freeman is said to have asked Flannery to kill Sayers, but Flannery refused. According to his wife Kath, Freeman was never the same with Flannery again.

Sayers was later shot dead outside his garage, but Flannery had a watertight alibi for the night of the shooting. Actually, there was no shortage of suspects. Sayers was allegedly one of the instigators of the infamous 'Fine Cotton' attempt to substitute a 'ring-in' horse in a Queensland race at Eagle Farm, and he'd also stolen drugs from a Sydney crime figure. Both these actions made him powerful enemies.

Sensing the approaching danger, Flannery left his Arncliffe home and took up residence under an assumed name in an apartment at the Connaught building in central Sydney, quite close to CIB headquarters, a move he kept to himself and his family.

In April 1985, another good friend of Flannery's, Tony Eustace, was shot dead. It has been reported that Flannery spoke with Eustace earlier the same day, telling him he needed to leave town quickly with some ready cash. He arranged to meet Eustace at the Airport Hilton, but when Eustace parked near the hotel, he was shot as he left his gold Mercedes. Some young footballers heard shots and went to investigate. They found Eustace lying on the ground and saw a brown Valiant leaving the scene.

Eustace was rushed to hospital, but he died a short time later, having refused to identify his killer to police. This murder was never solved. Flannery was credited with having committed it, but there was little evidence to support the claim.

On 8 May 1985, Roger Rogerson rang Flannery, asking him to come to a meeting with two other senior detectives at the New South Wales Cricketers Club. These detectives later said they didn't arrange the meeting, and it was obvious that Flannery was anxious to leave. When Flannery left the meeting, Rogerson followed immediately after. It was later surmised that Rogerson didn't know Flannery's new address and wanted to have him followed home.

Next morning, Flannery had arranged to meet his boss at Freeman's Yowie Bay home to look at some guns. He tried to start his Valiant in the car park of his apartment block, but it wouldn't start. He returned to his apartment and told Kath he'd go to Freeman's by taxi and be back around midday. He also told her to contact Marshall Batteries, as his battery was dead. A security officer at the apartment block saw Flannery walking out the front door, heading for the street. What happened next is unknown. His disappearance was to become one of Australian crime's most enduring mysteries, and the subject of great speculation.

There are several conflicting accounts of what might have happened. Colin Sefton, a taxi driver, was later to swear that he'd picked up a man around that time outside the Connaught apartments and driven him to the TAA terminal at Mascot airport. His passenger had told him he couldn't start his car that morning, and Sefton also said he was carrying a large sum of money. Sefton later recognised his passenger as Chris Flannery from newspaper photographs, and was positive it was him.

Supporting those who argue that this was a carefully planned disappearance, Kath Flannery later said she'd contacted Marshall Batteries and a man had come to take a look at Flannery's car. He had no difficulty whatever in starting it, which led to the theory that it had been temporarily immobilised in order to get Flannery out onto the street in search of a lift.

At the time of his disappearance, the strongest theory as to what took place was that Flannery had been picked up, taken to George Freeman's place at Yowie Bay, murdered and disposed of. Certainly, Kath was convinced that Freeman had killed her husband.

Although no charges have ever been laid in connection with his disappearance, it seems almost certain that Flannery was taken away and murdered. The criminal underworld and corrupt police have generally remained tight-lipped about the disappearance, but some of the main players and chief suspects have made public comment about it, a couple even offering versions of what took place. 'Neddy' Smith has given his version, told to him by 'reliable sources', in his books *Neddy* and *Catch and Kill Your Own*. He claims that Flannery was picked up by a couple of policemen he knew and trusted, but the car had only travelled a short distance to a set of traffic lights when two ex-policemen climbed into the back, on either side of Flannery. The car accelerated, and Flannery was shot several times in the head and chest as the car moved along. Smith also claims that at a later meeting with Roger Rogerson, the detective said to him, 'Chris had to go, mate. He was becoming a danger to us all.'

Most of the theories about Flannery's disappearance claim that he was killed either by underworld figures or by police, though it is also quite possible that both were involved. Among the many accounts are that he was shot and buried by a policeman at the Geelong Racecourse; that he was shot with a machine gun and disposed of in Sydney Harbour; that he was shot and buried at a beach at low tide; that a detective and two criminal associates met him at the airport, drove him away, murdered him, and disposed of his body at sea; even that he was shot and buried beneath the freeway to Newcastle. In most accounts, the names of disgraced former detective Roger Rogerson and major crime figure George Freeman crop up.

Probably the most widespread rumour about what took place is that Flannery was picked up by Rogerson and driven to Freeman's home, where Freeman and his criminal associate Lennie 'Mr Big' McPherson lay in wait for him. They had guns to show him all right – one in particular, an Uzi machine gun, with which he was shot. As Flannery's wife had raised the alarm a short time after he disappeared and revealed he'd gone to Freeman's, Flannery's body was kept in a secret room there until the heat was off, and then disposed of at sea.

If indeed George Freeman was involved in Flannery's murder, he took the secret to his grave, dying of an asthma attack in 1990. He maintained to the end that Flannery didn't arrive at his home that day. Roger Rogerson too has always denied any involvement. In February 2004, he told the television program *Sunday*: 'Flannery was a complete pest. The guys up here in Sydney tried to settle him down. They tried to look after him as best they could but he was, I believe, out of control. Maybe it was the Melbourne instinct coming out in him. He didn't want to do as he was told, he was out of control, and having overstepped that line, well, I suppose they said he had to go, but I can assure you that I had nothing to do with it.'

The New South Wales Coroner, Greg Glass, took a different view. Following an inquest that lasted for years, Glass found that Flannery had been murdered and that 'a strong suspicion prevails that [Rogerson] has knowledge of the events surrounding Flannery's death'. He said that the evidence before him raised a strong suspicion that Rogerson was involved in Flannery's disappearance and death, and that Rogerson had the motive and opportunity to cause harm to Flannery, the motive being to get him out of the way before the trial over the Drury shooting.

Glass noted that when he disappeared, Flannery was armed with a gun and was on total guard. He also said that he was satisfied 'that Flannery was betrayed, deceived, possibly lured into a motor vehicle by someone, or by some persons, whom he trusted, and was then killed, with the remains being disposed of in a manner unknown'.

Coroner Glass also examined the possibility that two other suspects, Tom Domican and George Freeman, had committed the crime. He concluded that there was no direct evidence to reach a firm view that either had a role in Flannery's demise, though the evidence 'raised suspicion that Freeman may have been connected with Flannery's fate simply because Flannery was said to be on his way to Freeman's household – and Freeman was one of the very few that Flannery trusted right to the end'.

Glass observed that, while Domican's conviction for Flannery's attempted murder had failed, there was 'some evidence that would support the view that it was Domican who fired the shots'. Coroner Glass described Domican as a 'witness of little or no credit'. He also made the point that there was a feud between Domican and Flannery, and both 'were prepared to used firearms in furthering the feud'. He described them as 'strong and stubborn personalities who would not back off from any dispute'.

In his remarks about the other prime suspect, Roger Rogerson, the coroner described him as 'a skilled witness with a ready answer, truthful or otherwise, to any question put to him'. He went on to say:

The court does not accept Rogerson's evidence that he has no idea who shot Drury. Rogerson further maintains that at no time did he regard Flannery as a potential witness at his trial for attempting to bribe Michael Drury, stating 'If I had concerns, why would I arrange a meeting between Flannery and senior police the day before he disappeared?' In answer to that question there is an obvious reason why Rogerson might have organised such a meeting. He may have wished to locate Flannery so that he could follow him, or have him followed, after he left the meeting, and so discover where he was living. This possibility has to be seriously considered when one bears in mind that, on the evidence, very few people knew where Flannery was living at the time, and that Flannery disappeared the next day.

Glass concluded his remarks about Rogerson by saying, 'Roger Rogerson is intelligent, cunning but devious. However, in respect of Flannery's death, the evidence, as it stands, is insufficient to establish a prima facie case against Rogerson under Section 19 of the Coroner's Act.'

To this day, Flannery's disappearance remains a mystery, as do his deeds as a gun for hire. He was only ever charged with two murders, despite allegations that he was responsible for up to a dozen killings, and in both cases he was acquitted. It isn't clear how many people he supposedly murdered, numbers varying from ten upwards. A further mystery was how he came by his nickname of 'Mr Rent-a-Kill'. Some maintain that it wasn't given to him until his disappearance, and only then to cover for the crimes of others. It's difficult to tell where fact ends and fiction starts.

Many don't believe that Flannery was murdered at all and claim that he faked his own disappearance, as did his old mate Laurie Prendergast. Some theorise that each had obtained a passport under an assumed name and disappeared in possession of a large sum of cash. There is no way of knowing whether this is true, but there is no evidence that they disappeared together. Almost all the principal players have died, and the true story may never be known, but the mystery lives on.

CHAPTER 16
LAURENCE JOSEPH PRENDERGAST

A young B Division prisoner of the early 1970s who was to graduate through the criminal ranks was twenty-year-old Laurie Prendergast. At age eighteen, when his future was at the crossroads, Laurie had been placed among the most dangerous criminals in Pentridge. Whatever chance he had at rehabilitation was virtually extinguished when he was placed in the high-security B Division to serve a sentence of seven years for rape. This illogical placement, apparently made because of his misbehaviour in court, was compounded when he was sent to H Division, from where he emerged totally embittered.

By the time of his release in 1972, Prendergast was fully educated in criminal matters. He'd soon be back in Pentridge again over a failed armed robbery attempt, and his criminal career would escalate. He'd acquire a long criminal record, but he'd gain his notoriety for alleged offences that either weren't on his record or weren't proven. For example, reputation, rumour and a client's reported confession to his barrister had it that Prendergast was one of the masked men who burst into the Victoria Club during Easter 1976, executing what is generally referred to as the 'Great Bookie Robbery', one of the greatest heists in Australian criminal history. Later, he was acquitted of the only capital charge he ever faced – the murder of painter and docker Les Kane – and afterwards Prendergast faded from the major crime scene until he disappeared.

Born in 1950, Laurence Joseph Prendergast was the second of nine children. At the tender age of twelve, he began his criminal career when he engaged in house-breaking and stealing with his older brother and became a ward of the state. During his teenage years, he took up wrestling and boxing. He was also sent to a youth detention centre for twelve months after he broke into a house and assaulted a woman there. By then, he'd become firm friends with Chris Flannery.

In 1968, Prendergast and Flannery were sentenced to seven years imprisonment for rape, as discussed in the previous chapter. Prendergast was released on parole in November 1972, after serving four years of his sentence, but his liberty didn't last long. He breached his parole conditions and returned to Pentridge in 1973. At the conclusion of that sentence, he was again in trouble with the law. In 1974, he and Flannery were foiled in an attempt to rob the Pascoe Vale branch of the Bank of New South Wales. As a result, Prendergast received a sentence of five years with a minimum of three for 'conspiracy, and larceny of a motor car with intent to commit a felony'. Shortly after he began this sentence, he was found guilty of assaulting a prison officer and sentenced to a further 21 days.

Events followed a similar pattern after that sentence ended. Prendergast hadn't been out of prison long when he was charged with possession of a pistol. During the hearing, a senior detective claimed that Prendergast had made a confession in the back of a police car. Incensed by this claim, Prendergast leapt from the dock, but was quickly subdued by a policeman. Not surprisingly, he perceived the detective's claim as a 'verbal'. In the event, the possession charge was dismissed, but he was again imprisoned for 'assault occasioning actual bodily harm'.

Again released from Pentridge, Prendergast joined up with leading armed robber and criminal strategist Raymond

Patrick Bennett. It would later be alleged that Prendergast and Bennett were among those involved in two of the most publicised crimes in Australian criminal history, the Great Bookie Robbery and the murder of Lesley Herbert Kane.

THE GREAT BOOKIE ROBBERY

Bennett was born with the surname of Chuck and was often referred to by that name. He was considered on both sides of the law to be one of the most accomplished and fearless armed robbers of his time. He was one of the 'Kangaroo Gang' of robbers who operated in Europe in the early 1970s, and had learnt all the tricks of the trade. After serving time in a British prison, he was eventually put on a pre-release program and used a false passport to return to Australia. He flew into Melbourne to set up the bookie robbery and 'case' the Victoria Club, then returned to Britain to finish his sentence.

When he came back to Australia permanently, Bennett organised several experienced armed robbers – of whom Prendergast was reportedly one – to join him in his audacious plan to hold up and rob bookmakers at the Victoria Club. He trained his accomplices military-style and planned the crime down to the finest detail. So thorough was the planning that it is believed the robbers didn't even have to take their vast haul of money from the building at 131 Queen Street at the time of the robbery. Instead, before they made their escape, they stored the money in an office they'd rented on a floor above the club and kept it there for some time, to be retrieved when the heat was off. A getaway van was stationed outside the building, but it played no part in the actual robbery. Bennett had also thoroughly familiarised himself with the bookmakers' procedures on 'settling' day, and it was rumoured that he had the club's scant security in his pocket.

The Victoria Club, situated on the second floor, was where bookmakers met their clients to pay outstanding bets from the previous weekend's racing. These bets often involved large amounts but weren't recorded on betting sheets to avoid turnover tax.

The club had long been considered a prime target for a major robbery, but nobody had actually attempted it, as the risks were considered too great. Bennett, however, was no ordinary bandit. He considered the heist a big challenge to his renowned planning skills and personal daring. Ever the strategist, he chose the date for the heist as 21 April 1976, when the money on hand was considerably higher than usual after the Easter holiday. He knew that triple the number of race meetings meant triple the cash holdings from the 116 bookmakers attending the race meetings, ensuring that a huge amount of money would be taken into the club.

Bennett chose six members of his team to make the final assault. These are believed to have included Bennett himself, Ian Revill Carroll, Norman Leung Lee, Laurie Prendergast and Anthony Paul McNamara, while Dennis 'Greedy' Smith is thought to have been the driver of the supposed getaway vehicle, a stolen laundry van. As final preparation, it is believed that Bennett took his accomplices to the club for a 'full dress rehearsal' over the long weekend, when there was nobody there.

Around midday on 21 April, a man believed to be Bennett appeared at the building and announced that he was there to repair a refrigerator in the bar on the second floor. On obtaining admittance, he stood watching as several cash boxes were pushed into the building. After the last of these boxes were delivered, he proceeded to the elevator and tampered with it, causing a breakdown and eliminating the normal access to the second floor. He then moved quickly to a doorway leading to a stairwell, where he donned a balaclava and was joined by five other balaclava-clad accomplices, heavily armed with automatic weapons and pistols.

At 12.07 pm, the bandits stormed into the club, ordering those in attendance to lie down on the floor. Most of the patrons quickly complied. In the pandemonium that followed, a security guard made a grab for his revolver, but was prevented from taking any further action by a bandit, who knocked him to the floor with the butt of a submachine gun. While this was going on, another bandit ripped the telephones from the walls. The bandits then used bolt cutters to open the cash boxes, which contained about a hundred bags filled with banknotes. The haul was a fabulous sum, though it has never been accurately appraised because of the unrecorded bets. Estimates of its value range from $1.3 million to $15 million.

Before making their getaway, the bandits jammed the lift with the empty cash boxes, then disappeared through a little-used door. It was all over in about eleven minutes.

There were suspicions about how such an audacious robbery could have been so readily accomplished. It was quickly established that the robbers had been assisted by a lack of security within the club. Normally, three detectives from the Consorting Squad were hired to keep an eye on proceedings at 'settling' time, but on this day they'd been sent elsewhere. It was rumoured that they knew what was about to happen, and that they'd been well looked after by Bennett. Strangely, the same detectives were also rumoured to be involved in Bennett's later demise.

Norman Lee became the only person charged over this robbery after his Chinese food business received a cash injection of $250,000, but a magistrate dismissed the charge. Most of those thought to be involved died violently. Bennett, Carroll and McNamara were all murdered, Prendergast disappeared, presumed murdered, and Lee was shot dead by police during a later robbery.

THE KANE MURDER

The next time Laurie Prendergast came into prominence was in October 1978, after underworld figure Lesley Herbert Kane disappeared from his Wantirna unit. Kane, a painter and docker, was 'employed' at the wharves. His busiest day of the week was payday, when he collected several pay packets under a variety of names, including that of his brother Brian, who was never seen at the wharves.

Brian Kane was a standover man whose main occupation was to collect debts for two-up school proprietors, from whom he drew a weekly wage plus a percentage. A renowned street fighter, Brian traded in fear and intimidation. Similarly, his brother Les once shot an off-duty policeman working as a bouncer at the Croxton Park Hotel, and on another occasion bashed a naval rating with a hammer in a road-rage incident. To add to his criminal record, Les had many convictions for larceny and assault.

After Les Kane disappeared, his wife Judith reported him missing, providing investigators with an address in Broadmeadows. She returned three days later, and this time she had a startling story: Les wasn't just missing, but had been murdered. In an interview with Detective Chief Inspector Paul Delianis, she now gave an address on the Mountain Highway in Wantirna and told an altogether different story. After this interview, police accompanied her back to the Wantirna unit, and warrants were issued for the arrest of three men: Ray Bennett, Vin Mikkelsen and Laurie Prendergast. By then, she had been granted an indemnity against prosecution in relation to the case.

A short time later, the three wanted men were in custody. Prendergast was arrested at his Essendon flat, Bennett was run down by police in a St Albans street, and Mikkelsen was interviewed and arrested at Karratha CIB in Western Australia. The trio was charged with Les Kane's murder, and their trial began at the Melbourne Supreme Court on 3 September 1979.

I attended this trial for several days. Security surrounding the court was extraordinary, with police marksmen occupying vantage points on the outside roof, while armed police lined the passageways and stairs. Other police put court observers through metal detectors, held identification checks and requested reasons for attendance. The reason for the security was that it was strongly rumoured that Les's brothers, Brian and Ray, would seek retribution of their own on the three accused. Another rumour sweeping Melbourne before the trial was that Kane's body had been taken to a northern Melbourne factory that manufactured Chinese food, put through a mincer and used as an ingredient in dim sims.

During the trial, Mrs Kane told the court that on the evening of 19 October, she, Les and their children had returned to their unit at about 9 pm after being out for dinner. Shortly afterwards, Les had gone to the bathroom while she took some ironing to the master bedroom. Switching on the light, she saw three men around the back of her bed. She immediately recognised two men she knew well, Ray Bennett and Vin Mikkelsen, who quickly headed for the bathroom. The other man, whom she'd later identify as Laurie Prendergast, grabbed her and pushed her towards her daughter Martine's bedroom. On the way there, she saw Bennett and Mikkelsen kick open the bathroom door. Mikkelsen went down on one knee while Bennett stood over him, both pointing their guns – which appeared to be machine guns with silencers attached – into the bathroom. Prendergast quickly forced her onto her daughter's bed, holding her face down. Muffled noises, which she presumed were shots, came from the bathroom, and she heard Les yell out, 'Oh no.' Prendergast then let her go and left the room.

She rushed out of the bedroom into the hallway and

saw her husband lying on the floor covered in blood. He'd been shot in the head and a big trail of blood ran from the bathroom, through the hallway to where he lay, groaning loudly. Suddenly, he lay still and stopped breathing. At this point, Prendergast forced her back into the bedroom with her children and slammed the door behind her. She then heard the engine of a car starting, together with the slamming of a boot and car doors, followed by the sound of the car being driven off. When she left the bedroom and returned to the hallway, she noticed that the telephone there had been pulled out, as had the one in the bedroom, and that her husband was gone.

She grabbed her car keys, left the bedroom and looked in the bathroom, which was in a mess, with a 'red carpet' of blood on the floor. She looked around for cartridge cases, but didn't see any. She then took her two young children out to her car and drove back to Les's sister's home, where her family had eaten dinner that evening. After spending the night there, she returned to the unit the following day and proceeded to 'clean up the mess', including the bloodied bathroom and hallway, using a mop, towels and some Chux.

Mrs Kane was to be the prosecution's main witness, and the success of their case hung on her credibility. She spent many hours in the witness box relating her story and being grilled by the defence counsel, which included Frank Vincent (later Justice Vincent), Colin Lovitt and Philip Dunn, all of whom cast doubt on her story. The defence was also able to exploit many holes in the Crown's case.

The defence revealed that Kane was a wife basher. Mrs Kane hadn't only been bashed by her husband, but had also been hung over a door. The defence suggested this gave her a motive to have killed him herself or arranged his disappearance. It was pointed out that, on her own admission, she'd fled the scene immediately after the alleged murder, without seeking the assistance of police or that of her next-door neighbour, whose unit adjoined hers. Instead, she'd gone to her sister-in-law's and spent the rest of the night there, during which she tried to telephone one of the men she'd later accuse – Mikkelsen, an old neighbour in Broadmeadows. She'd returned to the unit the next day and, without telling anyone she intended to do so, proceeded to clean it up so thoroughly that there was no sign of blood or fingerprints anywhere, including on the outside. She'd then gone to police the following day, providing a bogus address, which the defence claimed gave her time to 'further make detection difficult at the Wantirna unit'.

The defence hammered the point that only a few trusted close relatives knew where the Kanes were living. There was no sign of forced entry to the unit, and no damage anywhere. There were also no signs of a murder in the bathroom – no bullet holes or shell casings, no scratches on the door that Mrs Kane claimed was kicked in by the men, not even a chip off the wall or woodwork. Inside the bathroom, there was no trace of blood on the curtains, and no human tissue, bones or hair. In fact, only five small spots of blood were found in a recess of the lino, and they were consistent with a minor injury. Only one small spot of blood was found outside the unit.

The defence argued that there was no evidence of three men being in that unit that night, let alone two of them using machine guns to commit a murder. In fact, there was no evidence to support any part of Mrs Kane's story.

Mrs Kane's story also raised several questions to which there appeared no logical answers. Why would the alleged killers make no attempt to disguise themselves when she knew at least two of them well? Why didn't they harm her, or even threaten her? Why would she have gone looking for cartridge cases? Why didn't she seek help, and why didn't her neighbours hear or see anything unusual? Finally, why did she so meticulously clean the unit, destroying any evidence of the murder?

A further factor in favour of the defence was that the three accused men provided alibis for the night of the alleged murder. Bennett swore that he spent it with family, Mikkelsen claimed he was with his family at his sister's place, and Prendergast said he was listening to a band at a hotel with friends. Each received support from several alibi witnesses. It was no great surprise, then, that at the end of the three-week trial, after only a very short deliberation, the jury returned a verdict of not guilty and the accused men were released.

But the jury decision wasn't accepted in some quarters. The media would largely accept Mrs Kane's story and report that everything she told the court was true, but the jury at the time had to consider the improbabilities, if not the seeming impossibility, of her account of the murder.

This wasn't the end of the matter for the accused men. Mrs Kane had predicted during the trial that there would be war over what had occurred, and her brother-in-law Brian was reported to have told Mikkelsen's barrister, 'I'm going to cut your client's head off and leave it on your front doorstep.' Wisely, Mikkelsen did a disappearing act after the trial. Little is known of his movements, but it is believed he got his family together and flew out of Melbourne. If this is so, perhaps he survived, though his mates weren't to be so fortunate.

Laurie Prendergast made himself scarce around his usual haunts, but Ray Bennett was taken into custody to await trial for robbery, spending his time on remand in D Division. Bennett almost certainly knew he was a marked man, and that he was relatively safe in Pentridge. He was expecting a 'hit' and took precautions, including having his young son sent abroad.

When Bennett was taken to the Melbourne Magistrate's

Court for a hearing of his robbery charges, he asked his lawyer to make sure his wife was kept in a safe area of the court, warning that she should not stand about outside. In contrast to the security at his trial for the Kane murder, there was virtually none on hand on 12 November 1979, when Bennett was taken from the prison van to Court 10 of the Magistrate's Court for his committal hearing on the robbery charge. In fact, the manner in which he was 'escorted' and the events of that morning led to much speculation that police may have been involved in what was about to take place.

At about 10.15 am, Bennett was taken by two detectives through the courtyard and up the stairway to Court 10, where he was left to wait with a guard. As they stood outside the court, a man carrying a briefcase walked up to Bennett and shot him three times with a .38 pistol. Bennett, mortally wounded, staggered back down the stairway, tottering into a courtyard area where he fell, crying, 'I've been shot in the heart.'

He was taken to a nearby hospital, but he couldn't be saved. True to his undertaking to protect Bennett's wife Gail, lawyer Joe Gullaci had pushed her into the safety of an office when he heard the commotion, and he later took her to the hospital to see her dying husband.

Meanwhile, the killer fled unchallenged via a little-known rear stairway and corridor that led to the police garage. Once outside the court, he ducked through a hole where a sheet of corrugated iron had been removed from a fence. This gave him access to the car park of the Royal Melbourne Institute of Technology, at which point he vanished.

The assassin was heavily disguised and has never been identified. As newspapers of the time reported, it reeked of a setup. Many, including some police, believed that a detective was involved in the murder, but at a subsequent inquest, a coroner found no evidence of this. Another theory was that Brian Kane was the killer, though again there wasn't much evidence. Whoever he was, many still believe the killer received inside assistance. He certainly knew the court precinct thoroughly, including the virtually unknown stairways and corridors he used to make good his escape.

Three years later, almost to the day, Brian Kane was gunned down at the Quarry Hotel in Brunswick by a pair of balaclava-clad killers. Their identities have never been established.

GONE WITHOUT A TRACE

In late 1979, Prendergast had met a woman named Ursula, and eighteen months later they married. The pair took up residence in Warrandyte, a leafy outer Melbourne suburb, and Laurie became stepfather to her two children by a previous marriage. He still had some trouble with the law; in 1980 he received twelve months imprisonment for being a felon in possession of a pistol. Otherwise, there was nothing for the next three years. Ursula bore him a daughter, and Prendergast appeared to have gone straight.

'Neddy' Smith had a different story, though. According to Smith, during this period Prendergast again teamed up with Chris Flannery, and the pair performed contract killings while supplying alibis for each other. Smith's version of events is hard to believe. Prendergast's only brush with the law over that time was that he was fined in 1984 for making a false statement to obtain a passport, and again for being a felon in possession of a pistol.

Then, on 23 August 1985, three months after Chris Flannery disappeared, Prendergast did the same.

That morning, Prendergast had driven his stepson, Carl, to Doncaster Shoppingtown in their silver Volvo. Ursula was visiting her parents in Queensland with their daughter, and Laurie was looking after Carl. Prendergast dropped Carl off at 10.30 am and told him to catch a bus home and make sure he was back by 4 o'clock.

On his return, Carl phoned home from a public phone box in Warrandyte to see if his stepfather could give him a lift, but when the call was unanswered, he walked home.

Arriving at about 4.15 pm, Carl found the front door locked and the house empty. Inside, he found two plates and two cups in the kitchen sink that hadn't been there when he left. Otherwise, everything was normal. When his mother rang home at 5 pm, Carl told her what had happened. She said she'd ring back on the hour to see if Laurie had returned, but he never did.

Ursula Prendergast returned home the following evening and found newspapers dated 23 August 1985 on the kitchen table. As there was still no sign of Laurie, she contacted his solicitor, and together they reported his absence to police on Sunday 25 August at 1.30 am.

The following Tuesday, a resident of Cartmell Street in Heidelberg informed police that a silver Volvo had been parked opposite her house since about 5.30 pm on Friday 23 August, when she returned from work. A check on the Volvo's registration revealed that it was Prendergast's. The street was sealed off as a possible crime scene, and the Volvo was taken away for forensic examination, but the only unusual object found in the car was a cigarette butt. Prendergast was a non-smoker who didn't like others to smoke in his car. The forensic experts found no evidence of foul play, and there were no identifiable fingerprints in or on the car.

Laurence Joseph Prendergast, aged 35, had disappeared and – as far as is known – has not been seen or heard of since. Was he abducted and murdered, as was the popular theory at the time, or did he stage his own disappearance?

Five years later, a coronial inquiry into the disappearance was held before Coroner Maurice Gurvich, who took evidence from ten witnesses. During the hearing, Ursula revealed that she'd discovered Prendergast's pistol in his wardrobe, which she felt indicated that Laurie had believed he was safe when he left home, as he normally carried it if he sensed danger. Another witness, a builder working on a house next to Prendergast's home in Brogil Road, Warrandyte, noticed a Kombi van with the name Prendergast on the door parked near Laurie's home on the day of his disappearance. Laurie's cousin William owned such a vehicle, but he denied he was there. The workman also saw a Volvo leave the house during the afternoon.

Coroner Gurvich handed down an open verdict, observing that, on the evidence, he couldn't conclude that Prendergast was dead, and that there were a number of other possible reasons for his disappearance. The coroner noted that Prendergast had many criminal associates and many criminal enemies. He had a strong incentive to disappear, though that wasn't to say that he necessarily planned it. There was no credible evidence to give one conclusion greater force than the other, the coroner concluded.

Laurie Prendergast's disappearance, like Chris Flannery's, has long been the subject of rumour and speculation. When weighing up the accuracy of accounts by people such as 'Neddy' Smith – who had them as a pair of contract killers in partnership with each other – it's worth considering Smith's account of Prendergast's disappearance as given in his book *Catch and Kill Your Own*. Smith's account would have it that Prendergast disappeared from his car, which was left in his driveway, and that his wife reported him missing when she found the deserted car with the driver's door open. Very little of this account tallies with the known facts. Smith went on to report a rumour that four policemen had taken Prendergast away, though he doubted that Laurie would have gone voluntarily. His conclusion was that Prendergast was dead.

There are striking similarities between the disappearances of best mates Prendergast and Flannery. Each abandoned his car. Flannery said he couldn't start his – though it was later easily started – and left it in a car park. Prendergast left home in his, but it was later found parked in a small side street some distance from his home.

Neither of them was reliably sighted after he'd left his car. Flannery disappeared off the street outside his unit, and no-one saw Prendergast leave the street where his car was found. However, a taxi driver claimed to have picked Flannery up and taken him to an airport, and it is not difficult to imagine that Prendergast had his own 'taxi' waiting to take him to a similar destination. While both were reportedly taken away and murdered, there is no evidence of foul play in either disappearance.

Only three possibilities would seem worthy of consideration: that Flannery faked his own disappearance, and Prendergast followed suit; that Flannery was murdered, and Prendergast faked his disappearance to avoid a similar fate; or that both Flannery and Prendergast were murdered.

The third possibility is by far the most likely. All manner of reasons have been advanced for Prendergast's possible murder. It's been rumoured, for example, that he'd become involved in the drug scene and was murdered as a result of these connections. Another theory was that he was offered the contract on a well-known Sydney crime boss to avenge Flannery's death, but that the Sydney man's connections got to him first.

The second possibility – that Prendergast staged his disappearance after Flannery was murdered – has some merit. There were signs that Prendergast was making preparations for his departure before he disappeared. For example, a week earlier, his wife had borrowed $6000 and given the money to him.

Though the least likely, the possibility that both faked their disappearance can't be entirely discounted. They both had good reason to disappear, having made enemies on both sides of the law. However, with the passing of time it has become less and less likely that what happened to them will ever be revealed.

CHAPTER 17
TOWARDS CLOSURE

Alexander Whatmore, the great reformer, retired as Director-General of Social Welfare in 1971. His reforms had made a significant contribution to Pentridge, but years of government neglect had left the archaic prison overcrowded, and conditions remained harsh. The 1970s were a time of great unrest at Pentridge, with fires being lit and property damaged – particularly in H Division, where repeated rebellions caused a breakdown in control. Protests continued on and off throughout the decade. In 1978, B Division prisoners rioted, and the chapel there was badly damaged by fire.

Amid all these upheavals, some significant advances were made in prisoner welfare. A swimming pool was constructed in the mid-1970s, and a new hospital within the prison's grounds was completed in 1980. J Division, having failed as a dormitory section for young offenders, was converted into comfortable single-cell accommodation for long-term prisoners.

In 1974, the archaic C Division was closed and demolished. This decision had a tinge of ambivalence about it. On the one hand, C Division was long past its use-by date as part of a working prison. It had been built without sewerage or electric light, and prison authorities had been advocating its closure for thirty years. But it was also a unique, original structure that formed a significant piece of Australian penal history. Surely, shame must have played a part in the decision to demolish it; the preservation of the prison's history certainly didn't.

JIKA JIKA

During the mid-1970s, the prison authorities began to plan for a new maximum-security section, which they hoped would offer something to replace the quasi-military discipline that had broken down in H Division. The unrest and rioting around the prison, and the need for a facility to accommodate unruly prisoners, were also factors in the move. The need for tighter security was thrown into sharp relief in late 1976, when Edwin Eastwood escaped from prison in Geelong and kidnapped several children and a teacher from Wooreen Primary School in Gippsland. Recaptured, Eastwood was sentenced to 21 years imprisonment and sent to H Division.

In search of a 'solution' to the security problem, a new division called Jika Jika was built at a cost of $7 million to segregate high-risk inmates from the rest of the prison population. Jika Jika became fully operational in 1980. Prisoners were held in six separate units, connected through corridor 'spines' that led to a central administrative area. Each unit could accommodate twelve prisoners and was further divided into two 'sides' of six inmates each, separated by a thick wall of bulletproof glass. Prisoners were also separated from guards by bulletproof glass, and were kept under constant surveillance through the use of video cameras. The prison officers used electronic consoles to control prisoner access, power and heating. The entire structure sat on stilts, and there was no access to fresh air inside the complex.

Inmates of Jika Jika passed unescorted through remotely controlled doors or 'security locks' operated by the prison officers. This was often a source of frustration when prisoners had to wait for an inattentive or overworked prison officer to open a door and let them pass. Each unit had an escape-proof exercise yard with a cage-like roof, and the perimeter was protected by microwave technology and alarm systems. Built to keep staff costs to a minimum and security to a maximum,

Jika Jika was beset with problems. There were fires, self-harm and suicide attempts, assaults and murders. The fraught relations between prisoners and guards reached a low point in 1983, when the Pentridge prison staff went on strike for a week in protest after two prison officers were disciplined for their part in allowing four prisoners to escape from Jika Jika.

A prison within a prison, Jika Jika relied on disciplinary techniques of isolation and sensory deprivation, which bred boredom, tension and psychological problems. Prisoners there were offered few useful activities or opportunities for human interaction. Like H Division before it, the division embittered its inmates, who became a danger to the community on release.

THE BRIEF LIFE OF B ANNEXE

Prisoner unrest wasn't confined to Pentridge. During the early 1980s, there were protests by women prisoners at Fairlea, mainly over their housing in an old dormitory section. In 1982, a large fire in that section claimed the lives of three of its inmates – including the woman who had lit the fire. About forty female prisoners were relocated to Pentridge, where they were housed in a section of B Division known as B Annexe.

Conditions there were spartan. Women were locked up for sixteen hours a day, causing them much distress. Those at risk of suicide were placed in observation cells, which were subject to extreme conditions, particularly in winter. Female prisoners on suicide watch were dressed in canvas to prevent them from tearing their clothes into strips to hang themselves. Sometimes women were sent to Jika Jika for fighting and other disciplinary offences. This added to the strain on the prison's accommodation, and was a source of many problems for both male and female inmates. It was a relief all round when new facilities were opened at Fairlea in 1986, including cottage accommodation and an education centre, and the women were sent back there.

CRISIS AND RETREAT

After several escapes from Pentridge during the early 1980s, an American security expert named James Henderson was brought in to conduct an inquiry into the prison's security. The consultant's report that followed severely criticised the security measures employed at Pentridge and made many recommendations for improvement. Victoria's prisons were described as 'disgraceful places in which to house people', the worst of their kind in Australia.

Henderson said that Pentridge, in particular, was overcrowded and required massive expenditure to bring it up to reasonable standards of prisoner accommodation. The report also suggested that most prison officers be disarmed to prevent their weapons from being used against them by escaping prisoners.

Little was done to implement the Henderson report's more expensive suggestions, and the prison officers' association dismissed the report as 'useless'. The officers also opposed the recommendation that they be disarmed. The report, however, was a sign of the growing recognition that modern systems of rehabilitation and education couldn't easily be established within the oppressive, isolating structure of a nineteenth-century prison. To adapt it would be an expensive business, if it were possible at all.

But when the situation at Pentridge reached crisis point, the focus of the problems wasn't its older buildings but its newest one, the former Jika Jika, which had been renamed K Division in 1984. On 29 October 1987, prisoners in Unit 4 of K Division mounted a protest against their conditions that ended in total disaster.

The unit was divided into two sides by a bulletproof glass

panel, with half the inmates of the unit on each side. At about 3.30 pm, prisoners on both sides of the unit moved to block the unit doors. The prisoners on Side 1 piled a foam mattress, a table-tennis table and some books against their door, and the Side 2 prisoners concealed this activity by smashing security cameras and covering windows with newspapers. About half an hour later, the Side 1 prisoners set fire to their barricade, but the effects were much worse than they expected. The burning foam quickly spread toxic fumes through the unit. The five prisoners tried to breathe fresh air through some pipes, but the smoke poured in there as well, and all five were asphyxiated.

In the chaos that followed, a prison officer became trapped attempting to open the doors and had to be rescued, while other officers made futile attempts to gain access to the unit. Eventually, the prisoners on Side 2 were released, narrowly avoiding death.

The deaths brought an immediate response, and K Division was closed the following month. Announcing its closure, Victoria's Attorney-General, Jim Kennan, described it as a 'dehumanising electronic zoo'. A subsequent coroner's report was very critical of the Office of Corrections' response to the fire, and also recommended the removal of the remote-controlled doors.

When the division was reopened the following year, it operated under different rules. The remote-controlled doors had gone, and the division was now used to house assessment and treatment programs for drug-dependent prisoners and those with intellectual disabilities. It also provided programs to assist HIV-positive prisoners, and in some cases was used to provide protection for prisoners who were at risk from other inmates.

During the early 1990s, Pentridge's future again came under review, with the Kennett government flagging its intention to privatise Victorian prisons and, in particular, to replace the 'inadequate and costly' prisons at Pentridge and Fairlea. In 1994, H Division was closed, and the partitioned walls of H Division's labour yards were quickly demolished on closure, perhaps in an attempt to make the place appear a little less inhumane. The following year, Pentridge was downgraded to a medium-security prison, and the prison's six main towers were closed. In May 1997, the northern half of the prison was officially shut down and its inmates transferred elsewhere. The southern section closed the following year.

In 1999, the government sold off the north and south sections to property developers. In the first stage of the site's redevelopment, much of the great outer wall was demolished, as was Jika Jika, and a housing estate and business precinct were developed in the southern section.

The northern part of the site, which contains most of the buildings that form the core of the old prison, has been more problematic, and has repeatedly changed hands. The Valad property group, having acquired a 6.5-hectare section in 2001 after the original release was subdivided, proposed an ambitious redevelopment involving the construction of several high-rise residential complexes on the site. Burdened by debt, however, Valad listed the site for sale in 2011, and it was acquired by the Taiwanese-based Shayher group.

The historic divisions remain under the control and protection of Heritage Victoria. There was something of a panic in June 2014, when it was announced that the developers had been given the go-ahead to demolish most of the H Division labour yards to permit road access to other parts of the site. Former chaplain Peter Norden published a column in the *Age* calling for H Division to be 'retained and protected, although it holds so many bad memories'. Since then, the Shayher group has announced that there is no intention to destroy the labour yards, and that they will be carefully reconstructed from the original materials at their expense once road access is no longer required. This incident is a sign of how Pentridge's past and future are constantly being renegotiated.

PENTRIDGE NEW AND OLD

Since its closure, Pentridge has undergone a metamorphosis. Beginning at the old remand centre – which was converted into a very large wine storage facility – a prisoner walking into Pentridge would be shocked at the change of scenery. The old farm area with its endless rows of vegetables has been replaced by rows of suburban houses along thoroughfares with names such as Stockade Avenue, Pentridge Boulevard, Warden's Walk and Governor's Road.

Arriving at the gate to the Square, our prisoner would be amazed to find that the old industry areas have been turned into privately owned residences. In the old mat-yard area, the original building leans up against a new block of units. On the northern part of the site, however, most of his old stalking grounds still stand, and even in the cleared areas, there have been many archaeological digs. The foundations of C Division have been unearthed, along with some original cell blocks, courtyard floor surfaces and the drains used until the mid-1970s. Archaeologists have also uncovered the foundations of Champ's panoptical exercise yards. The bodies buried in the southern section of Pentridge have been exhumed, including those of Ned Kelly and other famous – or infamous – former inmates.

During a recent visit to the prison, I was amazed at the changes that had taken place there. The most noticeable aspect to me was how stark and grim the old place looked, probably because the gardens that once graced its buildings had now disappeared. This was particularly the case with A Division, which looked more forbidding than ever, though its interior was very little changed by the passage of time. At its eastern end lay H Division, which was reduced to a shadow of the house of horrors it once was. The partition that once divided it from A Division had gone, giving the appearance that its cells, which had brought so much misery to so many, were simply part of A. But there was no mistaking what lay beyond – the notorious tunnel to the labour yards. There, though the crosses remained on the floor, the partitioned walls and doors had gone, so that the place gave the impression of an open recreation area, leaving no trace of the physical and mental torture meted out there in the past. Most of these old labour yards were about to be bulldozed. And the reception area, where so many prisoners had been flogged and terrorised, stood barren and cheerless. If only those walls could talk!

Champ's panopticon, B Division, was impressive as always from outside, belying the soulless cell block within. Underneath a staircase, its 'blind cells', once terrible dungeons of human suffering, stood stark and bare. A central spiral staircase led up to the deserted chapel, where even the altar had gone. The walls were still marked with soot from the fire that burnt the chapel during the protests of 1978.

Standing where I'd once sat by the altar, I suddenly recalled a clattering at the door and saw a little 52-year-old man goose-stepping toward me, his arms swinging high and his body contorting. To me, the memory of William O'Meally embodies all that was wrong with the old regime at Pentridge. The physical and mental agonies that had left such obvious marks on him aren't part of a history that can be forgotten or swept away. No matter what its new owners do to lend Pentridge a sparkling new veneer, the dark, menacing structures at its heart remind us of how its inmates suffered in secrecy and silence behind those bluestone walls.

BIBLIOGRAPHY

Boyle, Damian, *Call Me Jimmy: The Life and Death of Jockey Smith* (Melbourne: Floradale Productions and Sly Ink, 2003).

Broome, Richard, *Coburg: Between Two Creeks* (Melbourne: Lothian, 1987).

Buckley, Bert, *HM Central Sub Prison Pentridge: Life Behind the Bluestone Walls from 1800's–1980's* (Pentridge: Department of Community Welfare, 1981).

Burns, Creighton, *The Tait Case* (Melbourne: Melbourne University Press 1962).

Carlton, Bree, *Imprisoning Resistance: Life and Death in an Australian Supermax* (Sydney: Institute of Criminology Press, 2007).

Chapman, Ivan, *Private Eddie Leonski: The Brownout Strangler* (Sydney: Hale & Iremonger, 1982).

Coroner's Court decision 557/1981, *Findings as to the Death of Raymond Patrick Bennett*, 1981.

Dillon, J. V., *Report of the Ombudsman on Investigation into Cause of Unrest in H Division Pentridge* (Melbourne: Government Printer, 1978).

Eastwood, Edwin, *Focus On Faraday and Beyond* (Melbourne: Coeur De Lion, 1992).

Ellem, Barry, *Doing Time: The Prison Experience* (Sydney: Fontana/Collins, 1984).

Fife-Yeomans, Janet, *Killing Jodie: How Australia's Most*

Elusive Murderer was Brought to Justice (Camberwell: Viking, 2007).

George, Amanda, and Jude McCulloch, *Women and Imprisonment* (Melbourne: Fitzroy Legal Service, 1988).

Glass, Greg, *Coroner's Bench Statement Following an Inquest Hearing Concerning the Disappearance and Suspected Death of Christopher Dale Flannery* (Sydney: New South Wales State Coroner's Court, 1997).

Grindlay, Ian, *Behind Bars* (Melbourne: Southdown Press, 1976).

Gurvich, Maurice, *Coronial Inquiry into the Disappearance of Laurence Joseph Prendergast*, 1990.

Hawkins, Gordon, *Beyond Reasonable Doubt* (Sydney: ABC Books, 1977).

Jenkinson, Kenneth J., *Report of the Board of Inquiry into Allegations of Brutality and Ill-Treatment at HM Prison Pentridge* (Melbourne: Government Printer, 1974).

Kerr, John, *The Hit Men* (Melbourne: Penguin Group/ Michael Joseph, 2010).

Lynn, Peter, and George Armstrong, *From Pentonville to Pentridge: A History of Prisons in Victoria* (Melbourne: State Library of Victoria, 1996).

Main, Jim, and Ben Collins, *Encyclopedia of Australian Crime* (Melbourne: BAS Publishing, 2006).

Mallon, Andrew, *Leonski: The Brown-out Murders* (Melbourne: Outback Press, 1979).

Marshall, Debi, *Lambs to the Slaughter* (Sydney: Random House, 2009).

McNab, Duncan, *Killing Mr Rent-A-Kill* (Sydney: Pan Macmillan, 2012).

Molomby, Tom, *Ratten: The Web of Circumstance* (Melbourne: Outback Press, 1978).

Mooney, Ray, *Everynight ... Everynight* (videorecording, Alkinoss Tsilimidos/Australian Film Institute, 1994).

Morgan, Kevin, *The Particulars of Executions 1894–1967: The Hidden Truth about Capital Punishment at the Old Melbourne Gaol and Pentridge Prison* (Melbourne: National Trust of Australia, 2004).

Morton, James and Russell Robinson, *Shotgun and Standover: The Story of the Painters and Dockers* (Sydney: Pan Macmillan, 2010).

Nagle, Justice J. F., *Report of the Royal Commission into New South Wales Prisons* (Sydney: Government Printer, 1978).

Norden, Peter, 'Behind the Walls of H Division', *Age*, 13 June 2014.

Norden, Peter, 'Prison Realities and the Need for Change', 2012, at <rightnow.org.au/topics/asylum-seekers/prison-realities-and-the-need-for-change/>

O'Meally, William John, *The Man They Couldn't Break* (Melbourne: Unicorn Books, 1980).

Pring, Jay, *Abo – A Treacherous Life: The Graham Henry Story* (Sydney: ABC Books, 2005).

Prout, Denton, and Fred Feely, *50 Years Hard* (Adelaide: Rigby, 1967).

Roberts, Gregory David, *Shantaram: A Novel* (Sydney: Picador, 2007).

Robinson, Doug, *H: The Division From Hell* (Melbourne: Dougbooks, 2005).

Robinson, Russell, 'Born To Be a Killer', *Herald Sun*, 30 September 2009.

Royal Commission on Penal and Prison Discipline, *Report No. 2* (Melbourne: Government Printer, 1871).

Sharpe, Alan, and Vivien Encel, *Murder! 25 True Australian Crimes* (Sydney: Kingsclear Books, 1997).

Silvester, John, 'Born To Be Badness', *Age*, 22 May 2012.

Silvester, John, 'Murder Witness Vanishes Suspiciously', *Age*, 4 February 2005.

Silvester, John, 'One Man So, Many Faces of Evil', *Age*, 22 April 2007.

Silvester, John, and Andrew Rule, *Gotcha: How Australia's Baddest Crooks Copped Their Right Whack* (Melbourne: Floradale Productions and Sly Ink, 2005).

Silvester, John, and Andrew Rule, *Underbelly: A Tale of Two Cities* (Melbourne: Floradale Productions and Sly Ink, 2009).

Simpson, Paul, *The Mammoth Book of Prison Breaks* (London: Constable & Robinson, 2013).

Smith, Arthur Stanley, *Catch and Kill Your Own: Behind the Killings the Police Don't Want to Solve* (Sydney: Ironbark, 1995).

Smith, Arthur Stanley, with Tom Noble, *Neddy: The Life and Crimes of Arthur 'Neddy' Smith: An Autobiography* (Sydney: Noble House Enterprises, 2002).

Smith, Jeremy, 'Losing the Plot: Archaeological Investigations of Prisoner Burials at the Old Melbourne Gaol and Pentridge Prison', *Provenance*, 2011, at <http://prov.vic.gov.au/publications/provenance/provenance2011/losing-the-plot>

Supreme Court of Victoria, *R vs William John O'Meally*, transcript 1952

Supreme Court of Victoria, *R v Bennett, Mikkelsen and Prendergast*, transcript, 1979.

Tog, Joe, *More Australian True Crime Stories* (Melbourne: Brolga Publishing, 2011).

Trove Newspapers, National Library of Australia.

Whiticker, Alan J., *Another 12 Crimes That Shocked The Nation* (Sydney: New Holland Publishers, 2007).

Whiticker, Alan J., *Derek Percy: Australian Psycho* (Sydney: New Holland Publishers, 2008).

Whiticker, Alan J., *Wanda: The Untold Story of the Wanda*

Beach Murders (Sydney: New Holland Publishers, 2003).

Wilson, Paul, Don Treble and Robyn Lincoln, *Jean Lee: The Last Woman Hanged in Australia* (Sydney: Random House, 1997).

IMAGE LIST

ACKNOWLEDGEMENTS

To my wonderful children Tania, Peter and Stuart without whose suggestions, encouragement and support this book would never have been produced, and to my wife Cheryl for all the hard yards she has put in to help me prepare the manuscript. Special thanks also to my two pillars of strength and support, my friends Ray Mooney and Marty Ryan, who encouraged me every step of the way.

Thank you also to Pam Warren for birth and death particulars regarding William O'Meally; Tom Molomby for his ready assistance with the Ratten case and Kenneth Allen for information regarding the conduct of an execution.

Special thanks go to Donna Squire for her extraordinary photography and to her husband, Brett, for his excellent graphic work.

I wish to express my gratitude to the people at Echo Publishing, especially to the ever-professional Julia Taylor. Special thanks go to Shaun Jury for his excellent page design and typesetting as well as to Luke Causby for his great cover design. Lastly, my thanks go to my wonderful editor, Jenny Lee.